Social Reconstruction

People, Politics, Perspectives

a volume in
Studies in the History of Education

Series Editor
Karen L. Riley
Auburn University Montgomery

Social Reconstruction

People, Politics, Perspectives

edited by

Karen L. Riley
Auburn University Montgomery

INFORMATION AGE
PUBLISHING

Greenwich, Connecticut • www.infoagepub.com

Library of Congress Cataloging-in-Publication Data

Social reconstruction : people, politics, perspectives / edited by Karen L. Riley.
    p. cm. – (Studies in the history of education)
  Includes bibliographical references.
  ISBN 1-59311-214-9 (pbk.) – ISBN 1-59311-215-7 (hardcover) 1. Educational soci-
ology–United States–History. 2. Progressive education–United States–History. 3.
Social change–United States–History. I. Riley, Karen Lea, 1946- II. Studies in the
history of education (Greenwich, Conn.)
  LC191.4.S655 2006
  306.43–dc22

                              2005034818

For our students

CONTENTS

ACKNOWLEDGMENTS

First and foremost, I would like to thank all of the contributing authors, without whose contributions this book would not have been possible. They were selected for their reputations in the fields of the history of education, social studies, and/or curriculum history. I would also like to thank the Midwest History of Education Society for having the vision to sponsor such a valuable contribution to the field of the history of education. While a book of this undertaking can never find its way to the printing house without the input of a number of key individuals, I would like to publicly acknowledge two of them: Melissa Reck and Murry Nelson. Melissa, at Auburn University Montgomery, assisted me in so many ways that I cannot begin to list them all. She is one of those treasures who completes a task in record-breaking time and always with a good heart and spirit. And Murry's reputation as a scholar on Harold Rugg and his support of this project have served as inspiration to all of us. His thoughtful and thought-provoking Introduction to this volume is an important addition. Murry, I thank you. Finally, I offer many thanks to my institution, Auburn University Montgomery, and the School of Education, for invaluable institutional support.

EDITOR'S FOREWORD

In a number of ways, this book was both a labor of love and a selfish endeavor. All of the contributing authors have examined and re-examined aspects of Social Reconstruction as intellectual challenges to understanding the American mind and what makes us tick. Perhaps we, as scholars, are drawn to "lessons" from the heyday of Social Reconstruction because those lessons constantly remind us that we haven't learned very much from them, thus causing us to delve further for answers that the Reconstructionists of the 1930s dealt with—poverty, ills of capitalism, and social justice—all in the hope of improving our lot. We, as author/educators, also possess a selfish motive for investing our time in the writing of this book. We are first and foremost teachers. Each year, we are charged with educating and acculturating a new group of preservice teachers, who know nothing or little of the history of education. Often they are surprised, even astounded, to discover that "once upon a time" teachers held the keys to a more vibrant, energetic, and socially-just America, at least according to the Reconstructionists. Therefore, we as teachers, search for the perfect text, pamphlet, or book that can capture the spirit of one of the most exciting times in American educational history—the Progressive Era. But, of course, it would be a difficult undertaking, even an arrogant one, to expect that one book could capture Progressive education in its entirety. Therefore, this book dedicates itself to the investigation and interpretation of Social Reconstruction and the individuals, politics, and perspectives that have endured over time.

As with any book, the author or editor must decide what to include and what to exclude. Such decisions are rarely easy. In the case of *Social Reconstruction: People, Politics, and Perspectives*, a number of worthy names are left out and for a variety of reasons—balance, time constraints on the part of contributing authors, existing materials. Individuals who would have significantly added a dimension to this volume are Paul Hanna, Jesse Newlon, and Mabel Carney, although there are many others whose careers and influence are just as important. Additionally, several fundamental and lucid articles on the subject of Social Reconstruction were omitted owing to the issue of balance. One is the history of the Rugg textbook controversy in Binghampton, New York. As for perspectives, what Murry Nelson, in his introduction to this text, pointed to as a crucial piece of the reconstructionist story that remains missing is the story of implementation. Which communities implemented the Rugg perspective? How was it received? Did the texts make a difference? What remains are chapters that illuminate some of the key figures of social reconstruction, some of the politics that surrounded the key ideas, which formed the constructs of social reconstructionist philosophy, and perspectives of how these key ideas were put into practice, obscured (see Watkins' chapter on Black Voices), or altogether neglected.

The vision of the editor and authors of this text is to provide preservice teachers, foundations of education professors, and historians of education with a book that sparks their interest in the topic, and challenges them to want to go farther and to explore those links that exist between the past and present. The history of education is a rich history. It is fraught with the same drama and intrigues as political history, social history, or any other branch of history. It is the hope of this editor that readers will find the stories and ideas contained within these pages as exciting and compelling as did the authors who have dedicated a large portion of their professional lives to researching and writing about social reconstruction, and delivering to you, the reading audience, their "once upon a time" stories of when teachers could have seized the day and created a just society, built by people educated for a better tomorrow.

INTRODUCTION

Murry Nelson

In this book Karen Riley and the various authors revisit Social Reconstruction, a philosophy of education that is inherently action-oriented. For those familiar with Social Reconstruction, the obvious question is "for what reason was this book conceived and published?" Surely this is an area that has been examined and reexamined over the past seventy-five years, beginning with the Social Reconstructionists themselves, who spend many hours and published many pieces that indicated their constant reassessment of what Social Reconstruction was, could be, and ought to be. Unless one is deeply immersed in researching this concept/philosophy/movement, it is unlikely that many of those works would be read today. Instead what have become the most widely read interpretations of Social Reconstruction are those offered by Lawrence Cremin and C.A. Bowers. Since Cremin's Transformation of the School: Progressivism in American Education, 1876–1957, was published in 1964, it has been the standard work to provide an insightful, analytical overview of educational Progressivism, of which Social Reconstruction is usually seen as a part. C.A. Bowers' The Progressive Educator and the Depression: the Radical Years, first published in 1969, takes a narrower and more critical look at Progressivism and Social Reconstruction and acts as a balance to Cremin's more "traditional" views. The two works complement each other and many of the authors in this book use one or both as anchors to ground further arguments or to establish a solid

Social Reconstruction: People, Politics, Perspectives, pages xiii–xx
Copyright © 2006 by Information Age Publishing
All rights of reproduction in any form reserved.

historical and philosophical foundation. Regarding the reliance on these volumes, Wayne Urban notes in his chapter that, "While an edited volume of Counts's work was published in 1980... the rest of that decade and the following decade fund no significant books or monographs devoted to Counts and other Rconstructionist educators and thinkers".[1]

My own academic interest in Social Reconstruction began more than thirty years ago and was the basis of my dissertation and numerous articles on the people and perspectives of the era. Many of the authors in this book have had as long or longer histories in writing and researching this topic and it initially struck me that there may be little left for them to say after all these years of reexamining the concept. But, after reading these chapters, I can say that I was wrong in making such a preconceived assessment. For the most part, these chapters represent new examinations by these authors, even though many draw upon their prior works for foundational development. Remarkably, what comes through to the reader in much of this book is the passion that still burns within these authors for the era and the ideas generated by that educational period and philosophy. There is an enthusiasm present that captures the reader and presents the social responsibility of Reconstruction as a prerequisite for American schooling. To many of the authors, the issue of Reconstruction is new again. Having been away from it for a time, they now see new possibilities because of their own growth through various experiences, but also because of stepping back and now returning with new perspectives. It is like working a difficult crossword puzzle. Sometimes one cannot progress and, rather, sees the same incorrect solutions for many of the clues. Returning hours later, the puzzle now is often solved in short order. The solver is no smarter; rather he or she has a clearer mind that connects in a different way to the problem at hand.

Nevertheless, this is not a book that simply lives in the past. Cremin offered the idea that Progressive education "died" in 1957, but many of these chapters illustrate the fallacy of that notion. Social Reconstruction is seen by many as the real foundation of critical theory in education and that base has led to similar calls today for the same kind of equality and social justice that drove the Social Reconstructionists in the period of 1930–50.

There are some basic themes and established notions in the book and reviewing them may act as a useful "advance organizer." First, the notion of what schools should do is important to consider. Why do they exist? A cynical answer is to keep children busy during the day, but even the cynic has more of a rationale than that. Our schools serve to present a basic idea of American values within the disciplinary content and assist another generation of children to understand why the American culture that exists today should be reproduced in the next generation. This, of course, is the "have" position in society. It is also related to some people believing that they deserve more or better things in the society and that is why they have them. Luck, power and control are obscured by this sense of entitlement.

It was, in large part, a response to this notion that led to the development of Progressivism, most specifically Social Reconstruction. As a number of authors discuss, the other "wing" of Progressive education, child-centeredness often was interwoven with the concerns of the Social Reconstructionists, but the advocates of the two positions clashed in their approaches and objectives. Interestingly, their basic desires were the same, i.e., the improvement of society. They both recognized that society was, and had to be, dynamic in order to remain vibrant and vital. The constant improvement of society would be the engine that drove the work of the schools. Their approaches differed, however. Adherents to child-centeredness felt that by helping individual children to grow in unique ways, children would become better and more self-satisfied and self-reliant individuals. Individuals who were happy and independent would, the theory went, work to improve society. Social Reconstructionists, however, were more direct. Their view was that society needed to be improved through constant reexamination and reconstruction and the aim of the school was to foster that. In other words, to make a better society, students needed to work at making a better society, tautological though that might seem. This end, a better society, is the ultimate goal of every educational approach—the difference in how to get to that end.

One of the major themes in Social Reconstruction—one that emerges in many of the chapters—is the idea of the social studies. Far beyond any curricular area, the social studies are reflective of much that characterizes Social Reconstruction and, for that reason, social studies is one of the controversial parts of Social Reconstruction as it is examined today. The field of social studies is at a critical juncture today and it is not unwise to examine social studies as it developed, through the lens of Social Reconstruction. In this manner it may allow educators to make a greater case for social studies in the curriculum, a content area both ignored by No Child Left Behind (NCLB) and excoriated by many who wish social studies to be abandoned in school altogether. Many of the chapters address these ideas in a variety of ways. Social studies grew out of various concerns for combining much of the information contained in social sciences and history as well as the social concerns of the Progressive Era of the late 1890s. The initial fights over the placement of social studies in the curriculum were most heated during the 1920s and 30s as many educational agencies commissioned reports on various aspects of the school curriculum.

The various commission reports—most significantly those from the National Educational Association, the American Historical Association, and the American Political Science Association—led to confusion, contradiction, and fragmentation in this period. However, the concession of the American Historical Association in the late 1920s (through its Commission on the Social Studies) that social studies was the best way to organize social sciences and history within the school curriculum seemed to lead to a "victory" for social studies. Even in victory, however, there was dissent and dissatisfaction since a number of the AHA Commissioners refused to sign the Final Report of the Commission, largely authored by Charles Beard and George Counts. Joseph Watras examines this most closely in this chapter, but a number of other authors also discuss this important work. (It should be noted that one chapter, that by Wayne Urban, does examine a Commission, the Educational Policies Commission, but this was a Commission with a larger scope than the curriculum committees.)

One of the early advocates of the social studies and a cofounder of the National Council for the Social Studies in 1921 was Harold Rugg and his presence in this book and within Social Reconstruction is enormous. Rugg appears and reappears in many of these chapters (those of Evans, Riley, Stern, and Ponder are the most obvious) because of his influence in social studies, curriculum development as a field of study at that time, and the later controversies that surrounded his textbooks in the early 1940s. Even when Rugg had no involvement, such as in the AHA Commission on the Social Studies, his absence was notable. Rugg was a lightning rod and his adherents were fiercely loyal while his detractors were just as fierce in their denunciation of him and his ideas. Trained initially as a civil engineer, Rugg believed in organized planning and disciplined thinking. He was a powerful advocate of so-called Frontier Thinkers, those on the "cutting edge" of the social science disciplines and the arts, but he was often dismissed by those who disagreed with him, because he was not "credentialed" in either area. Rugg's textbook difficulties, which led to the removal of his books from many school districts and the ultimate cessation of them as published works, are representative of the difficulties that Social Reconstruction faced as a movement. Ronald Evans traces much of that in his chapter and Barbara Slater Stern adds another perspective with her discussion of his concern with curriculum design.

Rugg also was strongly tied to the other people specifically profiled in this volume. William Bagley was Rugg's doctoral advisor while at the University of Illinois and the two were reunited when both later taught at Teachers College, Columbia. Rugg and Bagley were coauthors of a number of works in the late 1910s and had similar concerns for clear design and planning in curriculum. They deviated philosophically in the 1920s, although both never ceased to speak highly of one another, no matter what academic disagreements they might have had. In his chapter Wesley Null seeks to unravel this relationship and the frustration that William Bagley felt regarding his views of teacher education that he felt were unjustly ignored or misinterpreted by the other Social Reconstructionists.

Rugg is also linked closely to George Counts, originally viewed as the most radical of the Social Reconstructionists, but whose later views seemed to repudiate many of his earlier notions. Counts was an early observer of the Soviet Union and the efforts at communism to create a more just society. He was soon overwhelmed by the horrors of Stalinist policies and practices and became a staunch opponent of the Soviet Union. For years Counts and Rugg taught and fraternized at Teachers College. Gerald Gutek, who has studied and written about Counts, for most of his professional life, presents some revised insights on George Counts and Social Reconstruction in his chapter.

The last person specifically profiled, Theordore Brameld, was younger than most of the others profiled and discussed in this book, but was identified as a radical philosopher because of his ideas and his memberships in various Communist Party organizations in the 1930s. This, not coincidentally, was when the Communist Party was at its zenith in the United States as the great Depression drove many social thinkers to consider radical solutions to what seemed to be a failed American society. Brameld was a Visiting Professor at Teachers College in the later 1930s and studied with professors there, but left the city in 1939 for the University of Minnesota. By the time he returned to New York as a Professor of educational philosophy at New York University, most of the prominent Reconstructionists were retired or about to be retired and the United States was much different economically and socially. Craig Kridel provides insights into Brameld and his notions of Social Reconstruction in his chapter.

There is at least one presence here whose influence is often alluded to, and that is John Dewey. Dewey is seen as the font of much of Progressive educational thought and his work at Teachers College, with many of those profiled or discussed in this book, was highly influential in much of Social Reconstruction. Dewey is more often seen as a child-centered philosopher and, he was that, but his early linkages of Progressive education and the science of education also contained the "seeds" of Social Reconstruction. In his 1928 speech to the Progressive Education Association, he noted that "(I)f one conceives that a social order different in quality and direction from the present is desirable and that schools should strive to educate with social change in view by producing individuals not complacent about what already exists, and equipped with desires and abilities to assist in transforming it, quite a different method is indicated for educational science."[2]

Dewey was an active participant in the Social Frontier (later Frontiers of Democracy) as were Counts, Rugg, and others. This journal is discussed by Lynn Burlbaw in his chapter. In addition to that journal, Dewey was also active as the President of the People's Lobby, a kind of philosophical forerunner to Common Cause. In fact Dewey's activities with the People's Lobby were the only topic in his FBI surveillance file, unlike those of Counts and Rugg, which indicated that they were watched far more closely.

One omission from this book is any school-based chapter focusing on the implementation of Social Reconstruction in a school or district. This is unfortunate but not surprising since most school-based Progressives were more child-centered than Social Reconstructionist. In addition, the most well known school-based Progressives were usually at schools that were very well off and hardly the model for Social Reconstruction. Carleton Washburn at Winnetka, Illinois, springs readily to mind. A committed Social Progressive and an actively involved educator, Washburn worked for one of the wealthiest districts in the United States so he would hardly have been a "poster child" for social change. Jesse Newlon, later a professor at Teachers College, initially gained fame as a child-centered superintendent in Denver, Colorado, a small western city of only 250,000 in the late 1920s that had far fewer social problems than the older cities of the Northeast and Midwest.

There were African American educators concerned with Social Reconstruction and William Watkins describes and discusses their struggles in his chapter. One thing Watkins does not delve into is the Negro organizations that addressed Progressive education. Many of the most prominent educational groups, particularly in the South and the Border states were strictly segregated and African Americans did not hold many prominent positions in the larger national organizations. Watkins addresses the latter, but the parallel, shadow groups which were formed by African American educators, are not examined, mostly because the records of such organizations are very difficult to locate and examine. But this illustrates the limited scope that Progressive education and Social Reconstruction really had. The PEA was mostly composed of wealthy private schools, university-based lab schools, and well-off city or suburban schools. The schools of the poor were sadly missing.

In fact, this illustrates one of the overall problems of Social Reconstruction and that was its limited acceptance. William Stanley, in his chapter addresses this very well. He notes: "The mainstream rejection of Reconstructionism is one part of the more general conservative resistance to progressive political reform efforts in the twentieth century." Cremin notes this also in his aforementioned volume, i.e., the relatively small size of the Progressive Educational Association and the limited number of schools and districts, which seems to reflect active implementation of Progressive education ideas and ideals. Those reflective of Social Reconstruction were even smaller in number. Yet the PEA and Progressive education influence was far larger as evidenced by the President of the PEA, Fred Redefer, being on the cover of Time Magazine in October of 1938. The attention and influence of Progressive education was disproportionately larger than the actual size of the "movement."

Finally, the greatest reason for this volume and the best reason for doing and reflecting upon historical research is to provide better insights and arguments in educational matters today. The parallels to NCLB, the concerns for strict disciplinary, rote learning and the lack of concern for utilizing the school to improve society, among many other reasons, are striking. The lack of awareness of these arguments and differences being addressed 50, 60, or 70 years ago needs to be overcome in order to appreciate the worth and applicability of these Social Reconstructionists and their ideas today. The fear of Communism, then, while not totally vanished, has now morphed into the fear of terrorism, excuses for limiting the freedom of American society and teaching in school, under the guise of protecting freedom. As Stanley notes in his chapter, an additional threat is now to public education, itself, as conservatives seek to "deregulate and privatize public education.[3]

Thus there are compelling reasons to reexamine Social Reconstructionism as an aid to the problems of education today. The chapters in this book are not simply living in the past; rather each chapter contains insights into improving today's schools and society. The volume is an important and timely contribution to education today and in the future.

NOTES

1. Wayne Urban, "Social Reconstructionism and Educational Policy: The Educational Policy Commission, 1936–41."
2. Dewey, John, "Progressive Education and the Science of Education," Reprint of the Address Made at the Eighth Annual Conference of the Progressive Education Association, March 28, 1928. Washington, D.C. Progressive Education Association, 7.
3. William Stanley, "Education for Social Reconstruction in Critical Context."

CHAPTER 1

GEORGE S. COUNTS AND THE ORIGINS OF SOCIAL RECONSTRUCTIONISM

Gerald L. Gutek

It is a challenge to research the origins of Social Reconstructionism, an ideology that argues that American schools and their teachers could, and should, work for deliberate social reform. One might look to certain radical revolutionaries of the American and French Revolutions as early Social Reconstructionists, such as Thomas Paine. Reconstructionist themes are evident in nineteenth-century Utopian Socialism, especially in the ideologies of Robert Owen and Charles Fourier. Envisioning theorists, such as Edward Bellamy, the author of the didactic novel, *Looking Backward*, predicted the dawning of a new society. Historians of American education identify George S. Counts (1889–1974), as a founder of the Social Reconstructionist movement. This essay examines Social Reconstructionism's origins in terms of Counts' call for educators to construct a new society, his formulation of a reconstructionist strategy in the 1930s, his movement away from Social Reconstructionism after World War II, and his continuing significance in American education.

Counts consistently stated that education occurred in a context and was a product and a process of a particular people, living at a particular time and in a particular place. He wrote:

Social Reconstruction: People, Politics, Perspectives, pages 1–26
Copyright © 2006 by Information Age Publishing
All rights of reproduction in any form reserved.

1

The historical record shows that education is always a function of time, place, and circumstance. In its basic philosophy, its social objectives, and its program of instruction, it inevitably reflects in varying proportions, the experiences, the conditions, and the hopes, fears, and aspirations of a particular people or cultural group at a particular point in history . . . Education as a whole is always relative, at least in its fundamental parts, to some concrete and evolving social situation.[1]

To examine Counts' educational theory, we turn to the context in which he made his call for social reconstructionism: the Great Depression, the economic crisis of the 1930s, during which George S. Counts, like the American people, was facing a crisis of historic proportions.

THE CONTEXT AND THE MAN:
THE DEPRESSION AND COUNTS

The era of the Great Depression was no ordinary time in American history, if indeed any period is an ordinary time. When Counts launched his arguments for the schools to build a new society, Herbert Hoover, the great engineer and apostle of individualism and free-enterprise capitalism, was nearing the end of his troubled term as President of the United States. The newly elected President, Franklin D. Roosevelt, had promised the American people a New Deal, but its ideological contours and specific programs were still vague and undefined. In 1932, the year when Counts called upon the schools to create a new social order, unemployment had risen from one million in 1929 to eleven million in a nation whose population was then only 120 million.[2] Strident voices, on both the political Left and Right, demanded a revolutionary transformation of American political and economic systems. Abroad, Mussolini had installed a Fascist regime in Italy; Hitler and his National Socialists, determined to transform Germany into the totalitarian Third Reich, were consolidating power; in the Soviet Union, the Communist dictator, Josef Stalin, ruthlessly purging any opposition, had mobilized the country in the First Five Year Plan. The world prospects for parliamentary democracy were dim and some questioned the survival of capitalism and democratic institutions in the United States.

Who was this professor who dared the schools to build a new social order? A pioneer in the social foundations of education, Counts' scholarship crossed the disciplinary boundaries of history, political science, sociology, and comparative education to focus on educational issues. Earning his PhD in Education at the University of Chicago in 1916, Counts' program director was Charles H. Judd, a leader in the scientific movement in education. Unusual for Education students at that time, Counts took a concentration of sociology courses taught by Albion Small, a founder of modern sociology, and W. I. Thomas, a leader in the new field of social theory.[3] Though his career began in the scientific education camp of Judd and Franklin Bobbitt, who emphasized education's need for objectivity and efficiency, Counts moved steadily toward the interdisciplinary social-foundations approach that used history, philosophy, sociology, anthropology, and economics to examine educational institutions and processes. Later, Judd would criticize his former student's reconstructionist views as an attempt to impose an ideology on schools that threatened their scientific objectivity. As a professor at Columbia University's Teachers College from 1927 until 1955, Counts identified with the progressive wing of the faculty—William H. Kilpatrick, Harold Rugg, and John Childs—who were disciples of John Dewey's pragmatic Instrumentalism.

To establish Counts' position in education, we first examine his publications and activities in the 1930s. In 1929, the year of the Wall Street stock market crash, Counts addressed the topic of secondary education and industrialism in the Inglis lecture. The theme of the role and function of schools in industrial and technological society would resonate throughout his work in the 30s. In *The American Road to Culture* (1930), Counts used history, philosophy, and social theory to examine how public schools had transmitted and shaped American culture.[4] Prophetic of themes he covered in his later writing, he analyzed the American "faith in education," the ideal of "individual success," "the democratic condition," the rise of "mechanical efficiency," and the problem of "philosophic uncertainty." Although recognizing public schools' vital role in transmitting the cultural heritage from generation to generation, Counts found that Americans had an exaggerated faith in the schools' power to solve all kinds of social problems. Though schools were important elements in education, he argued that education was a far broader concept than schooling. In his expansive view of education, Counts anticipated Lawrence Cremin's and Bernard Bailyn's critique of the historiography of education; they saw it as overly celebrationist and too focused on schooling.[5] Throughout the 30s, Counts made the school's functions of cultural transmission and formation key features in his Social Reconstructionist ideology. He reformulated transmission to mean a highly selective process of identifying and passing on the parts of the heritage that were viable for an industrial and technological society. He defined cultural formation as integrating these parts with technology, the new cultural element that had not been integrated successfully into modern society.

Counts delivered two addresses in 1932 that are highly relevant to Social Reconstructionism's origins: "Dare Progressive Education be Progressive?" to the Progressive Education Association (PEA) and "Dare the School Build a New Social Order?" to the National Education Association (NEA).[6]

His NEA address was published as a small book that is frequently quoted in histories of American education and foundations of education textbooks. Although usually portrayed as the fiery educator who eloquently pleaded for schools and their teachers to build a new social order, the events of the 1930s were but one among many, rather than the defining phase in Counts' long life and career.

During the middle years of the Depression, Counts served on the American Historical Association's Commission on the Social Studies. Appointed to the Commission in 1928, Counts became its Director of Research in 1931. As the Commission's Director of Research, he developed a warm, personal, and close-working relationship with Charles A. Beard (1874–1948), the veteran historian who was a leading member of the Commission. Together Beard and Counts articulated a decided reconstructionist agenda for the social sciences and social studies curriculum. Counts' reconstructionism went far beyond the social studies to encompass the entirety of education—philosophy, administration, curriculum, and instruction. Counts' *The Social Foundations of Education,* one in the Commission's monograph series, expanded the social foundations beyond schooling and reached into the various aspects and agencies of culture and society—politics, religion, social class, economics, art, recreation, information, and the media.

From 1931 to 1937, Counts served as senior editor of *The Social Frontier,* a journal that examined the major social, political, and educational issues facing the nation. Advocating Social Reconstructionism, *The Social Frontier* featured articles by John Dewey, Charles A. Beard, Merle Curti, William H. Kilpatrick, Harold Rugg, and other recognized scholars who examined social, political, economic, and educational issues. Counts' *The Prospects of American Democracy* (1938), his most developed argument for the reconstruction of American life and institutions, brought his writings for Social Reconstructionism to a close. As the economic depression eased, he moved to other issues such as the threat of war in Europe and his struggle against the American Communist Party in teacher organizations and unions. During the 1940s, the war years, Counts dealt with the struggle of democracy against totalitarianism, the need for commitment to democratic education, and his growing antagonism to the American Communist Party as an obstacle to liberal reform.[7]

As an international educator, Counts made several extended research trips to the Soviet Union in the early 1930s.[8] In *The Soviet Challenge to America* (1931), Counts commented on his impressions of the Soviet Union, then in the midst of a concerted modernization campaign: the First Five Year Plan. The Plan impressed him as a carefully coordinated effort at total social planning, coordination, and implementation.[9] Despite his later enmity toward Stalinism and the Communist Party, Counts' opponents would use his comments on Soviet education made in the early 30s to label him as pro-Soviet and friendly to Communism. In the 50s, his works on Soviet education grew increasingly hostile to Marxist-Leninism, Stalinism, and to Communism in general.[10] With this background, we can examine Counts' role as an originator of Social Reconstructionism more closely.

CALLING FOR A NEW SOCIAL ORDER

In the early 1930s, Counts issued his highly dramatic call for American educators and schools to take a leading role in bringing about a new society. In his stirring addresses in 1932 to the PEA convention in "Dare Progressive Education Be Progressive?" and to NEA convention in "Dare the School Build a New Social Order?" Counts pointed out the contradictions in American political and economic life:

> Here is a society in which a mastery over the forces of nature, surpassing the wildest dreams of antiquity, is accompanied by extreme material insecurity; in which dire poverty walks hand in hand with the most extravagant living that the world has ever known; ...in which breakfastless children march to school past bankrupt shops laden with rich foods gathered from the ends of the earth; in which strong men by the million walk the streets in a futile search for employment, and with the exhaustion of hope, enter the ranks of beaten men.[11]

In these addresses, Counts urged America's educators to unite with progressive forces to build a reconstructed, more democratic, and egalitarian society. He urged teachers to "come to grips with the problem of creating a tradition that has roots in American soil, is in harmony with the spirit of the age, recognizes the facts of industrialism, appeals to the most profound impulses of our people, and takes into account the emergence of a world society."[12] He warned progressive educators that they could not ignore America's deepening economic crisis by escaping into a romantic child-centered sentimentality. He told his larger NEA audience that American educators could no longer plead neutrality on the issues facing the Republic but had to take a stand to work for a more just and equitable "new social order."

Counts' call to build a new society came from within the intellectual framework of American pragmatist philosophy, primarily from John Dewey's Instrumentalism. The concept of the reconstruction of personal and social experience permeated the philosophy of Dewey, the country's leading philosopher of education. For Dewey, socially intelligent persons continually reconstructed their ideas and values as they used their previous experiences as instruments to solve new problems. Intelligent societies, like intelligent persons, too, reconstructed their social, political, and economic experience when they faced problems. As individuals joined in communities and used open-ended experimental and democratic processes to solve their shared and mutual problems, they were on the way to creating the "great society," the great democratic community. Dewey's books *Individualism Old and New* and *Liberalism and Social Action,* addressed issues similar to those raised by Counts and other reconstructionist educators.[13] Counts and his progressive colleagues at Teachers College were closely allied with Dewey who argued for a reconstructed concept of individualism that recognized the corporate realities of a technological society. Like Counts, Dewey sought to reconstruct the concept of Liberalism away from its laissez-faire origins to a revitalized process of thinking and action that could solve the problems of an increasingly corporate industrial and technological society.

In 1932, when Counts asked "Dare the School Build a New Social Order?" the United States, as well as the world, faced an ever deepening economic crisis. Counts began to answer his own question by exploring the possibility that Americans could reconstruct their collective social, economic, political, and educational experience to solve the immediate problem of the Great Depression and in so doing create a more just, equitable, and truly democratic "New Social Order," the Great Society. This reconstruction, Counts argued, needed to be based on two necessary conditions: one, affirmation of the democratic values embedded in the American past, and two, recognition of the emergence of an industrial-technological society.[14] To analyze Counts' efforts, we examine his conceptions of the American historical experience and of education in the light of that experience.

COUNTS' INTERPRETATION OF AMERICAN HISTORY

Counts sought to construct an educational philosophy to provide educators with the theoretical foundations needed to reconstruct society. While he called his version of Social Reconstructionism a "civilizational philosophy" of education, it resembles an ideology more than a philosophy. Although concerned with moral and ethical considerations, Counts, unlike a philosopher, did not deal with broad metaphysical and epistemological issues. Instead, he developed a highly contextual ideology with its own heroes and heroines, version of the past, and program for deliberate social change. This educational ideology was to be an instrument to mobilize the nation's progressive and liberal educators to join like-minded allies in the struggle against vested special economic interests and the forces of conservatism and reaction. Moving the debate from academe to the political platform,

Counts urged teachers were to be partisan, not neutral, and committed, not aloof, to the momentous issues facing the nation and, indeed, the world.

In articulating his Social Reconstructionist ideology, Counts collaborated with Charles A. Beard as members of the American Historical Society's Commission on the Social Studies in the Schools. A leading revisionist historian, Beard's controversial book, *An Economic Interpretation of the Constitution of the United States,* examined the role of economic forces in shaping history and conditioning social and political control and change. The elder Beard, whom Counts affectionately called "Uncle Charley," acted as mentor to the younger Counts. In constructing an historical interpretation aligned with Social Reconstructionism, Counts was informed by Beard's historiography.

Together, Counts and Beard sought to move the Commission in a Social Reconstructionist direction. Beard, the nationally recognized historian, and Counts, growing in repute as an educator, believed their ideas would bring highly significant transformative reform to American society. Beard helped to contextualize Counts' reconstructionist principles into a theoretical framework that grew out of American rather than European models.

An historical relativist, Beard repudiated the idea that universal laws directed history's course. Rather, he believed that social, political, and especially economic forces of a particular period influenced or conditioned history. For Beard, writing objective history was an impossibility, as was teaching and studying an ideologically neutral history. The past is written and interpreted in terms of the present's problems and the future's possibilities.[15] Counts easily translated Beard's historiography into an educational principle: education, especially when organized as schooling, is an expression of a particular culture and society living at a given period of history in a specific geographical setting.

In Beard's economic interpretation of history, political institutions are largely shaped by the economic interests of those who established and controlled them.[16] Influenced by Beard, Counts saw the economy as a largely conditioning, but not necessarily determining, force. Here Beard's and Counts' orientation departed from Marx's insistence that all history, politics, and society are economically determined and subject to the universal law of dialectical materialism.[17] Referring to economic forces as a conditioning, rather than determining, process, Counts stated:

> It is contended here that man in history is neither wholly bound nor wholly free, that his life, though always conditioned, is never fated ... within the bounds of the possible human preference operates.[18]

Like Beard, Counts rejected the philosophy that history can be studied objectively or that it is a universal movement in time that operates independently of context. He was not sympathetic to the Hegelian concept of history as the unfolding of the great universal mind over time. Neither did Counts accept Marx's idea of the predestined inevitable dialectical clash of socio-economic classes for control of the means and modes of production. History, for Counts, was the story of a people working and struggling in the context of their lives, living in particular situations of time and place.

Counts' outlook on education was as relativistic as his history. Education was not, as Robert Hutchins and Mortimer Adler claimed, about eternal universal truths. It was always time and space specific to a people in their cultural and social contexts. To reconstruct a society implied that there were social, cultural, economic political, and educational elements embedded in a people's collective experience and memory that could be reshaped, reformulated, and indeed, reconstructed. To identify these elements, Counts constructed an interpretation of American history. Not neutral, dispassionate, nor academic, his history, written from an ideological point-of-view, constructed a perspective on the past committed to deliberately changing society. Rejecting his history as ideologically biased, Counts' critics contended his selection of evidence and conclusions were a politically motivated presentist argument rather than an historically accurate portrayal of the past.

In dialectical fashion, Counts interpreted American history as falling into two conflicting traditions or strands—one Jeffersonian and the other Hamiltonian. The Jeffersonian tradition, which Counts endorsed, provided the democratic and egalitarian elements that needed to be reconstructed into the new social order. The Hamiltonian strand, named for Alexander Hamilton, a Federalist leader in the early Republic, represented rule by an economic elite and its special interests. This dichotomy of two competing traditions in the American historical experience was neither unique nor original to Counts. What Counts did, however, was to reinterpret, or reconstruct, the dichotomy of conflicting traditions into an interpretation that fit the Depression-era of the 1930s and could be used as ideological ammunition in the struggle for directed social change.

For Counts, the Jeffersonian tradition was the history of the freehold farmers of the colonial and early national periods who constructed the foundations for a political democracy of one man, one vote and the economic foundations that produced rough frontier equality. The Jeffersonian tradition put human rights and liberties ahead of the sanctity of private property and rule by special interests. In the era of the Great Depression, these Jeffersonian elements—democracy and equality—needed to be reasserted against the special economic interests, big business titans and their conservative political allies.[19]

These formative tensions in the American historical experience, which began with Jefferson and Hamilton, continued throughout the nineteenth century, resurfacing in the conflicts between Jacksonian Democrats and their Whig opponents about the nation's destiny, political structures, and economic infrastructure. Jacksonianism carried forward the Jeffersonian legacy as the freehold farm ideal was transformed into the frontier homesteads that moved ever westward toward the Pacific Ocean. Promoting political equality, the Jacksonian Democrats reduced or abolished property requirements for voting in many states. Hamilitonianism, however, also continued to compete for national dominance in the Whig Party that pushed internal improvements, tariffs, and a national bank geared to the vested financial interests.

Then in the post-Civil War period, Hamiltonianism resurfaced as a powerful alliance of robber barons, the industrialists who monopolized the new industrial wealth, and their politically conservative allies in the Republican Party. The industrialist-conservative alliance of special interests ruthlessly exploited natural resources, oppressed the industrial and agricultural working classes, and created, often with government subsidies, huge corporate monopolies that concentrated wealth and power in the hands of an elite. The counter force represented by the Jeffersonian-Jacksonian tradition was on the defensive in the nineteenth century with the forces of resistance splintered. There was a moderate opposition in the Democratic Party but the main line of resistance came from new and more radical forces. The Farmers' Alliances and the Populists, in the rural South and plains and western states, called for the federal government to break up the trusts and monopolies, regulate railroads, and for the states to create processes for a more direct political democracy. Combatants in the struggle for the new social order were those liberal, progressive, and left-of-center groups struggling against vested economic interests. Counts, himself, was a founder of the American Labor Party and then of the Liberal Party, two significant third parties in New York state.[20] He advised teachers to form unions and join with organized labor in the struggle. Here, Counts, too, was an activist in the American Federation of Teachers, serving as its President from 1939 to 1942.

At this point in the discussion, socialism, as a political ideology, needs interpretation in terms of Social Reconstructionism's origins. While the American Socialist Party of the late nineteenth and early twentieth century represented a strong anti-Hamiltonian view, was it in the Jeffersonian–Jacksonian tradition? The American Socialist Party of Eugene V. Debs and later of Norman Thomas was in the tradition of democratic non-Marxist socialism. However, a powerful version of socialism that appealed to leftist intellectuals, especially during the 1930s, came from Karl Marx's scientific socialism or dialectical materialism. The tension between democratic socialism and Marxism would be a point of dissonance in the ideology that Counts was shaping and in the development of Social Reconstructionism, itself. Counts was often attacked as a Marxist and a Communist sympathizer by conservative opponents such as the Hearst press. In his editorials on class conflict and the rise of economic elites in *The Social Frontier*, Counts came close to a socialist analysis. However, Counts, like John Dewey, by the late 30s was strongly anti-Marxist and anti-Communist. He led the fight against Communists in the American Federation of Teachers. He and John Childs predicted that the American Communist Party and its support by the Central Committee of the Communist Party of the USSR would be a serious obstacle to peace in the post-World War II era.[21] Counts was definitely left of the political center. Had he been in the United Kingdom, he would most likely have been a Fabian socialist and a Labour Party supporter. Late in his career, when asked if he was a Marxist, he said, "No, I'm a Methodist." Efforts to position Counts and the origins of Social Reconstructionism in the Marxist ideological terrain need careful analysis and dissection, especially today when the educational foundations are heavily influenced by Neo-Marxism and Critical Theory.

In the early twentieth century, the Progressive movement revitalized the forces of the Jeffersonian-Jacksonian tradition. Progressives sought to identify and investigate corruption and malfeasance in government and society, and eliminate them so that the American system functioned according to democratic principles and processes. Progressivism in politics as well as in education called for incremental rather than transformative social change. Counts' call for a larger federal government role was more in the spirit of the progressive Herbert Croly's *The Promise of American Life* than the limited role Jeffersonians endorsed.

CULTURAL CRISIS

Counts identified Jeffersonian democracy as the viable element in the American heritage that could be transferred to, and maintained in, the new social order. Next, his reconstructionist strategy involved identifying and confronting the problem: in Dewey's terms, the "deviant particular," the new problem in need of resolution. Counts diagnosed the economic catastrophe of the Great Depression as a symptom rather than the underlying cause of the profound and pervasive cultural malaise. The crisis was caused by the inability to construct social and political institutions as well as ethical values that integrated democracy and technology.

Counts, in the late 1920s and 30s, commented frequently on the great crisis of culture, indeed, of civilization. Western civilization, he wrote, was in a profound transition from an agricultural to an industrial, urban, and technological society.[22] Counts relied on Ogburn's thesis that human intellectual and moral development lagged behind material and technological innovation. According to Ogburn:

> The inventions occur first, and only later do the institutions of society change in conformity. Material culture and social institutions are not independent of each other, for civilization is highly articulated like a piece of machinery, so that a change in one part tends to effect changes in others parts—but only after a delay. Men with habits and society with patterns of action are slow to change to meet the new material conditions.[23]

Counts believed a deep cultural chasm existed between technological change and social adaptation. A cultural lag developed when technological innovation outdistanced social organization, economic distribution, and moral consciousness. For Counts, a principal purpose of education was to narrow the breach between technology and social control. Narrowing the gap was insufficient, however. Human beings needed to make a bold leap in their thinking in order to strategize deliberate plans for directing technological change toward societal improvement—to construct a new social order based on equality and justice. According to Counts:

> The growth of science and technology has carried us into a new age where ignorance must be replaced by knowledge, competition by cooperation, trust in providence by careful planning, and private capitalism by some form of socialized economy.[24]

Technological change was to be welcomed, not feared. Like Reconstructionists such as Harold Rugg, Counts had faith in technology's power to improve the human condition. However, technology needed to be integrated with the viable elements in America's democratic heritage. After all, the totalitarians were adept at using technology as an instrument to enslave human beings, not liberate them. Like other Instrumentalists, Counts was committed to the scientific method, broadly conceived, as a method of intelligence and of education. Defining technology as the application of science to material culture, Counts closely identified technology with the scientific method. He saw technology as an instrument that was operationally functional, resourceful, dynamic, efficient, practical, purposeful, precise, and orderly.[25] To develop an attitude conducive to social planning, Counts wanted the study of technology infused throughout the school curriculum.

INDIVIDUALISM VERSUS COLLECTIVISM

Counts identified the powerful residue of individualism, embedded within the American social psyche, as a serious obstacle to progressive social and educational reform. The American ideal of the individual, part history and part myth, conjured a view of the person who alone conquered life's obstacles.[26] The popular version of American individualism recounted the epic saga of intrepid explorers and trappers who journeyed westward and charted the path to the Pacific; it told of rugged homesteaders who established their individual farms and then built towns and schools in the western territories. It was the story of enterprising inventors, like Thomas Edison and the Wright brothers, who in backyard workshops and laboratories developed the modern age's practical and applied technology. It was the story of innovative entrepreneurs who developed businesses and by their own initiative made fortunes. For Counts, the standard story of American individualism, the official version retold in many textbooks, was more myth than history. However, its grip on the American psyche was a key obstacle to creating the cooperative mentality needed in a technological society. Individualism—used by vested economic interests as an ideological smoke screen—blocked needed reform, regulation, and reconstruction.

Counts called for a new concept to replace the obsolete but nonetheless powerfully obstructive concept of individualism: "democratic collectivism." In a collective democracy, the people, through representative institutions, would develop plans to redirect the industrial-technological economy from selfish special interests to common needs. Progressive forces in the United States needed to join together and form a great coalition in order to create a collective and democratic society. Educators would lead in mobilizing this popular coalition for change. In schools, they would prepare the upcoming generation to understand technological change and the need for social planning. They would educate them in the methods of implementing the new society. Counts eloquently argued that:

> The familiar doctrine that the common good is best served if each individual is encouraged to pursue and safeguard his own interests will have to be rooted out of our mores and institutional life. This means that private capitalism with its dependence on the profit motive, the principle of competition, and private ownership of natural resources and the tools of production will either have to be abandoned altogether or so radically transformed as to lose its identity. In its place must come a highly socialized, co-ordinated, and planned economy devoted to the task of making science and the machine serve the masses of the people.[27]

Counts argued that the United States, along with western civilization had entered the age of collectivism. The challenge for Americans was to ensure that the collective future would be democratic rather than totalitarian, as in Italy, Germany, and the Soviet Union.[28] Counts' embracing of the concept of democratic collectivism placed Social Reconstructionism, at its very origin, in a highly and perhaps unnecessarily controversial situation. Counts' use of the term "democratic collectivism" was seized upon by conservative opponents to label him and his associates as reds, fellow travelers, Marxists, and Communists. These conservative critics connected Counts' endorsement of social planning and democratic collectivism with the Soviet Union's First Five Year Plan. In the early 1930s, Counts had found much to admire in the Soviet process of total planning in the First Five Year Plan. He contrasted the Soviet approach in which planning integrated political, economic, social, cultural, and educational aspects with the lack of, and resistance to, centralized planning in the United States. These criticisms against collectivism did not disappear but were used as allegations against Social Reconstructionism in later years when Counts was no longer pursuing a reconstructionist agenda.

While the conservative response was predictable, democratic collectivism also generated a negative reaction from some liberals and progressives. While sympathetic to Counts' general political and educational orientation, these liberals opposed his vision of a collective society as suggesting a closed rather than open-ended view of society. Child-centered as well some more experimentally inclined progressive educators argued that the agenda for democratic collectivism was a form of indoctrination that impeded experimental inquiry. Counts, himself, later agreed that the choice of the term had been unfortunate.[29]

DEVELOPING A STRATEGY TO RECONSTRUCT THE HERITAGE IN A TIME OF CRISIS

At this point, Counts had developed two key elements for the reconstruction of American society: one, a Jeffersonian interpretation of American history; two, an identification of the problem facing the United States—the larger cultural crisis and the more present economic crisis of the Great Depression—as the inability to integrate technology into social institutions and values. Similar to Dewey's "Complete Act of Thought," or problem solving according to the scientific method, Counts had defined the problem—the cultural crisis—and was engaged in how the American experience might be reconstructed to build the new social order.

By instrumentally using the American heritage, Counts had examined and identified two conflicting traditions—the Jeffersonian and the

Hamiltonian. The use of the heritage to reconstruct society required a deliberate act of selection. One of the two traditions, the Jeffersonian, was viable in resolving the cultural crisis. The Hamiltonian tradition needed to be rejected, exposed, and discarded because it contained elements that blocked needed reconstruction.

In identifying the Jeffersonian heritage as the viable historical tradition to be used in reconstructing American society, Counts had to reinterpret or reconstruct this tradition so that it incorporated a larger role for central planning by the federal government. Ironically, this larger central role of the government was better fitted to the Hamiltonian tradition. What Counts had to do was unite the egalitarian aspect of Jeffersonianism with his vision of governmental and educational institutions that would engage in the social planning and social engineering needed to create the cooperative commonwealth, the collective democracy.

What needed to be done to bring about the needed reconstruction of society? An answer to this question comes from Counts and Beard's recommendations for social science education, presented to the AHA Commission. For them, the social studies were not neutral bodies of knowledge but were to be deliberately selected, organized, and presented on the basis of a reconstructionist frame of reference.

Beard's *A Charter for the Social Sciences in the Schools* (1932) argued that history and the other social sciences, functioning in a context of time and place, could never be completely objective, nor even neutral, but were "organized around some central philosophy."[30] Instruction in the social sciences, like education itself, could, and should, not be isolated from social reality, but needed to be based on the dynamics of social change.[31] All education imposes a particular point of view, a social, political, and economic orientation. Organized education or schooling, especially the social sciences, needed to be based on the following realities about American society: one, it is gripped by profound change; two, it is an industrial society, resting on science and technology; three, rational planning and intelligent cooperation will grow in all social sectors, particularly in industry and government; four, the vitality of its elected and representative form of government requires public discussion, debate, and criticism informed by the social sciences.[32]

A key argument in Beard's *Charter* was that schools, like other social institutions, lag behind technologically generated change. A realistic social education needed to prepare people for life in a constantly changing society and to provide them with the rationality and methodology to plan and order that change in a democratic direction. In terms of national policy, it meant that American society and government had to throw off the residues of laissez-faire economic individualism and move rapidly to become a democratic and collective planning society. Engaged in social engineering, the progressive social science educator would be open to change and to choice, but always from a frame of reference.[33]

While Counts' dramatically charged ideological polemic, *Dare the School Build a New Social Order?* brought Social Reconstruction to the center of the educational stage, his more fully developed *The Social Foundations of Education* (1934) suggested implementation strategies. In reviewing the major changes that were transforming the United States from an agrarian and rural society into an urban, industrial, and technological one, Counts developed an early version of modernization theory, but it followed democratic and collectivist rather than capitalist lines. The emergent society, he envisioned, was to be interdependent, planned, highly integrated, and coordinated. The question was: will this emergent society be democratic or will it take some other political form, perhaps a totalitarian one?[34]

Counts took a very broad view of the social foundations of education, relating them to informal, nonformal, and formal agencies. The social foundations of education, he advised, were found in the family, the economy, media and modes of communication, health, recreation, science, the arts, law and justice, government, and in international relations as well as in education and schooling. According to Counts, social science education should: one, provide a history of ordinary people's lives, the arts of peace, and cultural development; two, trace the development of democratic institutions and processes; three, examine the development of industrial civilization and the emergence of an integrated technological economy and society; four, identify and describe the major contradictions in contemporary society; five, introduce the important proposals, programs, and philosophies that relate to social issues and provide the tools to make critical appraisals and intelligent choices in the light of democratic ideals.[35]

Counts' panoramic view of education was organized as a continuum that ranged from informal educational agencies to formal educational institutions. The media, he argued, should be a cultural instrument using communication for popular enlightenment rather than being subservient to special interests and crass consumerism. Art should not be relegated to galleries or museums but should heighten the aesthetic possibilities of industrial and urban society.[36]

The AHA Commission's *Conclusions and Recommendations* was to be written by a committee consisting of Beard, Counts, and August Krey, the Chairman of the Commission. Krey, who was ill, attended some meetings, but kept largely out of the discussions. In effect, Counts and Beard wrote *Conclusions.* Upholding the frame of reference that guided their work on the Commission, the two collaborators concluded that: one, the social sciences should provide "accurate knowledge" and "informed insight" about the human being and society; two, social creativity and planning cannot rest "on empiricism alone" but requires commitment to "ethical and aesthetic considerations;" three, the social sciences should affirm the ethical and aesthetic values of individual worth while recognizing the reality that the era of laissez-faire individualism had ended and that an interdependent and collectivist society and world were at hand; four, the social sciences should affirm commitment to democratic processes, improving living standards for all people, and creating a sense of toleration at home and abroad.[37]

Conclusions and Recommendations was strong on ideology but rather open-ended on specifics of social studies content and methods. Its authors recommended that social studies content be derived from physical and cultural geography, economics, sociology, political science, and history; that it should include classics and important contemporary works in these fields, and that teaching methods should emulate the great educators of the past and present.[38]

When *Conclusions and Recommendations* was put to the Commission for its endorsement, two key concepts generated controversy: indoctrination and collectivism. Challenging the term "collectivism," Charles Merriam saw it as unnecessarily provocative and ideologically biased.[39] When pressed on the meaning of collectivism, Beard defined it as "cooperative control with state facilitation or compulsion."[40] Objecting to the whole concept of indoctrination, Edmund Day said the report did not adequately address the major issues about "tolerance of conflicting social studies," "maintenance of freedom of speech," and the "freedom of teaching controversial social matters."[41] Counts rebutted, arguing that an "educational program" always involves "imposition on the mind" of the person being educated. Counts stated that "if you set up a school you set up a system of social relationships and transmit certain values. A certain outlook on life. There is a system of values in anything that is done."[42] Rejecting any idea that education could be totally objective, Counts argued:

> Any concrete school program will contribute to the struggle for survival that is ever going on among institutions, ideas, and values; it cannot remain neutral in any firm and complete sense. Partiality is the very essence of education, as it is of life itself. The difference between education and life is that, in the former, partiality is presumably reasoned and enlightened.[43]

The Commission's *Conclusions and Recommendations* provoked heated debate in the popular press and academic journals. Commentaries ranged from ringing endorsements that acclaimed it a major contribution of profound importance to critics who panned it as a polemic of evangelical ideological proselytizing. Essentialists in education said that it offered social studies teachers little in terms of specific objectives, methods, and materials.

Conservatives decried its use of terms such as "the masses," "collectivism," and a "new social order."

Although a progressive and experimentalist, Boyd Bode condemned *Conclusions and Recommendations* as an undemocratic manifesto to indoctrinate youth in a particular set of predetermined conclusions for social planning and the redistribution of wealth.[44] Charles H. Judd, Counts' former dissertation director at the University of Chicago, wrote:

> Inspired by the idea that schools must contribute in some way to social reform, certain radicals have gone so far as to advocate that teachers assume the role of leaders and direct the reorganization of the economic and political systems. These extremists have misconceived the function of the schools. The duty of education is to prepare people to make intelligent judgments on social problems."[45]

In 1934, Counts and other like-minded educators such as William H. Kilpatrick and Harold Rugg, launched *The Social Frontier*, a journal promoting Social Reconstructionism and social, political, economic, and educational criticism. Counts served as senior editor for its first three years, from 1934 to 1937. He affirmed that the *Social Frontier* would be committed to the "raising of American life from the level of the profit system, individualism, and vested class interests to the plane of social motivation, collectivism, and classlessness."[46] *The Social Frontier* restated the nature of the crisis facing the American people and continued to analyze the situation from a variety of theoretical perspectives. Counts' editorials in *The Social Frontier* focused attention on "class struggle" and cited gross inequalities as exacerbating class division. He urged teachers to align with the forces of labor and to use the school to improve economic conditions. While the journal charted a new path, it generated more theory than strategy for action. Social Reconstructionism, in the hands of Counts and his associates, Harold Rugg and William H. Kilpatrick, remained a theory that might reshape how people, especially teachers, thought about education. It enlarged the educational challenge by giving it a broader social and political dimension, but left the implementation stage largely underdeveloped.

DID COUNTS REMAIN A SOCIAL RECONSTRUCTIONIST?

Though influential in founding reconstructionist educational theory, Counts moved to other issues after the 1930s. Like his ideology of education, he was a highly contextual educator who moved with the times and addressed the changing issues of American education. By the late 30s, he had become strongly anti-Communist. In 1939, the European popular front movements in which socialists and liberals had cooperated with Communists against fascism collapsed after the Ribbentropp-Molotov nonaggression accords between Nazi Germany and the Soviet Union. Left-of-center liberals, such as Counts, already had grown increasingly disenchanted by Stalin's purge trials in the Soviet Union. Counts was fighting a continuing battle against Communist factions in the American Federation of Teachers. Counts, who once believed Soviet planning might be instructive for other countries, now saw the Soviet experiment as an unrelenting challenge to liberal democracy. He warned that those who looked to the Soviet Union for guidance would be severely disillusioned.[47] By the late 30s, his view of the Soviet Union changed as he recognized Stalinism's totalitarian nature and condemned the Soviet system as "revolutionary Machiavellianism." In 1939, Counts, running on an anti-Communist platform, was elected President of the American Federation of Teachers (AFT). During his three-year term, he took the offensive against Communist Party domination of some AFT locals. Under his leadership, the AFT amended its Constitution to eliminate members who belonged to totalitarian parties, be they fascist or Communist.[48] Though known as a radical and condemned as a "Communist " and "red" by the Hearst press, Counts had moved from a sympathetic view of the Soviet Union in the early 30s to a decidedly anti-Communist stance by the decade's end.

During World War II, Counts was preoccupied with the war effort and with affirming democracy and democratic education against Fascism and Nazism. Looking to the postwar world, he warned that unless the Soviet Union dropped its support of the American Communist Party that relations would be jeopardized between the USSR and the United States. He was concerned with postwar reconstruction and was a member of the educational mission in 1946 that advised General MacArthur on the democratic reconstruction of education in Japan.

In his book, *Education and the Promise of America,* published a year after World War II's end, the consistently left-of-center Counts moved away from reconstructionism to liberalism. He continued to call for an inspiring interpretation of American history that explored the promises of an industrial and technological society.[49] Reiterating his liberal interpretation of American education in *Education and American Civilization,* Counts called for the establishment of a stable economy, with full employment and full economic production, as fundamental to maintaining democratic institutions. In *Education and the Foundations of Human Freedom,* Counts contrasted the democratic ethic and democratic education with all species of totalitarianism, including Communism. Although he was concerned about the rise of the military-industrial complex, attacks on capitalism were either muted or absent from his postwar writing. His postwar works enlarged the context of American education by emphasizing it as part of Western Civilization and as being shaped by the Hebraic-Christian tradition and cosmopolitan humanism. Although he rejected the idea of a market economy based on forces of supply and demand and believed there was a continued need for national planning, the concept of "democratic collectivism" disappeared from his writing.

A RETROSPECTIVE CONCLUSION

The general outline of Counts' reconstructionism was that: one, the United States, as well as other industrially developed nations, had experienced a great transition from an agrarian economy and society to one that was industrial and in the process of becoming highly interdependent and technological; two, while the means and modes of production were industrial and technological, social-cultural beliefs and values had lagged behind in this great transformation; this lag had created a serious maladjustment between the material development of an industrial-technological order and the social-political institutions and the ethics that governed them; three, the most serious residue from the agrarian past was the concept of "rugged individualism," which in a technological era meant an avaricious and unregulated capitalism; the Great Depression and the rise of Fascist, Nazi, and Communist regimes were symptomatic of this unresolved cultural lag or maladjustment; four, it was imperative that the cultural lag be reduced and that the emergent industrial-technological society be reconstructed according to a humane cultural ethics based on collective intelligence and sociability; five, the new social order would need to be constructed along lines that were democratic, egalitarian, centralized, and planned; education had a central role and purpose in helping to build the new social order; six, education, including the social studies, could be neither neutral, nor objective, in facing the challenge of building a new social order; teachers needed to take a stand and, Counts asserted, this commitment should be for the new technological society framed in democratic, popular, egalitarian interests.

Perhaps, the following statement from the AHA Commission on the Social Studies was prophetic of Count's own work:

Education always has a geographical and cultural location; it is therefore specific, local, and dynamic, not general, universal, and unchanging; it is a function of a particular society at a particular time and place in history; it is rooted in some actual culture and expresses the philosophy and recognized needs of that culture.[50]

If the statement is correct, Counts' own version of social reconstruc-tionism was contextual and bound by its time and place. Certain aspects that related to the tensions of the 1930s, especially the language used by contending ideologists during the Great Depression, are marked by these contextual limitations.

When lifted from the context in which it was developed, Counts' call for educators to build a new social order still has a relevance and meaning for educators. Organized education, especially schooling, is always based on a frame of reference that is rooted in the cultural heritage. Curriculum and instruction always require selection. Counts' mode of social and educa-tional analysis remains a useful method for educational policy makers. His method involved an analysis of the heritage to identify the elements that were viable and those that were an anachronism in the contemporary situ-ation. The selective prisms of viability and obsolesce were changeable and relative to the social situation. Then, came an identification of the prob-lematic conditions, the deviant particulars that were impeding the progress of the society. When these were identified, the viable elements of the heritage could be used instrumentally to resolve the problematic con-ditions and reconstruct the society. What was key for Counts was democ-racy. The reconstructed society, for him, had to be democratic. Of course, the nature, content, and method of democracy and democratic processes also were subject to redefinition. For Counts, education was always a matter of relating the cultural heritage to the vital trends and challenges a civiliza-tion faces. However, still unanswered is the question of indoctrination and imposition. At what point does the educator's act of selection become indoctrination of students?

An important concept used by Counts was that of the "educational statesman." His vision of the statesman included a knowledge and interpre-tation of the past as well as a policy for the future. His vision remains appropriate to the educational foundations as it embraces educational-pol-icy analysis and policy making.

How would Counts' recommendations fare at the hands of today's Post-modernist and Critical Theorist educators. There is a similarity in Counts' cultural relativism with the Postmodernist view that contending groups and classes construct the record of past. In his arguments that history is contingent on those who interpret it and that their interpretation, in turn, reflects time, place, and circumstance, Counts was making the case that history is a construction. His dialectical examination of American history as the contestation of two competing interpretations, the Jeffersonian and the Hamiltonian, indicated the efforts of competing classes to control his-tory as a means of power. He also proceeded to deconstruct the Hamilto-nian version of history by indicating how powerful, vested interests, particularly in the exaltation of individualism, blocked needed reforms.

Critical Theorists would find much to applaud in Counts' contextual view of education and its relationship to socioeconomic issues. In his research and writing, Counts, like the contemporary Critical Theorists, did not confine himself to a particular academic discipline. He frequently crossed the boundaries of academic disciplines and used those, especially in history and the social sciences, that he felt were relevant to his work. Critical Theorists would likely praise his concern for the nation's unemployed and under-represented masses. They would agree that education should be a transformative force for popular change. Indeed, Paulo Freire's argument that all education is ideologically based would be retrospectively reaffirmed in the frame of reference developed by Counts. Both Postmodernists and Critical Theorists would agree with Counts that education is never completely objective, unbiased, and neutral. They would commend his call for teachers to be committed to an interpretation of history and to an analysis of social, economic, and political issues that would empower dispossessed and downtrodden groups and classes.

However, Postmodernists and Critical Theorists would find Counts overly impressed and overly committed to technology, which he saw as emanating from Enlightenment theory. Indeed, he was developing the concept of technology as a metanarrative—a transforming force that was working throughout the world. Counts was clearly preaching the merits of modernity and modernization. It was not modernity that he feared but rather that the engines of modernization would be controlled by special interests. For Postmodernists, modernity itself is a historical construct that originated in and still sustains oppressive power relationships.

How would Counts fare at the hands of contemporary neo-Conservative and neo-Essentialist educators? Neo-Essentialists would find his views as objectionable today as did their predecessors in the 1930s. They might argue that Counts' enlarged view of the role of the schools weakened the concept that the school is primarily an academic institution for the transmission of knowledge, as organized in skills and subjects, across generations. Further, they might contend that Counts blurred the distinction between education, in the general sense, and schooling, in the specific sense. While schooling might be contextual, education itself is trans-contextual and is a universal process of human growth and development. Neo-Essentialists would contend that Counts was foisting an ideology on the students and indoctrinating them in a particular version of history and the social studies. He was closing, rather than opening, the doors of critical debate. Further, they would believe that his cultural and ethical relativism would lead to the erosion of ethical and moral standards. For Diane Ravitch, Counts' ideological platform was another of the "failed reforms" of the progressives and reconstructionists that attempted to divert schools from their academic purpose.[51]

Perhaps George Counts' educational message rises and falls with his own words: education is always conditioned by the time and circumstances in which it occurs.

NOTES

' 1.   George S. Counts, *The Social Foundations of Education* (New York: Charles Scribner's Sons, 1934), 1.

2.   Basil Rauch, *The History of the New Deal, 1933–1938* (New York: Creative Age Press, 1944), 8.

3.   George S. Counts, "A Humble Autobiography," in *Leaders in American Education: The Seventieth Yearbook of the National Society for the Study of Education,* ed. Robert J. Havighurst (Chicago: University of Chicago Press, 1971), 151–174. Also see, Gerald L. Gutek, "George Sylvester Counts (1889–1974): A Biographical Memoir," *Proceedings of the National Academy of Education 3* (Stanford: National Academy of Education, 1976), 333–353.

4.   George S. Counts, *The American Road to Culture: A Social Interpretation of Education in the United States* (New York: John Day Co., 1930).

5.   Lawrence A. Cremin, *The Wonderful World of Ellwood Patterson Cubberley* (New York: Teachers College Press, 1965); and Bernard Bailyn, *Education in the Forming of American Society* (New York: W.W. Norton, 1972).

6.   George S. Counts, "Dare Progressive Education Be Progressive?" *Progressive Education* 9 (April 1932): 257—63; and Counts, *Dare the School Build a New Social Order?* (New York: John Day Co., 1932).

7.   For example, see George S. Counts, "Education for War and Peace," *American Teacher 26* (February 1942): 31; and Counts and John Childs, *America, Russia, and the Communist Party in the Postwar World* (New York: John Day Co., 1943).

8.   George S. Counts, *A Ford Crosses Russia* (Boston: The Stratford Co., 1930).

9.   George S. Counts, *The Soviet Challenge to America* (New York: John Day Co., 1931). Also see, Counts, "Education and the Five-Year Plan of Soviet Russia," in *Education and Economics*, ed. Harold F. Clark (New York: Teachers College Press, 1931), 39–46.

10.   For example, see George S. Counts and Nucia P. Lodge, *The Country of the Blind: The Soviet System of Mind Control* (Boston: Houghton-Mifflin Co., 1949); and Counts, *The Challenge of Soviet Education* (New York: McGraw-Hill, 1957).

11.   George S. Counts, "Dare Progressive Education Be Progressive?" *Progressive Education* 9 (April 1932): 259–260.

12.   George S. Counts, *Dare the School Build a New Social Order?* (Carbondale, IL: Southern Illinois University Press, 1978), 36.

13.   John Dewey, *Individualism Old and New* (1929). Reprint, New York: Capricorn, 1962; and Dewey *Liberalism and Social Action* (1935). Reprint, New York: Capricorn, 1963.

14. George S. Counts, *The Prospects of American Democracy* (New York: John Day Co., 1938), 318.

15. Lawrence J. Dennis, *George S. Counts and Charles A. Beard: Collaborators for Change* (Albany, NY: State University of New York Press, 1989), 19.

16. Charles A. Beard, *An Economic Interpretation of the Constitution of the United States* (New York: Macmillan Co., 1913.

17. Dennis, *George S. Counts and Charles A. Beard*, 2–4.

18. George S. Counts, *The Prospects of American Democracy*, 76.

19. Committee of the Progressive Education Association on Social and Economic Problems, *A Call to the Teachers of the Nation* (New York: John Day Co., 1933), 12.

20. Counts was chairman of the American Labor Party, from 1942 to 1944 and a founder of the Liberal Party, serving as its chairman from 1954 to 1959 and as its candidate for U.S. Senator in New York in 1952.

21. George S. Counts and John Childs, *America, Russia, and the Communist Party in the Postwar World* (New York: John Day Co., 1943).

22. George S. Counts, *Secondary Education and Industrialism* (Cambridge, MA: Harvard University Press, 1929), 9.

23. William F. Ogburn, *Recent Social Trends in the United States* (New York: McGraw-Hill Book Co., 1933), 166.

24. Counts, *Dare the School Build a New Social Order?*, 48.

25. Counts, *The Social Foundations of Education*, 55.

26. George S. Counts, "Presentday Reasons for Requiring a Longer Period of Pre-Service Preparation for Teachers," *National Education Association Proceedings* 73 (1935): 697.

27. George S. Counts, "Secondary Education and the Social Problem," *School Executives Magazine* 51 (August 1932): 519.

28. George S. Counts, " Collectivism and Collectivism," *The Social Frontier* 1 (November 1934): 3.

29. In an interview with the author, Counts reflected that the choice of the word, "collectivism" was most likely a mistake. He said that Beard and he had considered for a time the use of the word "associational," but fixed on the stronger term Collectivism. George S. Counts, interview by Gerald Gutek, Southern Illinois University, December 21, 1962.

30. Charles A. Beard, *A Charter for the Social Sciences in the Schools* (New York: Charles Scribner's Sons, 1932), 34.

31. Beard, *A Charter for the Social Sciences in the Schools*, 24.

32. Beard, *A Charter for the Social Sciences in the Schools*, 34–51.

33. Beard, *A Charter for the Social Sciences in the Schools* , 54–55.

34. Counts, *Social Foundations of Education*, 548–49.

35. Counts, *Social Foundations of Education*, 548–58.

36. Counts, *Social Foundations of Education*, 524–524.

37. American Historical Association, Investigation of the Social Studies in the Schools, *Conclusions and Recommendations of the Commission* (New York: Charles Scribner's Sons, 1934), 5–9.

38.   *Ibid.*, 46–83.

39.   *Conclusions and Recommendations* was sent to the Executive Committee of the AHA in 1933 which returned it for revisions. The revised report was resubmitted, approved, and published in 1934. Four Commission members refused to sign the final report—Frank. A. Ballou, Edmund E. Day, Ernest Horn, and Charles E. Merriam. Isaiah Bowman signed with reservations. In addition to Merriam and Day, Horn refused to sign, saying that *Conclusions* did not represent his point of view and would jeopardize the effectiveness of the other volumes in the Commission's series. Frank Ballou, the Superintendent of Schools in Washington, D.C., refused to sign, stating that "we say many things in the report which . . . should be left unsaid because they are destructive to no purpose." Despite his refusal to sign, Ballou was questioned and criticized during the U.S. House of Representative's deliberations on the 1937 Appropriations Bill for funding Washington's schools. Texas Congressman Thomas Blanton called the Commission's recommendations "a deliberate preconcerted plan to communize schools and colleges in the United States" masterminded by "the leading Communist professors, George S. Counts and Charles A. Beard."

40.   Dennis, *George S. Counts and Charles A. Beard: Collaborators for Change*, 87.

41.   Transcript of Meeting of October 12, 1933, in Dennis, *George S. Counts and Charles A. Beard: Collaborators for Change*, 88.

42.   Transcript of Meeting of October 13, 1933, in Dennis, *George S. Counts and Charles A. Beard: Collaborators for Change*, 87–88.

43.   Counts, *The Social Foundations of Education*, 535.

44.   Diane Ravitch, *Left Back: A Century of Failed School Reforms* (New York: Simon & Schuster, 2000), 229.

45.   Charles H. Judd, *Education and Social Progress* (New York: Harcourt, Brace, 1934), 268.

46.   George S. Counts, quoted in an interview to the *New York Times, 17 September 1934, p. 19, in* Dennis, *George S. Counts and Charles A. Beard: Collaborators for Change,* 118.

47.   George S. Counts, "Education and the Five Year Plan of Soviet Russia," *National Education Association Proceedings* 68 (1930): 20, 104, 146.

48.   Dennis, *George S. Counts and Charles A. Beard: Collaborators for Change,* 145.

49.   George S. Counts, *Education and the Promise of America* (New York: Macmillan Co., 1946), 103.

50.   American Historical Association, Investigation of the Social Studies in the Schools, *Conclusions and Recommendations of the Commission*, 31.

51.   Ravitch, *Left Back: A Century of Failed School Reforms*, 465–66.

REFERENCES

American Historical Association, Investigation of the Social Studies in the Schools, *Conclusions and Recommendations of the Commission*. New York: Charles Scribner's Sons, 1934.

Bailyn, Bernard. *Education in the Forming of American Society*. New York: W.W. Norton, 1972.

Beard, Charles A. *A Charter for the Social Sciences in the Schools*. New York: Charles Scribner's Sons, 1932.

Beard, Charles A. *An Economic Interpretation of the Constitution of the United States*. New York: Macmillan Co., 1913.

Cremin, Lawrence A. *The Wonderful World of Ellwood Patterson Cubberley*. New York: Teachers College Press, 1965.

Committee of the Progressive Education Association on Social and Economic Problems. *A Call to the Teachers of the Nation*. New York: John Day Co., 1933.

Counts, George S. *The American Road to Culture: A Social Interpretation of Education in the United States*. New York: John Day Co., 1930.

Counts, George S. *The Challenge of Soviet Education*. New York: McGraw-Hill, 1957.

George S. Counts, "Collectivism and Collectivism," *The Social Frontier* 1 (November 1934).

Counts, George S. " A Humble Autobiography," in *Leaders in American Education: The Seventieth Yearbook of the National Society for the Study of Education*, Robert J. Havighurst, ed. Chicago: University of Chicago Press, 1971.

Counts, George S. "Dare Progressive Education Be Progressive?" *Progressive Education* 9 (April 1932), 257–63.

Counts, George S. *Dare the School Build a New Social Order?* New York: John Day Co., 1932.

Counts, George S. *A Ford Crosses Russia*. Boston: The Stratford Co., 1930.

Counts, George S. *Education and the Promise of America*. New York: Macmillan Co., 1946.

Counts, George S. *Education and American Civilization*. New York: Teachers College Press, 1952.

Counts, George S. "Education and the Five-Year Plan of Soviet Russia," in *Education and Economics*, Harold F. Clark, ed. New York: Teachers College Press, 1931, 39–46.

Counts, George S. *Secondary Education and Industrialism*. Cambridge: Harvard University Press, 1929.

Counts, George S. *The Soviet Challenge to America*. New York: John Day Co., 1931.

Counts, George S. *The Social Foundations of Education*. New York: Charles Scribner's Sons, 1934.

Counts, George S. *The Prospects of American Democracy*. New York: John Day Co., 1938.

Counts, George S. "Teachers and the Class Struggle," *The Social Frontier* 2 (November 1935), 39–40.

Counts, George S. and Childs, John. *America, Russian, and the Communist Party in the Postwar World*. New York: John Day Co., 1943.

Counts, George S. and Lodge, Nucia P. *The Country of the Blind: The Soviet System of Mind Control.* Boston: Houghton-Mifflin Co., 1949.

Dennis, Lawrence J. *George S. Counts and Charles A. Beard: Collaborators for Change.* Albany, NY: State University of New York Press, 1989.

Dennis, Lawrence J. and Eaton, William E. *George S. Counts: Educator for a New Age.* Carbondale: Southern Illinois University Press, 1980.

Gutek, Gerald L. "George Sylvester Counts (1889–1974): A Biographical Memoir," in *Proceedings of the National Academy of Education* 3. Stanford, CA: National Academy of Education, 1976, 333–353.

Gutek, Gerald L. *George S. Counts and American Civilization: The Educator as Social Theorist.* Macon, GA: Mercer University Press, 1984.

Gutek, Gerald L. *The Educational Theory of George S. Counts.* Columbus, OH: Ohio State University Press, 1970.

Judd, Charles H. *Education and Social Progress.* New York: Harcourt, Brace, 1934.

Ogburn, William F. *Recent Social Trends in the United States.* New York: McGraw-Hill Book Co., 1933.

Ravitch, Diane. *Left Back: A Century of Failed School Reforms.* New York: Simon & Schuster, 2000.

CHAPTER 2

SOCIAL RECONSTRUCTION WITH A PURPOSE

The Forgotten Tradition of William Bagley

J. Wesley Null

Writing about William Bagley is a difficult task. The task is so difficult because Bagley's philosophy of professional education has been so radically marginalized, neglected, and misunderstood. Higher education has become what Bagley did not want it to become, and this radical transformation in the purpose of higher education has obscured who Bagley was, what he did with his life, and why he matters. His vision for democratic education, at both the K–12 and higher education levels, most certainly had the reconstruction of society in its sights, but it also should be understood that his idea of social reconstruction never neglected the question of purpose or the end of democracy.

This chapter has three purposes. First, I will provide a brief biographical account of Bagley's life in order to address the problem of coming to understand his forgotten vision for American education, specifically American higher education and the task of teaching teachers. Second I will explain Bagley's criticisms of Progressive education prior to the radical change that took place in Progressive educational philosophy following the stock market collapse of 1929. Third, I will compare Bagley's educational philosophy, which was remarkably consistent throughout his life, with the positions set forth by George Counts when Counts set out to rewrite Progressive education in 1932. Bagley, I will argue, always had the common good in mind with his writings, even when arguing for the social whole was not fashionable in the minds of his trend-seeking colleagues. A brief look at Bagley's background helps us to understand who he was and what he was doing with his work on behalf of the profession of teaching.

BRIEF BIOGRAPHICAL BACKGROUND

William Bagley was born in Detroit, Michigan, in 1874. He attended elementary school for a few years in Worcester, Massachusetts, but his family returned to Detroit in 1887. He graduated from Detroit's Capitol High School in 1891. Upon graduation from high school, Bagley set his mind on becoming a farmer. Thus, he enrolled and completed an undergraduate degree in agriculture from Michigan Agricultural College, in 1895. Upon graduation, however, he had no land and he had no money. He was a landless farmer, which did not bode well for someone with the training he had received in agriculture. As a result, he was looking for a job. To make matters worse, the economy was not doing well in the 1890s, so he was a landless farmer looking for a job in the middle of a depression.

Eventually, however, he found a job. Through a contact with his sister, Bagley was offered a position teaching in a one-room rural school in Upstate Michigan near Garth and Rapid River. He remained uncertain about what he wanted to do with his life, but teaching seemed like an interesting possibility at the time. He accepted the position without any intention of making teaching his life's work. In fact, he had some interest in law, and he thought the teaching position would allow him the opportunity to save a bit of money before he headed off to law school. This mindset of using the teaching position as a stepping stone, however, changed radically after he began to teach in the fall of 1895. His attitude toward teaching changed so much, in fact, that Bagley became ashamed of the idea that he once thought the teaching profession could or should be used like a doormat to something "more important" like law. This tendency to treat teaching as a means rather than an end was something that Bagley dedicated his life to changing.

The young people in Bagley's classroom during the academic years of 1895–96 and 1896–97 must have done something remarkable to him. The experience of teaching changed his life almost overnight. He decided that the profession of teaching would be his calling. He enrolled for a summer semester in 1896 at the University of Chicago, but, for whatever reason, he decided that Chicago was not the right place for his graduate studies. In 1898, he completed a master's degree in psychology at the University of Wisconsin in Madison, where he studied with Joseph Jastrow. Then, Bagley entered graduate school at Cornell University in Ithaca, New York. At Cornell, he studied with Edward Bradford Titchener, a German-inspired psychologist who was doing work that was quite at odds with the American psychology and philosophy that was emerging at the time.

Upon the completion of his PhD degree in 1901, Bagley had additional important decisions to make. Throughout his graduate student days, he remained deeply committed to the profession of teaching. He wanted to use psychology to make teaching and education better. Psychology was a means, not an end to Bagley. He also wanted to be a teacher who impacted students' lives directly, not merely a psychologist who published narrow studies of research. Consequently, he chose to remain a practitioner and accepted a position as an elementary school principal in St. Louis, Missouri. This was quite a shocking decision to make for someone who had just completed a PhD degree at Cornell.

Bagley's stay in Missouri, however, only lasted one year. His decision to leave St. Louis and move to Montana State Normal School in Dillon, Montana, was another significant landmark in his life. By moving to Montana State Normal School, he was now associated with an institution whose sole purpose was to teach teachers. During his four year stay in Montana, 1902–1906, Bagley found a calling that helped him to serve his profession in an important way. He found his identity as a teacher of teachers. Yes, he taught psychology in this new normal school in Montana, but, more importantly (from his perspective), he taught people who would teach others. The moral philosophy that came with the task of teaching teachers was what motivated his work. The goal he set up for himself was to be a teacher of teachers, not a producer of scientific studies. While in Montana, he also retained his close connection to public school practice by serving as superintendent of the Dillon Public School system.[1]

Bagley's first book, *The Educative Process,* brought him national fame.[2] He published the book in 1905 and, one year later, he departed Montana for Oswego State Normal School in Oswego, New York (today's State University of New York at Oswego). This move demonstrates Bagley's commitment to teaching teachers. Like Montana State Normal School, Oswego was an institution dedicated to the single purpose of teaching teachers. Oswego had a rich moral and intellectual tradition that stretched back well into the nineteenth century. It was one of the most powerful and well-known normal schools in the nation. Oswego's philosophical heritage was anything but the pragmatism that came to dominate American philosophy and psychology in the decades ahead.

Bagley's stay in Oswego, however, was short lived. He taught there for only two years, from 1906 to 1908, before he decided to accept a position at the University of Illinois. To understand who Bagley was and what he was doing, we must take into account the normal school tradition to which he dedicated his life. After teaching at normal schools in Montana and New York State, Bagley decided that he wanted to be a leader in the profession of teaching. He also made the decision that his goal was to become a leading figure in the field of teaching teachers. He was not sure, however, how best to provide this leadership for the profession. His view of curriculum for teaching teachers was quite different than the view that was being developed in some public and private universities, as opposed to the normal schools.

Bagley was committed to the idea that entire institutions should be dedicated to teaching teachers. These institutions, moreover, were to make no distinction whatsoever between the what of teaching and the how of teaching. The moral purpose of teaching teachers was what held the what and the how aspects of teacher education curriculum together. Normal schools were not institutions that were designed to do research. They also were not designed to separate knowledge into various disciplines in order to build these disciplines into pockets of specialized intellectual prestige. The institutions to which Bagley dedicated his life existed for one purpose, and that purpose was to teach teachers, primarily elementary school teachers.

Democratic education was to be achieved, according to Bagley and the normal school tradition, through the education and then placement of the brightest young people in the country in classrooms as teachers. In this respect, normal schools were socially revolutionary. They were being institutionalized at the same time that common schools were being created across the country.[3] The purpose of these normal schools, moreover, was to provide democracy with well-educated teachers. At the same time, however, normal schools were being created to raise the status of the teaching profession. Bagley must have dreamed about how the public's view of the teaching profession could be changed for the better if he and other teachers of teachers created powerful institutions that taught young people what, how, and why to teach. He wanted institutions for teaching teachers to become more powerful and visible within the public realm, but he also wanted them to retain their single purpose as institutions for the education of teachers.[4] The challenge for those who taught teachers was to become more powerful in the culture, while at the same time retaining their purpose.

The ideal that Bagley had in mind, moreover, was the ideal of universal liberal education. He was by no means against specialized, vocational training, so long as the vocational aspect of the curriculum came after students had mastered the core democratic culture that he thought held American democracy together. Teaching teachers was Bagley's purpose, and, at the time, the overwhelming majority of teachers in the nation were being educated within normal schools like Montana State and Oswego. As a result, Bagley was an outspoken advocate for normal schools.

NORMAL SCHOOLS VS. UNIVERSITIES

The challenge of democratic education, however, influenced not only the development of normal schools, but also universities. We cannot overestimate the difference between normal schools and universities within the context of Bagley's early career. Universities were selective institutions that provided social uplift to the students who attended them. They were not institutions that were created to teach teachers. Professional programs that prepared students for careers in law, medicine, and engineering existed in some universities, but universities in early twentieth-century America existed primarily to teach children of wealthy parents and, increasingly, to conduct research.

In the context of the early twentieth century, however, new questions arose for these selective institutions.[5] What were elite universities to do about public education? What role were they to play in the task of universal education? Should they have programs designed specifically to teach teachers as well as lawyers, engineers, physicians, and professors? If the universities were to teach teachers, how should they organize this work? Should universities have anything to do with elementary teachers? Or, should they only produce secondary teachers? What should be the relationship between the specialized disciplines and the task of teaching teachers? And what about research? Should the universities conduct research into educational questions? And, if so, how was research supposed to relate to the moral task of teaching teachers?

These were not easy questions to answer, but Bagley was forced to address them head-on when, in 1908, he chose to depart Oswego State Normal School and begin his career at the University of Illinois. His new context was radically different from the two normal school campuses where he taught previously. Before he arrived at Illinois, the institution's program for teaching teachers was virtually nonexistent. Illinois had a department of education, but the department produced only a few secondary teachers each year. Bagley's charge as a professor of education at the University of Illinois was to build up its program for teaching secondary teachers, while at the same time connecting the University to the local community of Champaign-Urbana. He helped give a public face to the University. This social and political dimension of Bagley's efforts was one of the main reasons why President Edmund Janes James was so pleased with, and supportive of, Bagley's work. Bagley helped President James to battle the charge that the University was an elitist enclave for wealthy children. Bagley and the other education faculty members he hired were proof that the University was *doing something* to help provide universal education. He and his colleagues were social servants as well as professors of education.

BAGLEY'S SOCIAL VISION

Now at Illinois, however, Bagley faced the twin issues of discrimination and research. Like others engaged in the work of building up the profession of teaching, Bagley faced discrimination because he was viewed as preparing students for the "women's work" of teaching children and youth. Law and medicine had strong, masculine-oriented traditions to support them as professions, but teaching, regrettably, was still viewed as a lower vocation fit only for those who could not make a career doing something else. Bagley accepted this challenge of building up the profession of teaching with energy, enthusiasm, and political skill.

He built a School of Education at the University of Illinois that thrived under his leadership. At one point, he even successfully petitioned the Illinois state legislature for funds to build the first School of Education building, which served as the University High School as well. Despite his new university environment, however, Bagley remained a teacher of teachers. That was his purpose. He was fervently committed to raising the status of the teaching profession, both within the University of Illinois and beyond. This was precisely why he did such things as create Kappa Delta Pi (KDP), an honor society in education. He wanted KDP to serve as a means through which the profession of teaching could rise in status and influence in the country.

The university in which Bagley now worked, however, was moving quickly away from teaching as its primary purpose. Research was becoming more powerful by the day, not just at the University of Illinois, but at universities across the country. Bagley, of course, supported research, but, above all else, he was committed to teaching and to teaching teachers. Nonetheless, he helped to create Illinois' first PhD degree program in education, which graduated its first students in 1915, one of whom was Harold Rugg. Throughout this time when Bagley was working to raise the status of the teaching profession at two normal schools and then at the University of Illinois, Bagley was arguing for a philosophy of professional education that integrated the what, how, and why dimensions of the vocation of teaching.

He was adamantly against the idea that the disciplines that teachers teach should be separated from the methods of how those disciplines are taught.

Bagley supported "special" methods coursework and not so much "general" methods. Courses such as "The Teaching of History" or "The Teaching of Mathematics" were acceptable to Bagley, but he remained skeptical of General Methods courses such as those that were inspired by William Heard Kilpatrick's "The Project Method." Rejection of General Methods courses, however, raised the question of whether pedagogical philosophy existed at all. To Bagley, it most certainly did, but what stretched across all of the disciplines to Bagley was the *moral commitment to doing something* about providing a liberal education to all young Americans. His position on this matter was most clear when he was writing on the subject of "professionalized subject-matter."[6] With this idea, Bagley was describing something similar to what Lee Shulman currently calls pedagogic content knowledge.[7] With professionalized subject-matter, Bagley, in effect, was working to reconstruct all of the traditional disciplines by professionalizing them. By professionalizing them, he meant to infuse them with a moral and social purpose by connecting them to everyday problems in American society. In short, he wanted his colleagues from the arts and science disciplines to *do something*—like he was—to help educate all Americans.

In making this argument, Bagley was drawing upon a rich philosophical legacy that stretches back at least to educational philosophers like John Amos Comenius as well as American founders such as Thomas Jefferson, Horace Mann, and Noah Webster.[8] The idea of the "diffusion of knowledge," which Jefferson crystallized in his Bill for the More General Diffusion of Knowledge, was quite similar to what Bagley was doing with his concept of professionalized subject-matter. In a democracy, Bagley (as well as Jefferson, Webster, and Mann) argued that knowledge could not, and should not, be the secret treasure of any one group of elite citizens. In a democracy, knowledge—like power—must be *diffused* as widely as possible. It must be shared equally among the population. That was the task of the normal schools as well as teacher education programs within universities. They were to diffuse knowledge more widely by educating and then supporting the teachers who went out and shared this knowledge with classes of people who had never had access to this knowledge before. The calling of teaching teachers, to Bagley, was the final and most critical link in making the ideal of diffusing knowledge throughout the American population a reality. He thought knowledge should be democratized by infusing it with a social and moral purpose that had the ideal of democratic community as its end.

BAGLEY'S SOCIAL VISION IGNORED

That, in a nutshell, was Bagley's vision for social progress. Teaching teachers was the key to the success of his vision. It did not, however, come to pass. Bagley lost. He lost because new educational thinkers came along, thinkers who had a different idea of what democratic education should mean. These individuals—most notably John Dewey, William Heard Kilpatrick, and Edward L. Thorndike—took it as their task to redefine knowledge as it had been traditionally understood. They were not interested in diffusing knowledge more widely in American culture. This new breed of educational reformers emphasized curriculum differentiation, individual differences, and a pedagogy that sought to "meet the individual needs and interests" of students. Working in universities rather than in normal schools, the Progressives (the most critical examples of which are Dewey, Thorndike, and Kilpatrick) rejected the idealism to which Bagley and others adhered. There was no distinction between knowledge and experience to these reformers. Bagley defined democratic education as liberal education for all—regardless of race, class, or gender. This ideal was to be achieved through well-designed institutions for teaching teachers, institutions that were supported socially, politically, and economically by state legislators and the general public. Bagley did not want to redefine knowledge by lopping off traditional subjects such as Latin, Greek, mathematics, and philosophy. Rather, he wanted to focus on teaching these subjects better and to a much wider population than ever before.

Democratic education to the Progressives, however, rejected the ideal of liberal education for all. Instead, the Progressives argued for the exact opposite of this ideal. They proposed that every child should receive a different curriculum based upon his or her felt needs and interests. Above all else, they believed that curriculum should be individualized. What each child wanted and needed should be the basis for her curriculum.[9] These changes with regard to how curriculum had traditionally been understood proceeded most rapidly following the 1901 publication of the Thorndike-Woodworth studies on the transfer of training.[10] The behaviorist psychology of Thorndike and Woodworth supposedly showed that all subjects were equal and that learning how to cook, for example, taught students how and why to think just as "efficiently" as did Latin, literature, or mathematics.[11] Thorndike's studies were taken as proof by many people that the traditional curriculum should be tossed out and replaced with individualized programs that presumably met the needs and interests of students.[12]

Bagley was a critic of these new ideas, although he accepted some of the new pedagogical methods proposed by the Progressives. For example, he thought Dewey's methods were okay, so long as they ultimately led students back to an organized curriculum that embodied the traditions of American culture. But Bagley did not want to toss out the traditional curriculum. He was interested in teaching it to a much wider segment of the population—namely, everyone.[13] The logical consequence of the Progressives' ideas, Bagley thought, would be that nobody, instead of everybody, would receive a robust liberal arts education. He also argued consistently that the "child-centered" aspect of the Progressives' ideas was reinforcing rather than challenging the extreme individualism that threatened to tear democracy apart.

Bagley argued that education should teach all young Americans that they should study and seek to perfect themselves in order to contribute to society as their talents allowed. The social good trumped the individual good in Bagley's philosophy. He also, however, respected the individual rights of students. He labored to find a balance between these two extremes. A well-thought-out core curriculum that was taught by committed, well-trained teachers would teach all young Americans that they should contribute to the common good in whatever capacity they found themselves later in life.[14]

This social commitment that Bagley taught and that the normal schools advocated was challenged by the Progressives. Instead, they trumpeted individualized curriculum, individual rights, and the individual wants and needs of students. Progressives of the 1910s and 1920s thought the social good was passé, whereas Bagley most definitely did not. This tendency toward extreme individualism is clear in the early writings of John Dewey and, especially, in the work of Dewey's disciple, William Heard Kilpatrick.[15] This change in emphasis by the Progressives also supported vocational training, specifically during the era of World War I. The Cardinal Principles Report and the Smith-Hughes Act, both of which were largely supportive of vocational training, are evidence that Progressives like Dewey and Kilpatrick—not Bagley—were winning the day with regard to the curriculum.

It was within this context of battles over American curriculum and the profession of teaching that Bagley taught Harold Rugg from 1913 to 1915. As a loyal fighter for social service and the common good, Bagley taught Rugg that there were certain aspects of the educational and political philosophy within Progressivism that were dangerous. They were dangerous because they deified individualism, rejected the idea of an organized curriculum, and, above all else, disconnected children from the cultural heritage of the past. Rugg also learned from Bagley that the transfer of training experiments conducted by Thorndike and Woodworth were flawed and that the jury was still out as to whether or not woodshop taught students to think as effectively as geometry.[16]

Bagley had argued, since 1904, that studying certain subjects like mathematics, Latin, and chemistry trained the *moral character* of students as much as it did their intellect. The moral virtues that students learned by engaging these challenging subjects, moreover, were difficult, if not impossible, to measure. Thorndike, however, rejected the idea that something beyond measurement could exist. Bagley believed in ideals, whereas Thorndike's radical materialism rejected them. These were the ideas that Rugg was grappling with when he wrote his dissertation in 1915, which he entitled "Descriptive Geometry and Mental Discipline." Both Bagley and Rugg were battling the idea that the traditional curriculum held little, if any, value. They, of course, thought that it did have value, whereas Dewey, Kilpatrick, and Thorndike did not.[17]

All of this background on Bagley matters because, if we are to understand him, we must think carefully about his vision for the profession of teaching. Democratic education, to Bagley, was not a theoretic problem. It was a moral one. It was not a problem that could be "fixed" with modern scientific research. He, of course, had faith in research, but disciplines like psychology and history, to Bagley, were means, not ends. Bagley studied psychology for the sake of improving the practice of teaching. He studied the history of American education not for the sake of only understanding the past. He studied the past, rather, to improve the practice of teaching.

In Bagley's view, democratic education, again, was as much a moral problem as it was an intellectual one. Traditionalists of the nineteenth century were wrong in that they did not have a social vision nor did they have a moral commitment to providing a liberal education to all children. Throughout the nineteenth century, traditionalists held power over American education. Yet, in 1890, only 3.5 percent of high-school age students nationwide graduated from either a public or a private high school.[18] In other words, 96.5 percent of American children were being left behind. Universal education was an ideal that was a long way from being realized, yet the traditionalists had held power for decades. The problem with making universal education a reality was one of doing, not merely one of knowing. Bagley recognized this fact and then set out to do the hard work that needed to be done.

Unlike Dewey and Kilpatrick, however, Bagley was not so concerned about criticizing the teaching methods used by traditionalists. Rather, Bagley's criticisms were directed toward the *amount* of teaching that the traditionalists did and the *audience* that they had in mind when doing so. To Bagley, pedagogy did not so much need to be redefined in the early twentieth century, but it did, however, need to be expanded, and expanded widely. Democracy demanded it.

PROGRESSIVE EDUCATION SUDDENLY BECOMES SOCIAL

The Progressive education movement, which exalted individualism and curriculum differentiation during the 1910s and 1920s, changed radically, however, when the stock market collapsed in 1929. Individuals like Dewey and Kilpatrick had argued for at least 20 years that American education could be fixed if traditional teaching methods could be replaced with their plan to differentiate curriculum based upon students' needs and interests. To Bagley, Dewey and Kilpatrick had contributed to the rampant individualism that caused the Depression.[19] If the teaching profession had followed Bagley's plan and provided young people with a core curriculum that taught them to contribute to the common good, then the problem of excessive individualism at least could have been battled, perhaps successfully. When capitalism was under fire in the early 1930s, developmental Progressives like Dewey and Kilpatrick had to find something else for which to argue in place of their previously individualistic programs. At that point, George S. Counts stepped up to the challenge.

With his 1932 "Dare the School Build a New Social Order?" address, Counts made many points that Bagley had been arguing for 20 years. But Dewey and Kilpatrick, however, had already pigeonholed Bagley as one of the "bad guys." Consequently, a message from Counts that was quite similar to what Bagley had to say on numerous occasions was acceptable because Counts was the person delivering it. Counts's main point with "Dare the School" was that the Progressive education movement had deified the individual and had made no room for the common good.[20] In Counts's words:

> The weakness of Progressive Education lies in the fact that it has elaborated no theory of social welfare, unless it be that of anarchy or extreme individualism. In this, of course, it is but reflecting the viewpoint of the members of the liberal-minded upper middle class who send their children to the Progressive schools. . . . These people have shown themselves entirely incapable of dealing with any of the great crises of our time—war, prosperity, or depression. At bottom they are romantic sentimentalists, but with a sharp eye on the main chance. That they can be trusted to write our educational theories and shape our educational programs is highly improbable.[21]

These words must have been quite shocking to the likes of William Heard Kilpatrick and his thousands of followers. Kilpatrick had become famous since 1918 when he published his "The Project Method" essay. Kilpatrick had spread precisely the ideas that Counts was pummeling with his 1932 address. How would he and the others who supported him respond to Counts's challenge?

This question certainly crossed Bagley's mind as he, too, wondered how American democracy should respond to the Depression. How Kilpatrick and the other Progressives reacted to Counts's challenge, however, shocked Bagley like nothing in educational philosophy had before. The same individuals who had been promoting individualism and radically differentiated curriculum *suddenly switched sides* and began to argue the exact opposite of their previous position. Bagley labeled this shocking turn of events as "one of the most amazing phenomena in the history of educational theory." In Bagley's words:

> We come finally to one of the most amazing phenomena in the history of educational theory. As Dr. (Isaac L.) Kandel has recently pointed out, the group that has been urging most insistently pupil-freedom and the planless curriculum, the group that has held to a theory which deifies the individual and his free choices, is now the group that is most ardently advocating a planned economic order, a central control of industry, and an abandonment of laissez faire. They cannot find words that are strong enough when it comes to condemning individualism in the body politic; yet for a generation they have taught that education should follow the course dictated by the learner's individual interest.[22]

Bagley could not understand how Progressives suddenly could switch to a theory that was exactly the opposite of what they had been promoting for more than 20 years.

The only answer he heard as to why this sudden switch was logically possible was that new situations demanded new answers. But this response was not sufficient to Bagley. He detected serious problems with the relativism that lay behind the idea that educational theories could change overnight. Did America and Americans not stand for principles that did not change depending upon circumstances? How was America to respond to challenges from totalitarian regimes like Communism and Fascism if Americans had no ideals upon which to stand? What were the principles that supported these so-called Progressive theories?

Bagley agreed with Counts that democratic education must have a social purpose. He also agreed that some amount of indoctrination into the principles of American democracy was necessary, if not unavoidable. He did not, however, follow Counts so far as to accept the planned economic order that he and others were supporting. Despite the drawbacks of capitalism (which Bagley had pointed out for 30 years by this point), Bagley accepted the idea that democracy and capitalism existed together. This does not mean, however, that he thought business ideologies should be applied to education and teaching. He had been arguing for a moral purpose to support public education in the face of economic reductionism for at least three decades. Capitalism, to Bagley, could be applied, for example, to the production of automobiles and the distribution of refrigerators, but education was a moral enterprise that should not be reduced to mere economic analysis. In 1914, he derisively labeled this tendency to treat education as a business with the phrase "production-consumption thinking."[23]

Bagley, let us not forget, was a political liberal. He should be considered one of the moderate political liberals at Teachers College during his career, but, nonetheless, he was a liberal with regard to political philosophy. He voted for the Democratic candidate in every presidential election for his entire career, with the exception of the 1932 election, when he voted for the socialist candidate, Norman Thomas. Bagley also was an outspoken supporter of Franklin Delano Roosevelt, as was Bagley's good friend at Teachers College, Isaac Kandel. What separated Bagley from his colleagues—like Dewey and Kilpatrick—was the fact that Bagley did not believe that the profession of teaching could, or should, be built without the support and participation of scholars from the traditional academic disciplines.[24] He wanted to draw upon traditional knowledge in order to teach the public, but he did not want to redefine traditional knowledge. That task was undesirable and misguided, not to mention impossible.

RECONSTRUCTION WITH A PURPOSE

Why William Bagley and his advisee, Harold Rugg, parted ways with regard to educational philosophy is not an easy riddle to solve. Perhaps their ideas were not as far apart as educational historians have sometimes painted them to be. But Bagley, above all else, was a teacher of teachers. Rugg did not make teaching teachers his sole purpose as a professor of education. This difference in purpose may have had something to do with their lack of agreement on certain matters. Rugg also took the social reconstructionism of the 1930s to an extreme with which Bagley did not agree. Bagley thought Counts and Rugg were taking the Progressive education movement in a direction that was not healthy for the profession of teaching or to democracy in the long run. Bagley was not convinced that socialism, at least in its extreme forms, would last as a political philosophy.

Rugg and Bagley, nevertheless, remained friends throughout their time together on the faculty at Teachers College. Rugg praised his mentor in the concluding pages of his text entitled *Foundations for American Education.* Rugg wrote:

I was with him almost continuously for thirty-five years . . . was his first Ph.D. in the University of Illinois. . . . saw him deliberately choose for himself the role of brake on what he always thought was the too rapidly turning wheel of educational innovation. . . . saw him question critically the junior high school reorganization of the grades, the intelligence tests in the 1910s, the hereditarians in the nature *vs.* nurture controversy in the 1920s. . . and for two decades the "broad fields" reorganization of the subject matter of the curriculum and the programs of the progressive schools. We came together again when I joined the Teachers College faculty in 1920. My hat is off to a loyal friend, an untiring fighter for what he believed in, a staunch defender of the community of culture, one who practiced democracy as he preached it, and—a rarity in American education during his lifetime—a master of the English paragraph.[25]

These words from Rugg should discount any attempt to categorize Bagley simplistically as either a "good guy" or a "bad guy" with regard to the story of American educational thought. Bagley was a complex thinker who put forward a deeply sound philosophy for the profession of teaching. He labored to reconstruct society so that every child in the nation would be taught by teachers who knew what, how, and why to teach. He wanted these teachers, moreover, to inspire students to learn from the moral and intellectual heritage that holds American democracy together.[26]

The democratic purpose that Bagley had in mind was universal liberal education, a tradition that he extended from such thinkers as John Amos Comenius, Johann Pestalozzi, and Edward Austin Sheldon. In time, Bagley's integrationist philosophy of professional education will gain a stronger presence in the minds and hearts of faculty members in schools, colleges, and departments of education. The time is right for his message.

First, however, education professors must make the decision to stop chasing the phantom that is John Dewey. There are other, better models for the profession of teaching. Bagley is one such example. Dewey's pragmatism can be used as a means to the end of providing a liberal arts curriculum to all young Americans. In this respect, it is valuable. Deweyan pragmatism, however, cannot and should not be viewed as an end in and of itself. The current serious challenges that face the teaching profession are representative of what pragmatism produces when that philosophy is used as both a means and an end for our profession. Higher education has radically marginalized the profession of teaching, as well as the moral and intellectual task of teaching teachers. We must do better, for the sake of teachers today as well as for the sake of teachers and students in the future. Bagley was bold enough to make teaching (as well as teaching teachers) an end in and of itself and not a means to something else that is supposedly more important. Only when the tradition that Bagley represents is restored within American educational thought and practice will true democratic social reconstruction—with a purpose—take root.

NOTES

1.   J. Wesley Null, *A Disciplined Progressive Educator: The Life and Career of William Chandler Bagley* (New York: Peter Lang, 2003).

2.   William C. Bagley, *The Educative Process* (New York: Macmillan, 1905).

3.   For Horace Mann's thoughts on normal schools and their relationship to the spread of public education, see Andrew J. Milson, Chara Haeussler Bohan, Perry L. Glanzer, and J. Wesley Null, eds. *Readings in American Educational Thought: From Puritanism to Progressivism* (Greenwich, CT: Information Age Publishing, 2004), 149–190.

4.   William C. Bagley, "The Problem of Teacher Training in the United States," in *Educational Yearbook of the International Institute of Teachers College, 1927*, ed. Isaac L. Kandel (New York: Teachers College Bureau of Publications, 1928), 571–606.

5.   For a view of how institutions such as Yale, Harvard, and Princeton responded to this challenge of serving the common good, see William Torrey Harris, "University and School Extension," A paper read before the National Educational Association, St. Paul, Minnesota, July 1890, (Syracuse, NY: C. W. Bardeen Publisher, 1890), 1–12.

6.   See, for example, William C. Bagley, "Twenty Years of Progress in the Professionalization of Subject-matter for Normal Schools and Teachers Colleges," *National Education Association Proceedings and Addresses* (1928): 906–912; William C. Bagley, "What is Professionalized Subject-matter?," *New York Society for the Experimental Study of Education Normal-School and Teachers College Section Proceedings* (1928): 155–166; and William C. Bagley, "Teachers Professional Study of Subject-Matter in Mathematics," *Mathematics Teacher* 31 (October 1938): 273–277; for a larger discussion of professionalized subject-matter, see J. Wesley Null, *A Disciplined Progressive Educator: The Life and Career of William Chandler Bagley* (New York: Peter Lang), 154–155; 209–210.

7.   See, for example, Lee Shulman, "Knowledge and Teaching: Foundations of the New Reform," *Harvard Educational Review* 57 (February 1987): 1–22; and Robert V. Bullough, Jr., "Pedagogical Content Knowledge Circa 1907 and 1987: A Study in the History of an Idea," *Teaching and Teacher Education* 17 (2001): 655–666.

8.   For essays in which all three of these notable figures in American history use the conception of the diffusion of knowledge, see Andrew J. Milson, Chara Haeussler Bohan, Perry L. Glanzer, and J. Wesley Null, eds. *Readings in American Educational Thought: From Puritanism to Progressivism* (Greenwich, CT: Information Age Publishing, 2004).

9.   For John Dewey on this point, see selections from his *School and Society and the Child and the Curriculum,* reprinted in Andrew J. Milson, Chara Haeussler Bohan, Perry L. Glanzer, and J. Wesley Null, eds. *Readings in American Educational Thought: From Puritanism to Progressivism* (Greenwich, CT: Information Age Publishing, 2004), 307–334.

10.   Edward L. Thorndike and R. S. Woodworth, "The Influence of Improvement In One Mental Function Upon The Efficiency of Other Functions," *Psychological Review* 8 (2001): 247–261.

11.   For more on the story of how this happened, see Diane Ravitch, *Left Back* (New York: Simon and Schuster, 2000).

12.   For works in which Dewey, Kilpatrick, and Thorndike supported these ideas, see, for example John Dewey, "The Primary-education Fetich," *Forum* (1898): 315–328; John Dewey, *The School and Society* (Chicago: The University of Chicago Press, 1899); John Dewey and Evelyn Dewey, *Schools of Tomorrow* (New York: E. P. Dutton, 1915); E. L. Thorndike, *The Principles of Teaching: Based on Psychology* (New York: A. G. Seiler, 1906); William Heard Kilpatrick, "The Project Method: The Use of the Purposeful Act in the Educative Process," *Teachers College Record* 19 (September 1918): 319–335; and William Heard Kilpatrick, *Foundations of Method* (New York: Macmillan, 1926); see, also, Samuel Tenenbaum, *William Heard Kilpatrick: Trail Blazer in Education* (New York: Harper, 1951).

13.   Bagley's argument for the *everyone* aspect of this philosophy can be found in his attacks against the fashionable idea in the 1920s that children of "lower" races could not learn a challenging academic curriculum. Bagley argued persuasively that all young Americans should be offered the good stuff. See William C. Bagley, *Determinism in Education: A Series of Papers on the Relative Influence of Inherited and Acquired Traits in Determining Intelligence, Achievement, and Character* (Baltimore: Warwick and York: 1925).

14.   See, for example, William C. Bagley, "Dewey's Individualism," *School and Home Education* 35 (September 1915): 4–5; and William C. Bagley, "Education and the Ideals of Social Service," *School and Home Education* 34 (February 1915): 200–201; see also J. Wesley Null, "Social Efficiency Splintered: Multiple Meanings Instead of the Hegemony of One," *Journal of Curriculum and Supervision* 19 (Winter 2004): 99–124.

15.   See, for example, Kilpatrick's *Foundations of Method: Informal Talks on Teaching* (New York: Macmillan, 1925).

16.   For one of Bagley's published critiques of the Thorndike-Woodworth studies, see William C. Bagley, "Ideals Versus Generalized Habits," *School and Home Education* 34 (November 1904): 102–106.

17.   For a glowing tribute to Kilpatrick, written by Dewey, see Dewey's introduction to Samuel Tenenbaum, *William Heard Kilpatrick: Trail Blazer in Education* (New York: Harper, 1951). After reading this introduction by Dewey, it is clear that Dewey accepted everything that Kilpatrick wrote. In short, Dewey says quite plainly that Kilpatrick interpreted his philosophy correctly, even brilliantly.

18. David B. Tyack, *The One Best System* (Cambridge, MA: Harvard University Press, 1974), 57.

19. For Bagley's critique of Dewey's *Schools of Tomorrow,* see William C. Bagley, "Two Types of Social Progress," *School and Home Education* 35 (September 1915): 3; William C. Bagley, "Dewey's Individualism," *School and Home Education* 35 (September 1915): 4–5; William C. Bagley, "Can All Dualisms Be Reconciled?," *School and Home Education* 36 (October 1916): 5; "Deweyism and Democracy: Replies from Mr. Dewey and Mr. McManis, with Editorial Comment," *School and Home Education* 35 (October 1915): 35–36; Letter from John Dewey to Bagley and the Editors of *School and Home Education,* September 20, 1915, published in *School and Home Education* 35 (October 1915): 35–36; see also John Dewey, *The Middle Works, 1899–1924 ,* 8, ed. Jo Ann Boydston (Carbondale, IL: Southern Illinois University Press, 1979), 414–415; William C. Bagley, "Editorial Comment," *School and Home Education* 35 (October 1915): 36–37.

20. For a republication of Counts' address, see Andrew J. Milson, Chara Haeussler Bohan, Perry L. Glanzer, and J. Wesley Null, eds. *Readings in American Educational Thought: From Puritanism to Progressivism* (Greenwich, CT: Information Age Publishing, 2004), 407–422.

21. Counts changed the title of his address when it was published as a book. See George S. Counts, *Dare the School Build a New Social Order?* (London: Feffer and Simons, 1932), 4–5.

22. William C. Bagley, "Modern Educational Theories and Practical Considerations," *School and Society* 37 (April 1933): 413.

23. William C. Bagley, "The Fundamental Distinctions Between Liberal and Vocational Education," *National Education Association Proceedings and Addresses* (1914): 161–170.

24. J. Wesley Null, *A Disciplined Progressive Educator: The Life and Career of William Chandler Bagley* (New York: Peter Lang, 2003).

25. Harold Rugg, *Foundations for American Education* (Yonkers-on-Hudson, NY: World Book, 1947), 607.

26. For more of Bagley's writings from this perspective, see William C. Bagley, *Education, Crime, and Social Progress* (New York: Macmillan, 1932); William C. Bagley, *Education and Emergent Man: A Theory of Education With Particular Application to Public Education in the United States* (New York: Thomas Nelson and Sons, 1934); and William C. Bagley and Thomas Alexander, *The Teacher of the Social Studies* (New York: Charles Scribner's Sons, 1937).

CHAPTER 3

SOCIAL STUDIES VS. THE UNITED STATES OF AMERICA

Harold Rugg and Teaching for Social Justice[1]

Ronald W. Evans

INTRODUCTION

In the late 1930s and early 40s a great deal of controversy and criticism centered on social reconstructionism as embodied in the Rugg social studies program. Critics viewed the Rugg materials as "against private enterprise," as a "subtle, sugar-coated effort to convert youth to Communism," as part of a "reconstructed" educational system teaching that "our economic and political institutions are decadent," or as "un-American." The extent of the controversy is exemplified by a pointed communique from a prominent leader of the National Council for the Social Studies, who described the growing controversy over Rugg and social studies as, "National Council for the Social Studies vs. 'United States of America, or the civilized world. . . .'"[2]

Given recent interest in education for social justice, Harold Rugg's work, and the textbook controversy he inspired, are an important and

Social Reconstruction: People, Politics, Perspectives, pages 45–68
Copyright © 2006 by Information Age Publishing
All rights of reproduction in any form reserved.

especially relevant episode in curriculum history. Like many present-day reformers, Rugg wanted a curriculum that would lead to social transformation. Rugg's story sheds some light on the possibilities for success and the potential obstacles or limitations reformers may face. Moreover, it is an interesting story in which differing values and conflicting visions of the good society played out in a millennial struggle over the social studies curriculum.

Who was Harold Rugg and why should we care about his story? Rugg was one of a small group of leaders of the Progressive education movement centered at Teachers College, Columbia University, and a leader among the social frontier group that emerged in the 1930s to argue that schools should play a stronger role in helping to reconstruct society. He was the author of an innovative and best-selling series of social studies textbooks which came under attack from patriotic and business groups in the prelude to the United States involvement in World War II. The story of his rise and fall encapsulates a significant and central story in the history of American education. When combined with subsequent events, the Rugg story reveals a great deal about the direction of schooling in American life, the many alternative roads not taken, and the possibilities for the future.

As Kliebard writes, Rugg's career "virtually represents in miniature the panorama of educational ideologies that characterized twentieth-century curriculum reform in America: scientific curriculum making, child-centered education, and most notably, social reconstructionism."[3] Moreover, Rugg's career, and the ideas of his detractors, embody elements of the entire spectrum of social studies ideologies that influenced the making of the social studies curriculum in the twentieth century: education for social efficiency in the form of scientific curriculum making, social studies as social science inquiry, social studies as traditional history and civics, social studies as an issues-oriented and integrated field of study, and social studies as education for social reconstructionism.[4]

Rugg's story remains important today chiefly because it reminds us that social studies as a broad and integrated field of study has potential for the development of thoughtful and caring citizens, and that it is possible for a social studies reformer to influence the course of events. Rugg's work had a real impact, not only on rhetoric among theorists but on schools. His work helped develop greater interest in Progressive approaches to social studies, it brought an integrated and issues-centered approach to the field to a large segment of American schoolchildren during the 1930s, and thus influenced the education of a generation of Americans. His textbooks and materials sold millions of copies and ultimately inspired a controversy that changed the entire course of the curriculum.

Rugg created an avant-garde social studies program, which was pedagogically advanced and instructive for those with an interest in teaching for social justice. He developed an approach to social studies instruction that integrated the social sciences and history in an issues-centered program focusing on understanding and social transformation. To this day his program serves as a useful prototype for a unified social studies program focused on issues and problems, and aimed at education for social justice.

Rugg envisioned an entire social studies curriculum centered around, "The American Problem," and aimed at leading a thousand-year march to a "cooperative commonwealth." Rugg's story is a reminder of the potential power of social studies reform—his materials were pedagogically sophisticated and somewhat daring. They asked tough questions on topics that need to be addressed in a democratic society: the role of business in controlling government, the influence of property on the constitution and our form of government, and a myriad of others. He was an American original, the progenitor of education for social justice in social studies education. Moreover, in educational thought and practice, rationale is of key importance. Rugg's work was built on a thoughtful rationale that combined student interest with social worth, a powerful combination that still has appeal.

The Rugg story is also important today because social studies, as a broad, interdisciplinary, and issues-centered field, is currently endangered: reports on classroom practice find a pattern of instruction focused on content acquisition and a fact-myth-legend approach to history; the revival of history and mania for standards and high-stakes tests are increasing the emphasis on traditional history and narrowing the range of issues and questions discussed in schools. Thus, Rugg's ideas are especially relevant in states such as California, where the history-centered California Framework for History and Social Science is the crown jewel of the revival of history—a major victory for educational conservatives in the century-long war on social studies.

In the late 1930s and early 40s Rugg was censured by a media storm fed by conservative patriotic and business groups who, in an un-American fashion, did not want schoolchildren, or their parents for that matter, raising questions about the basic structures of American life and the capitalist economic system. His story reminds us that education is always political and can never be neutral. It also reminds us of what can happen to a good idea and to precious freedoms in a society in which the media, public sentiment, and school policy are subject to manipulation—the manufactured crises that seem to beset our schools again and again and which have an inordinate influence on how we educate citizens. The attack on Rugg, his ideas, textbooks, and school materials was perhaps the first major battle of what I have previously termed the war on social studies.[5] It is a war many educators of Progressive mind are still fighting and, unfortunately, still losing.

Rugg's story also illustrates the point that being a social critic, or Progressive reformer, can be dangerous, especially so in education. The culture assumes and seems to support a mythical, "apolitical" view of education as socialization—suggesting that it is permissible to have some discussion in the curriculum of central issues in American life within a framework of absolute balance and teacher neutrality. However, to openly declare allegiance to ideas that challenge capitalism and its most basic assumptions can, and has—on many occasions—led to serious repercussions. Rugg's work and his ideas made it clear that he placed higher value on human rights than on profits and private property, and that he wanted students in schools to wrestle with the issues raised by the dilemmas of capitalism. In essence, Rugg wanted schools to teach about the social world, past and present, as if people mattered.

Rugg arrived at a set of beliefs and chose a course of action that, at a certain key time in our nation's history, raised the suspicions and the ire of many Americans. His textbooks were never as forthright as his speeches and other writings, yet, inevitably it seems, school materials take on a hue or tint, and lean toward either socializing or counter-socializing. When counter-socialization is emphasized, raising questions about the contradictions in American culture, exposing the hypocrisy apparent in a land of "opportunity" in which prospects for success are not presented on a level playing field and carry baggage of mythological proportions, it can raise the doubts and indignation of conservative activists.

Rugg's life and work have great resonance today, in the twenty-first century. The Rugg story raises serious questions about the rationale and purposes of schooling for citizenship. What kind of citizens and citizen education do we want? How far can and should schools go in providing opportunities for social criticism? What kinds of activities and materials are appropriate in support of education for social justice? What are its limits, if any? And, behind all of these questions, whose version(s) of the American way should schools support?

Rugg was one of the seminal thinkers in the development of education for social reconstructionism, a forerunner of education for social justice. Teaching for social justice has had many advocates over the years and seems a permanent interest group in the panoply of educational thought. The literature on social-justice–oriented schooling has mushroomed since the 1970s, an offshoot of critiques of society, and of schooling, developed in many quarters during the 60s and later.[6] To a greater degree than many recent advocates of teaching for social justice, Rugg's work achieved a strong presence in school. Thus, most importantly, the Rugg story, his life and work, challenges us to make a difference in schools.

DEVELOPMENT OF THE RUGG SOCIAL STUDIES PROGRAM

Harold Ordway Rugg, born in Fitchburg, Massachusetts on January 17, 1886, was the son of a cabinet maker, attended Fitchburg public schools, worked in a textile mill, and, through good fortune and his own initiative, attended Dartmouth College. He studied civil engineering and worked as a railroad surveyor, then taught civil engineering for two years and became interested in how students learn. He earned a PhD in Education at the University of Illinois under the mentorship of William C. Bagley in 1915, then held a teaching post at the University of Chicago.

During World War I, Rugg served on the Army Committee on Classification of Personnel and came in contact with intellectuals holding an aesthetic orientation, which led him to read the work of frontier thinkers and contemporary social critics including Van Wyck Brooks, Waldo Frank, and Randolph Bourne, who had written for *The Seven Arts*, a highly regarded literary journal. A colleague on the Army's Personnel Committee, John Coss, planned to develop an undergraduate course at Columbia University that would integrate the social sciences into a general introduction to the contemporary world. This seems to have started the process in Rugg's thoughts of developing a similarly integrated approach to social studies.

In January, 1920, he joined the faculty at Teachers College, Columbia University, serving as school psychologist for the Lincoln School, and developed his interest in the history and social studies curriculum. His contacts at Teachers College with John Dewey, William H. Kilpatrick, George S. Counts, John L. Childs, Jesse Newlon, R. Bruce Raup, and others had a profound influence on his intellectual development, as did his association with the avant-garde in the New York area, including creative artists such as Alfred Stieglitz and Georgia O'Keefe in Greenwich Village, and his later residence in the arts community of Woodstock, New York.

During his early years at Teachers College, Rugg decided to attempt to improve education through what he saw as its most influential element: school textual materials. He set out to create an alternative form encapsulating his vision for social studies. In 1921 he called for a social studies curriculum that would be entirely problem centered, and built around the "American Problem."

Rugg argued that:

I. "All units of work shall be presented definitely in problem-solving form."

II. "There should be one continuous social studies course from the first grade to the twelfth."

III. Problems shall be based on "personal appeals" (what would you do
    if? etc.) or "alternative proposals" to force comparison, "intellectual
    opposition," and "much concrete human detail to obtain interest."

IV. "Constant practice shall be given in analyzing, generalizing, and
    organizing, as material that pertains to the 'problems' is collected
    and studied."

V. "Problem-situations shall be presented first through current affairs.
   Only those historical backgrounds shall be developed which . . . are
   crucial for clear thinking about contemporary matters."

VI. "Problems, or the examples of generalizations and organization
    which contribute to them, should occur in many grades on an increas-
    ingly mature level . . . (through) some form of 'layer' scheme."[7]

Rugg would later argue that the entire social studies curriculum should be
organized around problems of contemporary life. Though not the only
experiment in unification in social studies at the time, these ideas were
clearly far ahead of their time, and were later to become central guiding
principles for reflective and issues-centered approaches to social studies.
Rugg hoped to create a fully integrated social studies curriculum, abolish-
ing the artificial divisions among history, geography, political science, economics, and sociology, and grouping all of the material under the general
rubric of social studies. He contacted former students and asked them to
subscribe, sight unseen, to his pamphlet series. The response was overwhelming. By June 1922 he had received orders for 4,000 copies of each.
The second edition of the pamphlet series resulted in about 100,000 copies of each unit being shipped to schools.[8]

The pamphlets were problem centered: virtually every topic was introduced through a contemporary issue or problem connected to students'
lives; the writing was lively and engaging; open-ended discussion questions
were prominently featured in "open forum" and "group discussions;" the
pamphlets made frequent use of photos, drawings, and cartoons; and provocative topics were given full coverage including potentially controversial
topics such as the influence of business on government, and the influence
of men of property on the development of the U.S. Constitution.

THE RUGG TEXTBOOK SERIES

The pamphlets were revised and published in textbook form, two texts per
grade for the junior high school (grades seven, eight, and nine), beginning in August 1929, by Ginn and Company, with publication of another
volume in the series every six months thereafter. The series became a huge

financial success, and represents the zenith of issues-centered social studies materials entre into classrooms in the twentieth century.[9]

During the 1930s, sales of Rugg's textbook series literally skyrocketed. For the ten-year period from 1929 to 1939, the series sold 1,317,960 copies at approximately $2.00 each, and over 2,687,000 workbooks. Rugg and his associates had created a unified social studies program and his books attracted worldwide attention and imitation. Through force of will, brilliance, hard work and fortunate timing, he had clearly become the leading social studies educator in the United States.[10]

The content organization of the Rugg textbooks was centered around guiding principles distilled from the "frontier thinkers" including the growth of modern cultures, development of loyalties and attitudes for decision making, and the synthesis of knowledge. The methodology for introducing this content included the dramatic episode, planned recurrence of key concepts, practice in skills of generalizing, and learning by doing. The six volumes of the junior-high-school program were "designed to provide a comprehensive introduction to modes of living and insistent problems of the modern world," with the purpose of "introducing young people to the chief conditions and problems which will confront them as citizens of the world," through a unified course in social studies. Rugg defended his development of a "unified" course by alluding to students' need to "ultilize facts, meanings, generalizations, and historical movement" in understanding modern institutions. He cited the need to tie various factors "closely together in their natural relationships" in order to help students understand the modern world. He wrote:

> Whenever history is needed to understand the present, history is presented. If geographic relationships are needed to throw light upon contemporary problems, those geographic relationships are incorporated. The same thing has been done with economic and social facts and principles.[11]

Though the books contained a great deal of historical narrative, not unlike many other texts, the overarching aim was to make the study of history and the social sciences relevant, interesting, and meaningful to students in service of the ultimate goal of social melioration. Material from history and the social sciences was framed with issues and problems of present concern. Also worthy of note, the writing was appealing and down-to-earth, a major factor behind the books' success. For example, the narrative for one text began with an imaginary meeting of the Social Science Club of "George Washington Junior High School of Anystate, U.S.A.," in which members of the club discussed the problems and issues to be taken up in group study.[12] The description is lively and engaging, and undoubtedly helped to interest many students in the remainder of the text.

The Rugg textbook series for the junior high school was titled *Man and His Changing Society*. Individual titles included: *An Introduction to American Civilization, Changing Civilizations in the Modern World, A History of American Civilization,* and *An Introduction to the Problems of American Culture*. The final volume of the first edition was published in January 1932. Revised editions appeared from 1936 to 1940.

RUGG'S SOCIAL RECONSTRUCTIONISM

By the early 1930s Rugg had established his credentials as a leading scholar in education. With the social studies program, and publication of a number of highly regarded books and articles, his activities during the hard times of the Great Depression largely enhanced his reputation. He remained energetic on the faculty at Teachers College, and was an active member of the Progressive Education Association. Also, during the early part of the decade, he came to be known, along with his colleague, George S. Counts, as one of the leading advocates of education for social reconstruction in the nation, and was a respected participant in debates over educational and social policy in the *Social Frontier* and other venues.

Rugg had been a long-term advocate of social reconstructionism through the schools, but in the 1930s his rhetoric became more strident. During the 20s Rugg's social thought was influenced in two main directions. He read social criticism and was feeling the thrust of arguments for social engineering, and at the same time, was investigating the views of those who held that artists and writers should lead the way to social improvement. These strands matured in his thinking in the 30s and stood behind his work on the textbook series and his books and articles calling for reform. Rugg's vision was of a better society, which he referred to variously as "the great society," "the great technology," and "the great new epoch." The reconstructed society was to be created through a combination of large-scale social and economic planning and a new education which would cultivate "integrated" and creative personalities.[13] Achieving widespread popular consent for democratic social planning could only take place if the public were made more aware of existing social problems and potential reforms, thus a focus on social problems and issues in schools.

In *The Great Technology*, published in 1933, Rugg called for social engineering in the form of technological experts who would design and operate, or "engineer," the economy in the public interest. Though he did not support all of its tenets, Rugg's thought was heavily influenced by the popular movement for technocracy during the early 1930s. For Rugg, the economic problem was to design and operate a system of production and distribution which would produce the maximum amount of goods needed by the people and would distribute them in such a way that each person would be given at least the highest minimum standard of living possible.[14] An additional share of our abundance would be permitted to those who made excellent contributions through "greater creative ability and initiative," but this would be restricted to only "a low multiple of the minimum."[15]

Rugg's central concern continued to focus on his hope that social education could be used to help in the "scientifically designed reconstruction of society" for the general benefit of all. He called for "a mammoth and creative program of educational reconstruction" facilitated by a program of adult education that would educate a minority to lead reform.[16] Rugg's "axioms" for the economic system postulated an economy of abundance, a shorter work week, redistribution of income through progressive taxation, regulation of business and industry, and creation of consent for social reconstruction.[17] He frequently described his vision as a "thousand-year march" of democracy toward a "cooperative commonwealth."[18]

Many of his critics later cited press reports of Rugg's appearance at the 1934 Cleveland meeting of the Progressive Education Association, which reported that Rugg had called for a campaign:

> to organize 14,000,000 persons into a "pressure group" to force more radical changes in the economic system within three months. He said funds were forthcoming, but would refuse to reveal the source. He outlined the plan—to include a "central planning agency," probably in New York—to tie together thousands of groups of citizens who believe[d] that the capitalist system should come to an end.[19]

In a confidential memorandum prepared in 1940 for his superiors at Teachers College, Rugg denied the claims that many of his critics were making regarding his statements at the Cleveland meeting of 1934, charging, "they lie straight out. . . . I have never said or implied that our adult education plans were to tie together thousands of groups of citizens who believe that the capitalist system should come to an end." Rugg branded the allegations, "unmitigated falsehood," and wrote, "Every statement ascribed to me and my motives is by the implication that somebody "is said to have said," etc; all was obtained from newspaper reporters' accounts, oral hearsay accounts, and the like."[20] Despite such reported rhetoric, whether real or imagined, Rugg's social vision was never as radical as his critics portrayed, but rather, it placed him somewhere between New Deal liberalism and democratic socialism. Above all, his was a democratic vision.

THE GATHERING STORM

Early criticisms of the Rugg social studies materials foreshadowed what would transpire during the late 1930s and early 40s. As mentioned above, Rugg's writings underwent a shift in the early 30s with a more pointed advocacy of social reconstructionism and the goal of moving toward some form of "collectivism." It was, in part, these writings and subsequent media coverage of speaking engagements that attracted the attention of self-appointed censors to Rugg's work. His success as an author combined with his affiliation with unpopular causes to make him a target for criticism. In 1934, Rugg was listed as a "Communist" in Elizabeth Dilling's *The Red Net-work.*[21] During 1935 Rugg spoke out against American Legion attempts to censor a classroom magazine. For the balance of the decade, in a series of major speeches, Rugg attacked patriotic societies, the Advertising Federation of America, the National Association of Manufacturers, the United States Chamber of Commerce, and the New Deal itself. His comments and outspoken views, critical of the American Legion and other groups, had the effect of making him the chief target of their attacks.

By 1939, against the backdrop of dictatorship and war, controversies over the Rugg textbooks flared anew, and the American public was treated to a spectacle that received continuing national media coverage. The attacks centered in the New York metropolitan area and represented an intense campaign orchestrated by relatively few people. The bulk of the attacks came from a combine of business writers and publicists, retired military of the American Legion, professional journalists, and a few loose cannons. The flames were fanned by extensive coverage in the Hearst press. Attacks on the Rugg materials began as part of a blanket attack on American writers and texts, with Rugg gradually becoming the chief target.

Bertie C. Forbes, in his own magazine, attacked the Rugg textbooks in an article titled "Treacherous Teachings" in which he charged Rugg with being against private enterprise and urged boards of education to "cast out" the Rugg books. The Advertising Federation of America, led by Alfred T. Falk, attacked the books for carrying "anti-advertising propaganda." Merwin K. Hart, president of the New York State Economic Council, charged Rugg with "making a subtle sugar-coated effort to convert youth to Communism," and suggesting that capitalism "has been a failure and that socialism should be substituted in its place."

Controversies over the books in a number of cities and towns followed a typical pattern: a complaint, followed by appointment of a committee to investigate, then debate and, frequently, public hearings. In a number of well-publicized cases, Rugg appeared in person to defend the textbook series. The outcome of the controversy varied from place to place. Binghamton, New York, and Englewood, New Jersey had major controversies, which were covered extensively by local and national media. In a number of cities and towns, including Binghamton, the books were removed. In Bradner, Ohio, the Superintendent ordered the books taken down to the furnace room and burned.

During 1940, attacks on the Rugg social studies program continued to increase. The next round of controversy was generated by two articles which appeared in widely read, nationally circulated magazines. The first of these was an article by Augustin G. Rudd which was published in the April 1940 issue of *Nation's Business*, and was titled, "Our 'Reconstructed' Educational System." Rudd posited that the growth of radical youth organizations, such as the American Youth Congress and the Young Communist League, was inspired by an "entire educational system" which had been "reconstructed" with textbooks and courses teaching "that our economic and political institutions are decadent." He blamed the widespread teaching of "'Social science,' . . . (instead of) . . . history, geography and U. S. Government." Rudd cited the Rugg textbooks as the major culprit, and argued that Rugg "subtly but surely" implied a need for a state-planned economy and socialism. Rugg, he argued, used "dramatic episodes" to emphasize the worst aspects of our institutions. "Time after time," Rudd wrote, "he uses half-truths, partisan references, and an amazing liberty with historical facts, the net effect of which is to undermine the faith of children in the American way of life. The constantly recurring theme is an effort to sell the child the collectivist theory of society."[22]

The second article, by Orlen K. Armstrong, was titled, "Treason in the Textbooks," and appeared in the *American Legion Magazine* for September 1940. This was the official journal of the Legion and was distributed to one million homes. The article contained a bitter denunciation of the writers and teachers of the "new history," and quoted extensively from Rugg's text, *A History of American Government and Culture* and from its teacher's guide. He used these and other books by the "frontier thinkers" to document that the books sought:

- To present a new interpretation of history in order to "debunk" our heroes and cast doubt upon their motives, their patriotism, and their service to mankind.
- To cast aspersions upon our Constitution and our form of government, and shape opinions favorable to replacing them with socialistic control.
- To condemn the American system of private ownership and enterprise, and form opinions favorable to collectivism.
- To mould opinion against traditional religious faiths and ideas of morality, as being part of an outgrown system.

Armstrong also attacked fused courses which consolidate "history, geography, civics, and social science," and stated flatly that "these courses form a complete pattern of propaganda for a change in our political, economic, and social order." The author also went a step further and published a list of "subversive" books and magazines, which was later reprinted elsewhere. Once again, Rugg's textbook series was the central target.[23]

The Legion article created an immediate storm of controversy. Authors, educators, and even some Legionnaires attacked it, and a number of the blacklisted publications received an immediate retraction from the Legion. The associate secretary of the NEA wrote that the attack had "no adequate basis in fact." He argued, "It is not 'treason' to teach that American ideals require a fair chance for everyone in terms of economic, social, and educational opportunity," and that it was not treason "to teach that these ideals are not yet fully achieved," and to inspire youth to attain them.[24] Armstrong admitted, in the wake of the controversy, that he had not investigated a number of the publications he listed.[25] Yet, as is so often the case, the damage was done. Rugg, who had once boasted that "the only way to get somewhere in education was to attack someone big," had apparently met his match.[26]

The Legion campaign did not end after the partial retraction, but instead gathered steam. A campaign that had begun with the personal animus of Legionnaires Amos Fries and Augustin G. Rudd evolved into a major national campaign, led from national headquarters, and fought out town-by-town in hand-to-hand combat. In the fall of 1940 the Legion announced the hiring of R. Worth Shumaker, a school superintendent from West Virginia, to research and prepare a solid analysis of the Rugg materials. The hiring led to a series of articles and pamphlets which made a stronger case against Rugg and gave it a scholarly patina.[27]

Meanwhile the entire controversy garnered increasing national attention. According to an article in *Time* magazine, by the end of the Spring term in 1940, the Rugg textbooks had been banned from a half-dozen school systems. Critics objected to the Rugg texts, the article reported, "for picturing the U.S. as a land of unequal opportunity, and giving a class conscious account of the framing of the U.S. Constitution." The books were increasingly under attack "in the small town American Legion belt," the article reported, citing two fresh book "burnings" in the towns of Mountain Lakes and Wayne Township, NJ.[28]

THE STORM UNLEASHED

The next major development in the Rugg story raised the stakes considerably as it involved the activities of the National Association of Manufacturers, a mainstream organization with considerable resources. On December 11,

1940, the *New York Times* reported that the National Association of Manufacturers announced that it would initiate a survey of textbooks then in use
in the schools to see if it could find evidence of subversive teaching. The
activities of the NAM received extensive coverage from George Sokolsky in
the Hearst papers and were featured prominently and regularly in the *New
York Times*. Ralph Robey, an assistant professor of banking at Columbia
University and a columnist for *Newsweek,* was hired by the NAM to prepare
a series of abstracts of some 800 currently used social studies textbooks to
show the author's attitudes toward government and business.

On Saturday, February 22, 1941, a headline at the top of the front page
of the *New York Times* read:

UN-AMERICAN TONE SEEN IN TEXTBOOKS
ON SOCIAL SCIENCES

Survey of 600 Used in Schools Finds a Distorted Emphasis on Defects
of Democracy

ONLY A FEW CALLED RED

The article reported:

A "substantial portion" of the social science textbooks now used in
the high schools of this country tend to criticize our form of government and hold in derision or contempt the system of private enterprise, Dr. Ralph Robey, assistant professor of banking at Columbia
University, said yesterday in summarizing his personal conclusions
from abstracting the textbooks for the National Association of Manufacturers. . . . There is a notable tendency, he said, for books to play
down what has been accomplished in this country and to stress the
defects of our democracy. Only a few of the textbooks are actually
subversive in content and follow the Communist party line, according to the study. On the whole, the books do not bow to any "line" as
such, but tend to create discontent and unrest by their approach and
treatment of government and business questions, the educator found.

Next, the article reported:

During the last year or so a controversy over subversive textbooks has
disturbed the educational world. The social science textbooks by Dr.
Harold Rugg of Teachers College have come in for a particularly severe
attack. Several school systems have banned his books from the classroom, charging them with being too critical of our existing form of government. In one or two communities they were publicly burned.[29]

All of this, including the reference to Rugg, appeared on the front page. The abstracts provided selected and provocative quotations from the texts, segments in which textbook authors critically described, or raised questions about, the functioning of government, the distribution of wealth and incidence of poverty, or the interplay of power and wealth. The quotations were provided without any sense of the remainder of each text, much of which would be found utterly innocuous. Yet, the selected evidence cited did suggest, quite strongly, that many textbooks were raising difficult questions about the real functioning of American institutions.[30]

Development of the NAM abstracts and subsequent communications were shaped and influenced, in part, by members of the publicity office, administration, and office staff of the NAM. The organization had a long history of interest and concern regarding the general portrayal of American business in schools and textbooks, prior to involvement in the textbook controversy. The organization's general hope was that schools, teachers, and materials would inculcate patriotism by a focus on "the historical and spiritual foundations of the American system of government, free enterprise, and religious liberty."[31]

By April 1940, the NAM had clearly outlined a set of possible activities for "educational cooperation" aimed at stimulating better understanding of the business point of view. By late summer, concerns over schoolbooks had evolved through preliminary investigation and discussion into a plan to develop textbook abstracts. The abstracts were ostensibly prepared in an effort to provide unbiased information regarding the texts, so that interested persons could decide whether to read, or investigate further, any particular book.[32]

Internal memoranda from the files of the NAM suggest that many in the organization's offices were rather squeamish about the entire enterprise, and that it was considered a "ticklish subject." Because of the nation's tradition of academic freedom, and previous business association miscues, which had led to negative publicity, many staff members believed that it could result in negative publicity for business and the NAM. As it turned out, these worries were well founded.[33]

Protests, corrections, and replies to Dr. Robey's findings came quickly. Leaders of the National Council for the Social Studies made immediate contact with leaders of the NAM asking whether it "repudiates or endorses" Robey's statement. The NAM President, Walter D. Fuller responded with a press release stating that Robey's criticisms were his "personal opinion only." Later, after a storm of stories and editorials in the press, the NAM attempted to further distance itself from the controversy and expressed regret that "distorted" impressions of the project had been given such wide currency.[34]

THE AFTERMATH

The defense against the attacks on the Rugg textbooks was mounted on several fronts. The Academic Freedom Committee of NCSS issued a statement supporting academic freedom, and later prepared "a packet of reading matter on freedom of teaching in the social studies area," which included a sixty-six page booklet on fending off attacks on textbooks.[35] The Council of the American Historical Association asked Professor Arthur M. Schlesinger to draft a statement regarding controversial issues in textbooks. The statement, which was approved by the Council, gave strong support for the inclusion of controversial questions in "the historical account," and for encouraging a "spirit of inquiry" in young people.[36]

Rugg himself was undoubtedly the chief advocate for the defense of social studies, and the Rugg textbooks, against the attackers, and numerous friends and colleagues rushed to his defense. One of the most active groups was the American Committee on Democracy and Intellectual Freedom organized in the late 1930s to address a range of intellectual freedom issues, and chaired by Franz Boaz at Columbia.[37] Among other groups that furnished support were the Association of Textbook Publishers, and Rugg's associates on the journal *Frontiers of Democracy*. Even John Dewey came to Rugg's defense in an op. ed. piece which appeared in the *New York Times*. Like several groups and individuals, Dewey defended Rugg on the grounds of intellectual freedom even though he didn't always agree with Rugg's ideas or actions, and clearly did not think of Rugg as a major thinker.[38]

Rugg gave an able defense of his work, and attempted to meet every attack directly, appearing in person "whenever and wherever possible." Rugg's confrontations with his accusers followed a familiar pattern. First, he would be accused of being a Communist, then he would be criticized over his plan for a socialistic society in *The Great Technology*. When pressed, critic after critic would admit that they had not read the books. Under siege on every side, Rugg wrote an autobiographical work to tell his side of the story. *That Men May Understand* was published in April 1941, and received generally favorable reviews. *The New York Times Book Review* scoffed at the idea of Rugg being a communist, and described his generation of educational reformers as having "imbibed the antique liquor of utopianism which was always turning New England heads." *The Nation* compared Rugg to St. Paul carrying the gospel, and Teachers College to the early church. *Publishers Weekly* endorsed the book and joined Rugg in attacking his critics, accusing Dilling, Forbes, and Hart of preying on "the prejudices of the American people" and calling Rugg's book "a vigorous and adequate reply to his critics."[39]

After a little more time had passed, discussion of the attacks continued in the professional literature. One article, written by a school superintendent, argued that many of the attacks were part of a deliberate effort to undermine "public confidence in the schools so that school appropriations may be reduced." Another author provided a larger historical context for the attacks and suggested that they were part of a larger "War on Social Studies." The real animus of the critics, he wrote, "is against the whole modern conception of the social studies as a realistic approach to life. ..." In opposition to the critics, he argued that young people have "the right to know what the world is all about and to learn what can be done about it."[40]

As it turned out, February 22, 1941, the date of the Robey story, was a watershed in the war on social studies. Up to that point, tension built while the movement for integrated social studies and a focus on issues and problems with a meliorist or reconstructionist purpose gathered steam. After the Robey article, the tide had turned. The struggle over the Rugg textbooks continued in many communities, aided and supported by national campaigns orchestrated by the American Legion, the Advertising Federation, The Guardians of American Education, and others. In a few cases, the attempt to censor the texts was successful. In others, they were retained for some time, then quietly dropped when it came time for the adoption of new books. In 1943 Shumaker and the Legion officers believed that they had ousted the textbooks in approximately 1,500 communities.[41] Workbooks for the series continued to sell well after the attacks, an indication that the books were still being used for some time in many schools well into the 1940s.[42] However, by the middle of the decade, the Rugg textbook series and program had fallen from prominence and had virtually disappeared.

Though he never admitted it publicly, or with colleagues, the loss of his textbook series and the leadership and prestige it had given him, left Rugg deeply hurt.[43] Rugg continued to teach and write, but focused on scholarly work and college-level textbooks, giving up his efforts to revolutionize social studies in schools. Following the textbook dust up, controversy continued to haunt Rugg's life. He was at the center of another controversy in 1951, sparked by his reputation as a "radical" following a speaking engagement at Ohio State University. Also, during his remaining years he was the subject of an in depth FBI investigation.[44] Despite the controversies and unfortunate fate that befell him, Rugg continued to maintain his beliefs, and continued to support education for social reconstruction, though his public profile was forever altered and subdued. He died of a heart attack on May 17, 1960, at his home in Woodstock, NY.

In the larger picture, by the early 1940s, social studies, it seemed, was on the defensive. The possibility of critical, reflective social studies was seriously in doubt, and attacks on progressive educators continued to mount throughout the decade. Though Progressives would have both proponents and defenders, criticism of Progressive education seemed a rising tide that no seawall could restrain. Despite, and perhaps partly because of the lasting fame generated by public uproar over his textbook series, Rugg's achievement remains, to this day, the high point of Progressive reform in social studies. The attacks on the Rugg textbooks, and the war against social studies of which they were a part, were pieces of a much larger pattern of criticism that would have a lasting impact on educational rhetoric in the United States and on the shaping of the curriculum.[45]

CONCLUSION

What can we learn from an account of Rugg's life? His is certainly a story full of drama, with a cast of heroes and villains, and key turning points which capture, in microcosm, many of the basic ideological conflicts in American political and cultural life, as well as conflicting positions in American education and curriculum history.

Since the uproar over the Rugg textbooks, there have been many similar episodes. One of these occurred on the heels of the Rugg controversy. Allan Nevins' article in *New York Times Magazine*, which charged that United States history was no longer sufficiently taught in the nation's schools, inspired a spirited and protracted episode of controversy during the Second World War. Another prolonged episode of attacks on social studies developed in the 1950s as part of an assault on Progressivism writ large. Intellectual critics such as Arthur Bestor called social studies an anti-intellectual "social stew," while red-baiting critics characterized it as a forum of propaganda for Communism. Yet another round of criticism came in the aftermath of the new social studies reforms of the 60s and 70s and took the form of a series of academic freedom cases involving individual teachers, followed by the larger controversy over MACOS, an innovative project of the new social studies. Most recently, attacks on social studies were a core ingredient of the revival of history during the 80s and 90s, which led to dramatic growth in history offerings in schools and a narrowing of the social studies curriculum.[46]

During all of this, critiques of Rugg have continued, usually in the background, with Rugg portrayed as the poster boy for everything that is wrong with social studies education in schools. Contrary to the critics of Rugg, of recent or more distant vintage, Rugg's achievement was the high point of progressive reform in social studies. Moreover, there are several important implications stemming from an examination of Rugg's life and work, and the controversies he inspired.

The Rugg controversy, and the general failure of issues-oriented social studies to have greater success in social studies classrooms, has inspired more than one scholar from the issues-centered camp to reflect seriously on the future prospects for reform.[47] Clearly, one of the main reasons that issues education, broadly defined as attention to social issues of past and present in the curriculum, has had relatively limited success in the nation's classrooms is that we seem to have something of a cultural taboo against raising certain questions in the public schools, especially when they touch on some of the basic and sacred pillars of American economic and cultural success (e.g., capitalism, the Constitution, the founding fathers, etc.). The Rugg textbook controversy illustrates that a significant and vocal segment of the American populace does not want such questions aired in schools, and instead prefers imposition of an "our country right or wrong" mentality. Also, there seems to be a generally high level of support for history as the core of social studies among historians, and among many citizens, thus eclipsing visions of an integrated synthesis, as represented by Rugg and many other Progressive reformers. Historians are a strong and prestigious interest group when compared with teachers and teacher educators. Advocates of any alternative to traditional, discipline-based approaches face an uphill battle, in part because so little knowledge and understanding of the alternatives exists among the general populace.

The Rugg textbook controversy was an especially dramatic and important episode—the turning point at which criticism of social studies became a sort of national pastime. Prior to the Rugg tempest, critical and issues-centered approaches to social studies appeared to be headed for greater prominence in the nation's classrooms. Afterward, social studies itself appeared to be on the run, in a defensive posture and losing ground to advocates of more traditional approaches to learning and to more conservative visions of the American way.

One of the key implications of the controversy is that criticisms often stick, despite defense and counter-arguments. The sensationalistic charges of subversion and un-Americanism that critics attached to Rugg frequently appeared in prominent spaces, while Rugg's defense was too often relegated to the back pages. Over the years, similar criticisms of educators, and especially of social studies, have taken their toll on the vitality and public impression of the field and have contributed to the decline of Progressive social studies, the revival of traditional history, and a narrowing of the social studies curriculum and the range of ideas and questions which may be considered in the nation's classrooms. The sum total of criticisms over the years may have left the general impression that social studies is an unsound educational idea, developed by second rate scholars in schools of education, and dominated by radicals with an inclination to use the schools to subvert the social order.

A number of additional implications might be drawn from Rugg's life and the controversies he inspired. First, and perhaps most important, Rugg's example illustrates the importance, and the potential impact, of dreaming big and bold visions of reform, not only as a wellspring for inspiration, but as a source of ideas for practical action, praxis, with the aim of social improvement. Rugg had a worthy vision that was pedagogically advanced and forward looking. It seriously questioned capitalism, its apparatus and influences. Rugg's basic critique is largely still relevant. We need a renewed questioning of capitalism and of the mainstream institutions in American life. I believe it is healthy to ask such questions, and to ask school children, beginning at an early age, to begin wrestling with questions of fairness and equity. In short, today's education can benefit from the contributions of both past and present advocates of education for social justice.

Second, though his textbooks and ideas were sure to inspire some criticism, Harold Rugg did not deserve his fate. On the contrary, Harold Rugg was a seminal thinker who fully deserved to receive the recognition and financial fortune that sometimes accompanies a brilliant idea combined with hard work. The controversy that engulfed Rugg, and the defense offered by Rugg and those who rose to support him, suggests that some dreams are worth fighting for, even though the struggle may come at a cost and may take its toll. The Rugg episode tells us that the forces of reaction are always with us, and that the price of freedom, of free speech and academic freedom in schools, is, as Rugg himself once wrote, "eternal vigilance."

In the present era, we have seemingly entered a time period during which respect for the professional intelligence, knowledge, and choices of teachers and the freedom to choose alternative paths has reached a low ebb. Curriculum reform is increasingly mandated by centralized authorities and driven by a conservative corporate agenda for which the kinds of questions raised by Rugg and other similar social studies reformers are no longer welcome. During this era, it is especially important to keep alternative visions alive, to nurture deep dreams of justice and fair play, and to make sure that critics of liberal or issues-centered social studies are met with a stout defense. The attacks on Rugg, and especially the sustained campaign carried on by the American Legion, present early examples of the power of interest-group financing and organization. More recently, with the revival of traditional history, foundation supported interest-group financing has proven to have, once again, a significant influence on the direction of social studies in schools.[48]

Third, Rugg did make a few mistakes. Education for social justice can take many forms. In the Rugg materials, it seems there was some justification for the charge that he presented more evidence on the side of the questions which he supported than those he opposed. After all, it was a reflection of the frontier thinkers, those on the cutting edge of knowledge.

So, it seems, we must learn to include a balance of materials, sources, and interpretations, and challenge students to make up their own minds about the meaning of past and present institutions and societal dilemmas. Though this may not silence all critics, it is more easily defensible as part of the "American way," and as a clear example of John Dewey's method of intelligence applied to the social studies arena.

Fourth, in interpreting the meaning of the Rugg textbook controversy for today's social education, it is important to note that we now have a textbook machine by which certain books are approved, but only after they are altered, sanitized to reflect "a vision of America sculpted and sanded down."[49] This is, in part, a direct legacy of the Rugg textbook controversy. We have reached what amounts to a state of perpetual censorship of school materials, partly as a result of the Rugg censure. This situation requires serious and sustained attention. It is one of the few areas of agreement among liberal social studies theorists and neo-conservative critics.[50] This dilemma, along with the other central questions and issues raised by the life and work of Harold Rugg, deserve the continued attention of educational professionals at all levels as well as a high level of public awareness and discourse.

Given the interest among social studies professors in critical and social justice approaches to education, the continuing national support for standards, centralized curriculum making, and high-stakes testing, and the present climate of national and international crisis, it behooves us to be aware of, or be defeated by, the successes, the failures, and the mistakes—the "lessons"—of Harold Rugg.

NOTES

1. This manuscript is drawn from a book length draft manuscript, Ronald W. Evans, *This Happened in America: Harold Rugg and the Censure of Social Studies*, in preparation, and from Ronald W. Evans, *The Social Studies Wars: What Should We Teach the Children?* (New York: Teachers College Press, 2004).

2. Edgar Dawson postcard to Wilbur Murra, 22 December, 1940, box 5, series 4B, Archives of the National Council for the Social Studies, Milbank Memorial Library, Teachers College, Columbia University.

3. Herbert M. Kliebard and Greg Wegner, "Harold Rugg and the Reconstruction of the Social Studies Curriculum: The Treatment of the 'Great War' in His Textbook Series," *The Formation of the School Subjects: The Struggle for Creating an American Institution*, ed. Thomas S. Popkewitz (New York: Falmer), 268-287.

4. Ronald W. Evans, *The Social Studies Wars: What Should We Teach the Children?* (New York: Teachers College Press, 2004).

5. Evans, *Social Studies Wars.*

6. William Ayers, Jean Ann Hunt, and Therese Quinn, ed., *Teaching for Social Justice: A Democracy and Education Reader* (New York: The New Press, Teachers College Press, distributed by W. W. Norton, 1998).

7. Harold O. Rugg, "On Reconstructing the Social Studies: Comments on Mr. Schafer's Letter," *Historical Outlook* 12 (October 1921): 249–252.

8. Murry R. Nelson, "The Development of the Rugg Social Studies Materials," *Theory and Research in Social Education* 5 (1977): 64–83; George Allen Kay, "Harold Rugg: Social Reconstructionist and Educational Statesman" (Ph.D. diss., State University of New York, Buffalo, 1969).

9. Elmer A. Winters, "Man and His Changing Society: The Textbooks of Harold Rugg," *History of Education Quarterly* 7 (Winter 1967): 509–510.

10. Winters, "Man and His Changing Society," 509–510.

11. Harold Rugg, *An Introduction to Problems of American Culture* (Boston: Ginn and Company, 1931), vi, vii.

12. Rugg, *An Introduction to Problems of American Culture*, 3–10.

13. Peter F. Carbone, Jr., *The Social and Educational Thought of Harold Rugg* (Durham, NC: Duke University Press, 1977), 4.

14. Harold O. Rugg, *The Great Technology: Social Chaos and the Public Mind* (New York: The John Day Company, 1933), 106.

15. Rugg, *The Great Technology*.

16. Rugg, *The Great Technology*, 18, 233.

17. Rugg, *The Great Technology*, 171–182.

18. Michael E. Price, "A Thousand Year March: The Historical Vision of Harold Rugg," Paper presented at the annual meeting of the National Council for the Social Studies, 20 November 1983.

19. Augustin G. Rudd, Hamilton Hicks and Alfred T. Falk, eds., *Undermining Our Republic: Do You Know What the Children Are Being Taught in Our Public Schools? You'll Be Surprised* (New York: Guardians of American Education, Inc., 1941), 41.

20. Harold O. Rugg, "Confidential Analysis of the Current (1939–1940) Attacks on the Rugg Social Science Series, Prepared by Harold Rugg in May–June 1940," pp. 16–19, "Harold Rugg" folder, box 58, William F. Russell Papers, Milbank Memorial Library, Teachers College, Columbia University.

21. Elizabeth Dilling, *The Red Network: A Who's Who of Radicalism for Patriots* (Kenilworth, IL: The Author, 1934).

22. Augustin G. Rudd, "Our 'Reconstructed' Educational System," *Nation's Business* (April 1940): 27–28, 93–94.

23. Orlen K. Armstrong, "Treason in the Textbooks," *American Legion Magazine* (September 1940), 51, 70; Elmer A. Winters, "Harold Rugg and Education for Social Reconstruction," (Ph.D. diss., University of Wisconsin, Madison), 179–182. The article listed 21 books, 16 of them by Rugg.

24. Reprint of William G. Carr, "This Is Not Treason," *The Journal of the National Education Association* (November 1940), file 7, box 45, series 4C Director's Correspondence, NCSS Archives.

25. The blacklist was initially submitted to Legion headquarters by Rudd, but was prematurely published without his prior knowledge or approval. See Augustin G. Rudd to Homer L. Chaillaux, September 20, 1940, Legion dead letter files as cited in, Orville E. Jones, "Activities of the American Legion in Textbook Analysis and Criticism 1938–1951" (Ph.D. diss., University of Oklahoma, Norman, 1957), 61.

26. The Rugg books remained on the list. Armstrong was active in the Legion when the article was written and stated to Winters that his interest in the "socialist views" in the textbooks was stimulated by his participation in the Americanism Committee of the Legion. Interviewed in the late 1960s, Armstrong stated, "I still feel that Rugg was the leader of the pack who tried to influence the thinking of young Americans away from the ideals that made our nation strong and great." See Winters, "Harold Rugg and Education for Social Reconstruction," 182, footnote #90.

27. R. Worth Shumaker, "No 'New Order' for Our Schools" *The American Legion Magazine* (April 1941): 5–7, 43, 44–46; *Rugg Philosophy Analyzed* Vol 1–4 (Indianapolis, IN: American Legion, 1941).

28. "Book Burnings," *Time 9* (September 1940).

29. Benjamin Fine, "Un-American Tone Seen in Textbooks on Social Sciences," *New York Times* Late City Edition (22 February 1941) , 1.

30. Author, "Excerpts From Various Textbooks Criticized in the Survey," *New York Times* (22 February 1941), 6.

31. Committee on Educational Cooperation, National Association of Manufacturers, Official draft of a memorandum of industry's recommendations for the improvement of American educational methods in the preparing of students for citizendhsip in a republic, (28 June 1939): 3–5, "Robey Textbook Survey" folder, series 111, National Industrial Information Committee, Subject Files, box 847, NAM Papers, Accession # 1411, Hagley Museum and Library, Wilmington, Delaware.

32. NAM Educational Cooperation Meeting, "Suggested local activities to stimulate better understanding between industrialists and educators" (22 April 1940), Waldorf-Astoria, New York City, "Robey Textbook Survey" folder, series 111, National Industrial Information Committee, Subject Files, box 847, NAM Papers.

33. C. E. Harrison, inter-office memo, to W. B. Weisenburger (25 July 1940), C. E. Harrison to H. W. Prentis (10 January 1941), and attached inter-office memo, C. E. Harrison to W. B. Weisenburger (10 January 1941), C. E. Harrison to H. W. Prentis (19 March 1941), all contained in "Robey Textbook Survey" folder, National Industrial Information Committee, Subject Files, box 847, series 111, NAM Papers.

34. Erling M. Hunt, "Dr. Robey Versus the NAM?" *Social Education* 5 (1941): 288–292; Walter D. Fuller telegram to Wilbur Murra (24 February 1941), file 1, box 2 series 7, Committee Records, Academic Freedom Committee Correspondence, NCSS Archives; Evans, *Social Studies Wars;* Erling M. Hunt, "The NAM Restates its Policy," *Social Education* 5 (1941): 328.

35. Merle Curti to Wilbur Murra (14 October 1941), file 1, box 2, series 7, Committee Records, Academic Freedom Correspondence, NCSS Archives.

36. American Historical Association, "Freedom of Textbooks," *Social Education* 5 (1941), 487–488.

37. ACDIF Press Release, "A committee of ten outstanding social scientists ..." (23 February), American Committee for Democracy and Intellectual Freedom, New York. Franz Boas Professional Papers, B61p, sub collection 2, box A-Bend, ACDIF folder, American Philosophical Society, Philadelphia. See Jonathan Zimmerman, *Whose America?: Culture Wars in the Public Schools* (Cambridge: Harvard University Press, 2002).

38. John Dewey, "Investigating Education," *New York Times* 6 (May 1940); John Dewey to Sidney Hook (25 April 1944), Correspondence with Sidney Hook, John Dewey Collection, box 10, series 1, Dewey Papers, Dewey Center, University of Southern Illinois at Carbondale.

39. Harold Rugg, *That Men May Understand: An American in the Long Armistice* (New York: Doubleday, Doran and Co., 1941). Winters, "Harold Rugg and Education for Social Reconstruction," 187–189.

40. C. M. Dannelly, "Facing a Major Threat," *The School Executive* 60 (1941): 32; Kenneth M. Gould, "The War on Social Studies," *Common Ground* (Autumn 1941): 83–91.

41. Jones, "Activities of the American Legion in Textbook Analysis and Criticism."

42. Winters, "Harold Rugg and Education for Social Reconstruction," 510.

43. Alf Evers. (2003). Interview with Alf Evers, Woodstock resident, town historian and author, and a personal friend of Rugg, Woodstock, New York, June 14, 2003, conducted by the author, and Katharine Alling. (2005). Interview with Katharine Alling, Rugg's step-daughter, January, 2005, conducted by the author.

44. "Campus Probe in Order," *Columbus Dispatch* (23 July 1951), "Rugg" folder, box 69, faculty files, Public Relations Office, Archives, Milbank Memorial Library, Teachers College, Columbia University; "Ohio State Trustees Assail Rugg Speech," *New York Times* 5 (September 1951): 29; Rugg FBI Memorandum. Office Memorandum, SAC, Cincinnati, to Director, FBI (J.Edgar Hoover), 1 October 1951, Rugg FBI files, obtained from Federal Bureau of Investigation under Freedom of Information Act in 2003, Washington, DC, material unclassified, November 6, 2003; Murry R. Nelson and H. Wells Singleton, "FBI surveillance of three progressive educators: Curricular aspects," Paper presented at the Society for the Study of Curriculum History, Annual Conference, 1977.

45. Evans, *Social Studies Wars.*

46. Evans, *Social Studies Wars.*

47. Ronald W. Evans, Patricia G. Avery and Patricia Pedersen, "Taboo topics: Cultural restraint on teaching social issues," *The Social Studies* 90 (1999): 218–224; Richard E. Gross, "Reasons for the Limited Acceptance of the Problems Approach," *Social Studies* 80 no. 5 (September/October 1989): 185–186; Donald W. Oliver, "Reflections on Peter Carbone's 'The Social and Educational Thought of Harold Rugg,'" *Social Education* 42 no. 7

(November/December 1978): 593–597; James P. Shaver, "Lessons From the Past: The Future of an Issues-Centered Curriculum," *Social Studies* 80, no. 5 (September/October 1989): pp——.

48. Steven Selden, "The neo-conservative assault on the undergraduate curriculum," Paper presented at the annual meeting of the American Educational Research Association, San Diego (April 2004).

49. Frances Fitzgerald, *America Revised: History Schoolbooks in the Twentieth Century* (Boston: Little, Brown, 1979).

50. James S. Leming, et al., ed. *Where Did Social Studies Go Wrong?* (Washington, DC: Fordham Foundation, 2003); Webcast panel discussion: "Reclaiming Social Studies," sponsored by The American Enterprise Institute (Fall 2003).

CHAPTER 4

THEODORE BRAMELD

Reconstructionism for our Emerging Age

Craig Kridel

I have never been comfortable in the inner sanctums of pure scholarship for too long a period. The air is not sufficiently saturated with
the oxygen of everyday human life. So all the way through my professional years, I have found time both to study philosophy and to relate
theory to practice.

Theodore Brameld

Theodore Burghart Hurt Brameld (1904–1987) could easily have led a distinguished career in a university department of philosophy. Trained at the
University of Chicago with the well-known and highly-regarded American
Progressive philosopher and politician, T. V. Smith, and versed in early
twentieth-century Russian social-political thought, Brameld instead
wished to breathe the oxygen of everyday human life and made the field
of education his professional home. Following a distinguished line of Progressive educators who left university philosophy departments to become
members of colleges of education, Brameld sought to implement Progressive ideals and to strive for cultural renewal through education.[1] His quest

---

Social Reconstruction: People, Politics, Perspectives, pages 69–88
Copyright © 2006 by Information Age Publishing

to redefine the *means* of Progressive education and to designate Reconstructionist *ends* for educational reform proved a lifelong theme from his first major work in 1950, *Ends and Means in Education—A Midcentury Appraisal*, to his 1961 publication, *Education for an Emerging Age: Newer Ends and Stronger Means*, and concluding with his final work on education, *The Climactic Decades: Mandate to Education*, published in 1970.[2] In his effort "to relate theory to practice," he directed his considerable analytical abilities to address many of the classic educational issues of the day: fostering democracy in schools and society, integrating the subjects of the curriculum, reconciling free inquiry with the inculcation of values, and establishing broader cultural and international awareness.

As a junior colleague of the Social Reconstructionists of the 1930s, who nurtured his entry into the field of education, Brameld became actively involved with the activities of the Progressive Education Association (PEA) and embraced a vibrant Reconstructionist ideology from the 40s through the 70s. His beliefs, in keeping with the rudiments of Progressive education, were "ever searching, ever experimenting, ever moving on towards higher ideals and more complete realization of them."[3] As a charismatic speaker and shrewd promoter of this educational movement, Brameld used all means to popularize and further promote the ends of reconstructionism. His legacy is apparent today as generations of education students who enroll in educational foundations courses are introduced to Reconstructionist thought. For educators who are now in search of ways to improve schools, Brameld serves as a model for those who wish to transform education and to initiate educational change with carefully considered ends and means.

BIOGRAPHICAL OVERVIEW

Theodore Brameld was born in Neillsville, Wisconsin. After graduation from Neillsville High School in 1922, he continued on to Ripon College, in his native Wisconsin, where he completed an AB degree in English in 1926. Following two years in an administrative position at his alma mater, he entered the doctoral program in philosophy at the University of Chicago, where he studied with T. V. Smith, distinguished philosopher, activist, and politician. Brameld was graduated in 1931 after completing one of the first scholarly examinations in English of the writings of Lenin. His dissertation, "The Role of Acquiescence in Leninism," was revised and later published in 1933 as *A Philosophic Approach to Communism* by the University of Chicago Press.[4] Brameld took a faculty position in the department of philosophy at Long Island University in 1935 and later taught at Adelphi College. He also enrolled in post-graduate studies at Columbia University and served as a Visiting Associate Professorship at Teachers College before moving to the University of Minnesota in 1939 as a professor in the College of Education.[5]

Establishing himself as an educational philosopher during his eight years at the University of Minnesota, from 1939 to 1947, Brameld experimented with a high school curriculum project, conducted race-related research for the Rosenwald Fund, and edited a John Dewey Society yearbook.[6] He returned to New York in 1947 to accept a professorship in educational philosophy at New York University, a position he held for the next ten years. During that time he published four textbooks—*Ends and Means in Education, Patterns of Educational Philosophy, Philosophies of Education in Cultural Perspective,* and *Toward a Reconstructed Philosophy of Education.*[7] These "introductions to educational philosophy" redefined and fully substantiated Reconstructionism as a recognized educational movement in education, to be understood alongside the traditional "isms" of Perennialism, Essentialism, and Progressivism. The final years of Brameld's New York University appointment were spent at the University of Puerto Rico where he participated in an action research project to help redesign the educational program for Puerto Rico.[8]

Brameld accepted a professorship of educational philosophy at Boston University in 1958, a post he held until 1969 on the occasion of his official retirement. While in Boston, his interests took on more international dimensions. During the 1960s, he published *Education for an Emerging Age, The Use of Explosive Ideas in Education, Education as Power,* and, stemming from research conducted on a Fulbright research grant, *Japan: Culture, Education, and Change in Two Communities.*[9] Brameld became an active lecturer and teacher during his emeriti years. He published *The Teacher as World Citizen* and formed the Society for Educational Reconstruction with some of his former students, an active organization publishing the *Cutting Edge* and staging conferences at Brameld's summer home, Hardscrabble, near Hanover, NH. Journal contributors and conference participants included a distinguished array of educators including Michael Harrington, Rene Dubos, Maxine Greene, Myles Horton, Herbert Kohl, David R. Conrad, and Frank A. Stone, editor of *Cutting Edge* and author of the recently released biography, *Theodore Brameld's Educational Reconstruction.*[10] *Cutting Edge* developed a loyal following of readers, including educational reformer John Holt, *Saturday Review* editor Norman Cousins, and Harold Taylor, activist and former president of Sarah Lawrence College.

Throughout his career Brameld seemed to have a disposition for coining rather unique educational terms: anthropological philosophy, educology (the study of the field of education in contrast to education as teacher preparation), anthropotherapy (the planned improvement of human life by integrating cultural analysis with normative values and ethical actions), and culturology (the philosophical examination of the influences upon members of a culture).

EDUCATIONAL RECONSTRUCTIONISM:
"A PHILOSOPHY OF MAGNETIC FORESIGHT"

As Brameld became more prominent in the field of education during the late 1940s, the controversy between Progressives and Social Reconstructionists (George Counts, Harold Rugg, Goodwin Watson, John Childs, and Norman Woelfel) subsided. This permitted Brameld to make the necessary distinction between his philosophy, Reconstructionism, and 30s Social Reconstructionism. Brameld regarded the adjective "social" as too restrictive and viewed the period writings of Counts and others as representative of a dramatically different domestic and world situation. Influenced primarily by the Great Depression, the Social Reconstructionists were concerned with domestic ills and with ways education might help to change the political and economic systems. In reaction to the more conservative members of the Progressive Education Association, they were trying to focus on "social ends" rather than on what had been the traditional focus—personal needs.

During the 1930s and 40s, Brameld aligned himself with the Social Reconstructionists and approached education from more domestic and economic perspectives. His 1935 article in *The Social Frontier*, "Karl Marx and the American Teacher," is often cited to note his interest in class struggle and economic critique of American education.[11] In fact, Brameld seemed more involved in articulating the potential "agential power" of schools and exploring new roles for teachers to engage in social action. Brameld would later assert, in 1952, that his Marxist writings were a "fumbling inquiry into what Marx might have contributed, if anything, to the democratic thought of the time" and claimed that Marxism was an inadequate, dogmatic doctrine.[12] What held true in Brameld's work during this period, however, was his belief in the teacher's role for social action and the importance of educators and students to examine their beliefs.

In conjunction with this *Social Frontier* article, Brameld, in an earlier essay, had surveyed college students to ascertain not just their political and economic views but also their ability to adopt new ideas and convictions while still embracing open-mindedness and critical inquiry. This research would permit Brameld to later urge teachers to set aside their docility and timid criticism of American capitalism and to introduce new ideas to students who were capable and willing to question principles and prejudices. For Brameld, the survey data indicated that students were accepting of radical ideas, and introducing such information became a necessary role of the social sciences, and implicitly, of the teacher.

By the 1950s, Brameld turned his focus away from domestic and economic topics. The cultural setting for American education had changed dramatically and Brameld, whose writing recognized the improving technology in the fields of transportation and communication, acknowledged an ever-shrinking planet. He had come to view the community for reconstruction as encompassing the entire world. A cultural transformation was underway and, for Brameld, post–World War II planning and reconstruction must be aimed "toward the desperate plight, growing power, and emerging goals of the underdeveloped areas of the world, inhabited by the bulk of the world's population."[13] Brameld continued to emphasize social ends, similar to the earlier Social Reconstructionist, but he shifted from an economic to a more anthropological, cultural critique of society and redefined his educational philosophy to include a utopian vision for "health, abundance, security for the great masses;" an emphasis upon community, democracy, and collectivism ("group mind") for a "world in which national sovereignty is utterly subordinated to international authority;" and social action to achieve clearly defined, yet ever-changing, social ends attainable through the development of powerful, technological means.[14] With this changing focus, Brameld also distanced himself from his contemporaries, the University of Illinois Social Reconstructionists (Kenneth Benne, William O. Stanley, and B. O. Smith), who drew upon a more political and human relations approach for social change.

Brameld first introduced his version of Reconstructionism not in a focused polemic but, instead, in comprehensive, synoptic textbooks where other educational philosophies were discussed. Drawing heavily upon the ideas of Dewey, Reconstructionism became a coalescence of Progressivism with a concern for "planetary transformation;" however, this was not "another species of eclecticism" articulated by Brameld merely for the sake of trying to be distinctive.[15] His synthesis was achieved, in part, by depicting Progressivism as antiquated. As early as 1950, Brameld recognized the ultimate demise of Progressive education—"thoroughly misrepresented, hated, and sometimes honestly opposed"—and saw no way for this formerly vibrant educational ideology to change schools. While somewhat unjust, Brameld chastised Progressives for "the silly extremes to which 'child-centered schools' have occasionally gone" and an emphasis upon means and individual ends rather than focusing upon social ends.[16]

Though Progressive education was proper for an age of nationalism, capitalistic democracy, and individualistic liberalism, Progressivism was now too dated for the quickly changing contemporary times. For Brameld, Progressivism represented "the educational effort of an adolescent culture suffering from the pleasant agonies of growing up."[17] Reconstructionism, in contrast, represented a contemporary, refined form of Progressivism (along with certain positive attributes from Essentialism and Perennialism), offering a design during times when the present culture lacked meaning. Reconstructionist education, stated Brameld, "encourages students, teachers, and all members of the community not merely to study knowledge and problems crucial to our period of culture but also to make up their minds about the most promising solutions and then to act concertedly."[18]

An underlying premise of Reconstructionism redirected one of the most fundamental roles of education—namely, the transmission of culture. Brameld asserted that schools could no longer merely reflect society (i.e., transmit culture), but, instead, that education must become a process of cultural reconstruction and renewal. The specific educational ends were not identified by Brameld; however, throughout his career, he identified themes (some later called "explosive ideas")—democracy, power and control, class, culture, evolution—that would constitute the conversation for reconstruction. Brameld would later help to determine the four goals of the Society for Educational Reconstructionism—democratic socialism, global order, cooperative power, and self-transformation—that would serve to articulate the operations of the educational activist.[19]

Brameld was still left with the difficulty of assuring that acceptable ends could be predetermined during the process of cultural renewal. For this, "operational consensus" became a way—a means—to determine the fruitfulness of shared ends. Brameld, similar to the Progressives, placed great faith in the intelligence of the common person and in democratic dialogue and critical inquiry in order to reach cultural ends that served to better the human condition. Of course, some viewed Brameld's philosophy as being educationally and politically naïve. Nonetheless, he called for educators to construct "blueprints of a new social order, adequate enough to eliminate the tragedies of our present system, desirable enough to inspire fervent devotion to it as an achievable ideal, and implemented by a method powerful enough to reach the objective."[20] Later, he would avoid "blueprint" and dissociate himself from the term that he viewed had taken on an invidious use of a rigid, predefined pattern. Instead, Brameld turned to "design" as a way to suggest flexible ends.[21] In essence, Brameld altered and reinvigorated the purposes of education from mere transmission to renewal. His call for schools not to impose a blueprint, but instead to develop designs for living, offered a direction for educational ends without being overly rigid and predefined.

For Brameld, Reconstructionism—a "philosophy of magnetic foresight"[22]—could now be placed alongside other educational traditions and treated as first among equals. Brameld's promotional abilities came forth clearly as he proceeded to popularize his educational movement. In his textbooks, he constructed a conceptual scaffold to introduce four educational philosophies: Reconstructionism, Progressivism, Essentialism, and Perennialism. Brameld's "isms" were aligned with conservative/traditional, eternal/reactionary, liberal, and radical perspectives all brought to life by descriptions and fictional narratives. Reconstructionism became an accepted dimension of any introductory conversation of educational philosophies and, thanks to Brameld, served as a legitimate choice for a legion of preservice teachers who were asked to compose their teaching values, creeds, and beliefs.

THE IMPOSITION CONTROVERSY
AND DEFENSIBLE PARTIALITY

[Reconstructionism's] emphasis on commitment to agreed-upon, future-looking goals thus raises once more the old problem of bias and indoctrination.[23]

Although Brameld may have successfully distanced himself from the Social Reconstructionists, he nevertheless needed a response to the major criticism of their position—namely, if educators engage in the reconstruction of society with defined social ends, would not their actions constitute an imposition of values and represent a form of indoctrination? Brameld could not overlook the importance of articulating a clear rejoinder to this charge since, in many respects, indoctrination split the Progressives and may well have assisted in the demise of the Progressive Education Association.

The topic was debated by Boyd Bode and John Childs in the pages of *The Social Frontier* and came to be known as "the imposition controversy," representing one of the most thoughtful dialogues on the subject.[24] Childs (and later Brameld) called upon educators to build a guiding social philosophy for education and, in turn, to adopt a definite point of view that permitted for the development of distinct social ends. As Bode maintained, however, if such social ends were determined and the schools become the means for their implementation, was not this a form of dogmatism and authoritarianism, an anathema to democracy? Could democracy and the spirit of free inquiry, a basic goal of education, be embraced by the schools if social ends have already been determined?

Childs countered by acknowledging the fundamental biases inherent in all school settings and viewed education as being implicitly and necessarily partisan. For Childs, values were already being imposed in the educational system, and educators were irresponsible if they did not examine, and then emphasize, more appropriate values. In response, Bode objected saying that Social Reconstructionists believe "imposition is not really a crime but a high moral obligation, provided, of course, that it is of the right kind and done in the right way."[25] Bode called for a reconstruction of society, too, however the schools must inculcate democracy "as a way of life" and should not become a tool for social purposes. Any imposition of values represented an abomination to democracy.

Bode's resolution did not particularly satisfy the many Social Reconstructionists calling for societal change since, fundamentally, he placed considerable trust in "essential democracy," faith in intelligence, and confidence in the general sensibilities of the common person. "What is required of progressive education is not a choice between academic detachment and adoption of a specific program for social reform, but a renewed loyalty to the principle of democracy."[26] Educational dilemmas are rarely resolved, and the indoctrination exchange concluded with Bode stating, "The extraordinary thing about the whole business is that, with pretty much the same premises, we reach widely divergent conclusions with respect to education. How can such things be? It all seems to reduce discussion to the level of taking rabbits out of a hat."[27] Childs had already dismissed Bode's faith in the common person, acknowledging the irresponsible uses of power and illiberal, intolerant intelligence of those in control. The imposition controversy would lay silent and unresolved among members of the Progressive Education Association.

By the time of Reconstructionism's introduction in the 1950s, Brameld, a former professional touring magician during his college years, was ready to "pull another rabbit out of a hat." He asserted, "I have never understood why it is less legitimate for, say, a well-educated teacher to hold and express reasoned out convictions, than it is for a scientist to become enthusiastic about a hypothesis he then endeavors to prove true by a due process which, by definition, leaves the door wide open to the contingency that it may prove to be false."[28] While he objected to indoctrination, a one-sided form of communication to inculcate beliefs "so supremely true" that there is no need for further critical inquiry, [29] he believed teachers should be willing to discuss ideology in the classroom. In fact, Brameld was implicitly supporting Bode's faith in intelligence by asserting that educators' beliefs and convictions should undergo "public inspection and communication of all pertinent and available evidence and by exhaustive consideration of alternative convictions."[30] Only through open discourse and the critical examination of ideas could teachers hold beliefs that were also defensible.

From this perspective Brameld proposed a resolution to the imposition controversy, the concept of "defensible partiality:" "What we learn is defensible simply in so far as the ends we support and the means we utilize are able to stand up against exposure to open, unrestricted criticism and comparison. What we learn is partial in so far as these ends and means still remain definite and positive to their majority advocates after the defense occurs."[31] One might question whether "defensible partiality" would lead to an ideological rigidity, but Brameld suggested otherwise. While educators could embrace ideological positions, "partiality paradoxically increases in defensibility only as it is tested by the kind of impartiality provided through many sided evidence [irrational as well as rational], unrestricted communication by group learning, complete respect for criticism and minority dissent."[32] Teachers, students, and community members would seek out and encourage debate and criticism as the necessary prerequisite for maintaining beliefs.[33] In essence, the discussion and critique of ideas would become, for Brameld, a commonplace activity of schooling, as defensible partiality remained a basic construct for him throughout his career.

RECONSTRUCTIONISM IN PRACTICE: THE FLOODWOOD PROJECT

Theodore Brameld, even as a professor of educational philosophy and foundations, always took an active interest in curriculum development and the implementation of Reconstructionist ideas into school programs. Many of his foundations textbooks included sections on curriculum design at the secondary and post-secondary levels. Perhaps most unique, however, was Brameld's curricular experiment, "Design for America," now viewed as the first educational program based upon Social Reconstructionism and cited for decades to suggest the promise of Reconstructionist thought in the classroom. While a professor at the University of Minnesota, Brameld received a small stipend from the Graduate School in 1944 to initiate a curricular experiment in post–World War II, future planning at Floodwood High School in Minnesota. He developed with administrators and teachers a general education program for the junior and senior high school students "to build by cooperative thinking and exploration a blueprint of our future society."[34] For three and one-half months, fifty-one students met with core teachers for two hours a day, five days a week; the project followed a conventional "broad problems" core program popularized throughout the United States.

By examining economic, political, and cultural issues, Floodwood students set out to plan a utopian community and to reaffirm their commitment to democracy by addressing the issue of "what kind of society do we wish to build for tomorrow?" Two initial questions were posed: "Is it important to build a plan for the future of America? And is it possible to get the goals of such a plan so clear that the plan itself, in form and content, will be definitely indicated?"[35] The project was exploring open-ended means and predefined ends as Brameld, during his predefensible partiality days, attempted to experiment with open inquiry in contrast to the imposition of values. The Floodwood Project included many of the finest aspects of Progressive education at the secondary school level: integrating the separate subjects of the curriculum; focusing upon students' interests as a way to select curricular experiences; and placing responsibility upon students to become self-directed learners. Since Floodwood High School was a "community school," common in the 1930s and 40s, students and teachers drew heavily upon the resources from the area. High school studies were directly related to pressing local issues and affairs, and students were active participants in community activities.[36]

While the Floodwood students did not, nor could not, implement their utopian design, the project was more of an experiment to determine whether students could embark on an "adventure in learning" and re-examine their social, economic, and political ideals. Students reaffirmed their belief in democracy while also recognizing that "socialism and communism belong in the libertarian stream of democratic thought."[37] They also approved of long-range national public-works programs, although they believed capitalism and private enterprise "should be given every opportunity to provide as much employment as possible," and they embraced egalitarian treatment toward minorities, especially for African Americans, and "international as well as intercultural equalitarianism of races and groups."[38]

Many students supported federal aid to equalize educational opportunity; increased adult education programs and education programs for war veterans; better teacher training; increased vocational education; work experiences as a part of the school program; and more emphasis in the curriculum upon contemporary problems. The assessment of the program indicated its success; however, as one recent examination of the study by Thomas has noted, the findings "read more consistently as promotion rather than analysis."[39] Brameld maintained "perhaps the best test of its significance is whether or not it works reasonably well in communities like Floodwood itself."[40] In this regard, perhaps an unfair condition, the project may have been a disappointment since seemingly there were no other schools adopting the suggested syllabi recommended throughout *Design for America*.

As a demonstration of open-ended inquiry, the project was not imposing values but, instead, permitting students to examine and determine their own beliefs, a conclusion supported in a 1976 follow-up survey of the participating Floodwood High School students.[41] Unfortunately, most of the students were not particularly enamored with the underlying theory of the experiment. But few felt "certain beliefs [were] presented in such a way that caused you to prefer one over another" and few believed that they had been indoctrinated by the project.

Actually, Brameld did not need to impose values upon the Floodwood students since, what became rather apparent, the students and community at the time of his project were already in alignment with many of his beliefs. Brameld had selected a community of predominately Finnish families that was a center of strong cooperatives, then considered a form of economic socialism. Several socialist clubs provided a place for discussions, speakers, and political meetings. The former superintendent of Floodwood schools remembers, "These old socialists would sit around those halls and study, read, and debate; they were really very academic. They weren't too practical—they wouldn't get out and vote. But I was amazed to find the sophistication of some Finn lumberjack talk about economics or labor history."[42]

Brameld could easily have selected one of the schools within the nationally recognized Minneapolis school system, a noted Progressive education school system. Instead, he selected a school many hours away from his place of work, an educational setting obviously in philosophical accord with his beliefs and overseen by an affable superintendent who he very much liked. Does this diminish the "findings" of the Floodwood Project? To a certain degree it does; however, the *Design for America* program represents less an educational experiment in today's terms and more an example of an "implementative study" of the 1930s made famous in the Eight Year Study. These types of experimental programs implemented educational ideas rather than conducted research in order to test outcomes for future replication.[43] Many educators questioned whether high school students would be willing to participate in a program of utopian planning and the examination of economic and cultural issues. Brameld was exploring whether an open-ended secondary school core program—in this instance, one addressing issues of post-war planning—could be implemented in schools. While one must question the "objective" selection of his experimentation site, the project does adequately suggest that Reconstructionist thought could be introduced and that students, when committed and interested in the curriculum, could take on quite ambitious programs of study. Whether the Floodwood Project "proved" conclusively the non-imposition of values or the strength of democratic socialism seems of less consequence than the willingness of Brameld and others to go to such great lengths to initiate this unique program of curriculum development.

THEODORE BRAMELD AS PHILOSOPHICAL GADFLY AND CONSTRUCTIVE CRITIC

Brameld enjoyed his role as cultural critic and often referred to himself as an educational gadfly. He sought opportunities to publish exchanges with opponents and, no doubt stemming from his collegiate experience as a debater, looked forward to those occasions when he could dispute and argue the work of others. In fact, the rudiments of defensible partiality called for such an open exchange of ideas and certainly Brameld was willing to extend and accept criticism. No opportunity was left unattended. For example, after a Yale professor lectured in Brameld's class, he responded by critiquing the lecturer's book for not adequately treating Reconstructionism. Brameld requested a reply so that both statements could be distributed to the students. A rejoinder was received with the comment, "In much of your writing, I think you are still fighting a battle against those who don't realize the importance of social reconstructionism,"[44] and, for Brameld, his work did comprise a battle with those colleagues who wished not to accept the responsibility of taking Reconstructionist action.

This is not to suggest, however, that his classroom became the place to impose values. Maxine Greene, who was enrolled in Brameld's doctoral seminars at New York University in the early 1950s, recalled his great intellectual acumen and believed his knowledge of existentialism and contemporary European philosophy surpassed others in the field of education. No doubt his charisma and extensive reading in the humanities and social sciences aided what many describe as a brilliant and inspiring career as a teacher. Greene goes so far as to attribute her career in the field of educational foundations to have been inspired by Brameld.[45]

Not all educators, of course, were as enamored with Brameld's educational positions, and critiques of Brameld's work took many forms. In what became known as the 1952 Red Bank Incident, Brameld, who had been invited to talk to the teachers of the Red Bank, NJ school system, was banned from lecturing by the Board of Education on the grounds of maintaining affiliations with organizations and conferences deemed by the House Un-American Activities Committee (HUAC) to be "completely under the control of the Communists." Brameld, in response to the publicity, stated that he was not and never had been a member of the Communist party. "I am, in fact, a severe critic of the Soviet Union and the Communist party, and one of the main reasons I am is that they do exactly the same thing that happened in Red Bank; they demand unanimity and do not permit dissent and close their schools to views that may not be popular."[46] Later, when Brameld and other academics were called Reds in an article by a former investigator for HUAC, Brameld exclaimed that "he was honored to be included anytime with such distinguished American Philosophers."[47]

Yet, even within the context of the red baiting and conservative times of the 1950s, Brameld received positive publicity at the national level. Few professors can say that their philosophy of education textbook was featured in *Time Magazine*, as was *Toward a Reconstruction Philosophy of Education*. Defensible partiality and social self-realization were described to the nation as Brameld was introduced as "one of the chief spokesmen for an extraordinary doctrine called reconstructionism—a philosophy that wants to revolutionize the world's whole concept of education."[48] Rather than branded as "red" or "pink" by *Time*, Brameld was described as a "constructive critic" and applauded for his bold new experiments for the public schools.

Brameld participated in rather heated exchanges with his colleagues in the field of educational foundations. From his 1966 review of Reconstructionist criticism, he prompted George Kneller to reinitiate an exchange begun eight years earlier when he charged Kneller of "erecting impressive facades of sophistication."[49] In response, "The Angels and Demons of Theodore Brameld," Kneller speaks of Brameld with personal affections and high regard as a scholar and productive thinker; however, he also proceeded to dismiss defensible partiality as a mere euphemism and questioned the many criticisms Brameld originally directed at him and others. For today's education academics accustomed to stereotypical praise and predictable accolades in journal reviews, the exchange is a refreshing reminder of when academics of different ideologies critiqued one another's work with civility and thoughtfulness.

Few exchanges in the field of education, however, can compare to James McClellan's 1968 invective, "Theodore Brameld and the Architecture of Confusion."[50] The chapter defies description and while certain criticisms are legitimate, the argument is more reflective of the misconnections among educational philosophers of the 1960s and 70s. Brameld who intentionally wrote in a normative, persuasive, and even emotional style, sought to clarify and illuminate the dilemmas of the time and challenged educators to reexamine their beliefs. Further, Brameld sought to persuade and inspire and, at times, to willingly engage in hyperbole and propaganda—what has been called journalistic writing—in order to confront readers. He would have been easy prey for any educational analytical philosopher, such as McClellan, who brought conceptual analysis to the exchange. "Is/ought" differences quickly created irreconcilable differences, and any analytic philosopher would have questioned and condemned most Reconstructionist claims.[51] Little wonder that McClellan's diatribe would ridicule Brameld for confusion, fuzzy logic, and "contemporary eccentricities" that were nothing more than "mere curiosities."[52]

CONCLUSIONS: A DESIGN FOR EDUCATIONAL FOUNDATIONS

At a time when schools are placed under the burden of increased federal and state testing, when teachers are reduced to the role of clerks, when parents turn to litigation as a response to school policies, when few students are asking "what kind of world do we want to live in?" and when grant support is given to examine why the field of educational philosophy has become superfluous, Theodore Brameld would not be saddened or dismayed. He would identify the many important tasks for Educational

Reconstructionists and then ask how the assembled group wished to proceed. In so doing, Brameld would assume a much overlooked role for the educational philosopher that he proposed years ago. In *Education for an Emerging Age*, Brameld described the educational philosopher/Reconstructionist as a "liaison officer," a role now applicable for all educational foundations and history professors as well.[53] In this liaison role, he challenges us to become active in service activities and school-related projects since, as educators, we too have vowed "to apply fundamental theory to the eminently practical field of education [and] be eager to bring [our] training and experience to bear in as many concrete ways as possible."[54] Our responsibility, however, would not be as coordinator or administrator. The liaison officer functions in specific ways, all greatly needed today during a time of acquiescence and passive compliance within the professoriate and among the schools. One dimension of this role was to serve as a resource person who would pose those difficult yet crucial issues often overlooked or swept aside during planning sessions, i.e., the "obligation not to take for granted what other people often do take for granted."[55] Other functions included the liaison officer as a researcher engaged in inquiry from a foundations perspective, as an individual participating in conversations with policy makers, and as an interdisciplinarian who would seek out connections with other spheres of knowledge. In essence, Brameld was suggesting a means to reinsert philosophical and Reconstructionist thought back into educational and public discourse.

In addition to this liaison role, Brameld suggests another course of action of equal if not more importance today during a time of standardization and uniformity: the importance of "pilot projects." Brameld seems to have first suggested the importance of the pilot project in 1951 in a four-point agenda for education appearing in the edited collection, *The Battle for Free Schools* (and first published in *The Nation*).[56] Brameld maintained, "Instead of retreating, the school system of America must take the offensive in advocating and testing new designs for education."[57] The pilot project became the method to determine these designs, similar to what was initiated by the Floodwood Project. Brameld later coupled this practice with his belief "that a large number of typical parents, teachers and children in America and abroad would support [Reconstructionism's far-reaching proposals] if given the opportunity. It suggests that beginnings can be made by means of 'pilot projects'—experiments in curriculum, in teacher organization and training, in adult education, and in other ways."[58] In fact, perhaps one of the greatest outcomes of the *Design for America* project was the realization that pilot projects could influence the doubtful and persuade the unconvinced. Such advice should be well heeded today during a time when true educational experimentation is rare and the many examples of "innovative" charter schools are mere transplantations and demonstrations.

Theodore Brameld's career was a battle—a struggle to promote Reconstructionist thought, to challenge the complacent, and to build and renew disparate cultures. He called for educators to join the struggle for cultural renewal. Such participation did not require ideological "impartiality" but, instead, called for educators who were "inspired with enthusiasm for research, for diffusion of knowledge, for humanly realized beauty, goodness, and truth—an education which, through the schools of America and of all other democracies, will at last demonstrate its capacity to play no longer a minor but a major role in the reconstruction of civilization."[59] This was Brameld's hope and this becomes today's design, means, and ends.

NOTES

1 . Two examples, both connected to Brameld's home state of Wisconsin, are Boyd Bode and V. T. Thayer. Bode and Thayer added greatly to arena of progressive thought and both decided, as did Brameld, to leave academic positions in departments of philosophy for careers in education. As mentioned by the Bode biographer, Robert V. Bullough, "Bode's turn toward education was also encouraged by his growing dissatisfaction with teaching logic courses, 'horse sense made asinine,' as he called it, and his desire to develop a philosophy that made a difference—'philosophy brought down to earth, and centered in education' (Letter, Bode to Otto, March 3, 1922, State Historical Society of Wisconsin, Archives, Otto Papers).

2. Theodore Brameld, *Ends and Means in Education: A Midcentury Appraisal* (New York: Harper & Brothers, 1950); Theodore Brameld, *Education for an Emerging Age: Newer Ends and Stronger Means* (New York: Harper & Brothers, 1961); Theodore Brameld, *The Climactic Decades: Mandate to Education,* (New York: Praeger Publishers, 1970).

3. Eugene Smith, "A Message from the President of the Progressive Education Association," *Progressive Education* 1 (April 1924): 5.

4. Theodore Brameld, "The Role of Acquiescence in Leninism" (Ph.D. diss., University of Chicago, 1931); Theodore Brameld, *A Philosophic Approach to Communism* (Chicago: University of Chicago Press, 1933).

5. Theodore Brameld, Biographical File, New York University Archives, Bobst Library.

6. The Floodwood Project is described later in this chapter. Theodore Brameld, *Minority Problems in the Public Schools* (New York: Harper and Brothers,1946); Theodore Brameld (ed.), *Workers' Education in the United States* (New York: D. Appleton-Century,1941).

7 . Theodore Brameld, *Ends and Means in Education: A Midcentury Appraisal;* Theodore Brameld, *Patterns of Educational Philosophy: Divergence and Conver-*

gence in Culturological Perspective (New York: Holt, Rinehart and Winston, 1950); Theodore Brameld, *Philosophies of Education in Cultural Perspective* (New York: Holt, Rinehart and Winston, 1955); Theodore Brameld, *Toward a Reconstructed Philosophy of Education* (New York: the Dryden Press, 1956).

8. Theodore Brameld, *Remaking of a Culture: Life and Education in Puerto Rico* (New York: Harper & Row, 1959).

9. Theodore Brameld, *Education for an Emerging Age;* Theodore Brameld, *The Use of Explosive Ideas in Education* (Pittsburgh: University of Pittsburgh Press, 1965); Theodore Brameld, *Education as Power* (New York: Holt, Rinehart & Winston, 1965); Theodore Brameld, *Japan: Culture, Education, and Change in Two Communities* (New York: Holt, Rinehart & Winston, 1968).

10. Theodore Brameld, *The Teacher as World Citizen* (Palm Springs, CA: ETC Publications); for more information about Brameld, see the wonderful new biography, Frank Andrews Stone, *Theodore Brameld's Educational Reconstructionism: An Intellectual Biography* (San Francisco: Caddo Gap Press, 2003). Also, fine, succinct overview of Brameld's career, prepared by David Conrad, appears in the *Macmillan Encyclopedia of Education second* edition, ed. J. W. Guthrie, (New York: Gale Publishing, 2002). Brameld's archival papers are housed in Special Collections, Bailey/Howe Library, University of Vermont.

11. Theodore Brameld, "Karl Marx and the American Teacher," *The Social Frontier* 2:2 (November 1935): 53–56. Although not lessening the importance of this essay, Bowers notes that "Brameld did not, as some authors have argued, introduce the subject of a class struggle into the educational discussion. He merely stated in bolder terms the same ideas implicitly contained in Counts's *Dare the School Build a New Social Order?* As many readers could attest, class conflict had also long been an editorial theme of *The Social Frontier.* In fact, the idea was fast becoming conventional by the time Brameld raised the specter of a class struggle." C. A. Bowers, *The Progressive Educator and the Depression: The Radical Years* (New York: Random House, 1969), 143.

12. Theodore Brameld, "Dr. Brameld breaks silence, gives his side," *NYU Commerce Bulletin* (5 March , 1952): 1, 4.

13. Brameld, *Education for an Emerging Age,* 15.

14. Brameld, *Education for an Emerging Age,* 15.

15. Brameld, *Toward a Reconstruction Philosophy of Education,* 25.

16. Brameld, *Ends and Means in Education,* 35.

17. Brameld, *Patterns of Educational Philosophy,* 204.

18. Brameld, *Ends and Means in Education,* 86.

19. Theodore Brameld, "What is Democratic Socialism?" *Cutting Edge* 7:3 (Spring 1976): 45–46.

20. Theodore Brameld, "Metaphysics and Social Attitudes," *The Social Frontier* 4:35 (May 1938): 258.

21. Brameld, *Education for an Emerging Age,* 236.

22. Brameld, *Ends and Means in Education,* 16.

23. Brameld, *Ends and Means in Education,* 86.

24. The editors, "Introductory Remarks on Indoctrination," *The Social Frontier* 1:4 (January 1935): 8–9; 30–33. Boyd H. Bode, "Education and Social Reconstruction," *The Social Frontier* 1:4 (January 1935): 18–22. John L. Childs, "Professor Bode on 'Faith in Intelligence'," *The Social Frontier* 1:6 (March 1935): 20–24. John L. Childs, "Bode at the Crossroads," *The Social Frontier* 4:35 (May 1938): 267–268. Boyd H. Bode, "Dr. Childs and Education for Democracy," *The Social Frontier* 5:39 (November 1938): 38–40. John L. Childs, "Dr. Bode on 'Authentic' Democracy," *The Social Frontier* 5:39 (November 1938): 40–43. Boyd H. Bode, "Democratic Education and Conflicting Culture Values," *The Social Frontier* 5:41 (January 1939): 104–107. I am indebted to my colleague, Robert V. Bullough, Jr., for his insights into the Imposition Controversy. See R.V. Bullough, Jr., *Democracy in Education: Boyd H. Bode.* (Bayside, NY: General Hall Publishers, Inc., 1981).

25. Bode, "Dr. Childs and Education for Democracy," 39.

26. Bode, "Dr. Childs and Education for Democracy," 40.

27. Bode, "Democratic Education and Conflicting Culture Values," 104.

28. Theodore Brameld, "Reconstructionist Theory: Some Recent Critiques considered in Perspective," *Educational Theory* 17: 2 (Spring 1967): 338.

29. Brameld, *Ends and Means in Education*, 88.

30. Brameld, *Patterns of Educational Philosophy*, 563.

31. Brameld, *Ends and Means in Education*, 92.

32. Brameld, *Ends and Means in Education*, 93.

33. Brameld recognized that inherent power structures in school would deter open dialogue and believed defensible partiality, as a theoretical construction, was appropriate only for teaching adolescents and young adults rather than elementary age children who most likely would be unable to engage in critical discourse. He would later articulate a series of beliefs about indoctrination in response to a proposal of dismissing teachers proven of indoctrinating students. Brameld abhorred any doctrine that was presented in schools as infallible and subjected to no critical inquiry. Yet he also recognized the pervasiveness of indoctrination in schools and, as an example, pointed to the presentation of capitalism as an integral component of democracy as a commonly imposed belief. Brameld was less condemning of the techniques of propaganda when appropriately used. (Certain PEA colleagues were openly involved in agitprop workers' theater and documentary filmmaking as propaganda during Brameld's time in New York City.) Further, he distinguished, as he had implied before, between those teachers who hold convictions that they freely express to learners versus those teachers who indoctrinate beliefs. And in what may have frightened his critics, he separated thoughts from actions, i.e., teachers may accept doctrine and advocate indoctrination but remain blameless as long as they do not themselves practice indoctrination in the schools. Brameld was drawing fine distinctions between acceptable promotion and inculcation of values in contrast to the blatant imposition of doctrine that occurred daily throughout the nation, in his estimation, with the promulgation of capitalism. See

Theodore Brameld, "What is Indoctrination?" *School & Society* 85:2119 (9 November , 1957): 326–328.

34.   Theodore Brameld, *Design for America: An Educational Exploration of the Future of Democracy for Senior High Schools and Junior Colleges* (New York: Hinds, Hayden & Eldredge, 1945), 3.

35.   R. B. Raup and B. O. Smith, "High School Students Work on "A Design for America'," *Teachers College Record* 46:4 (January 1945): 250.

36.   The curriculum was quite flexible. No detailed outline of the course of study was presented to the students. Instead, Brameld assumed that as the experiment progressed, the curricular direction would be determined cooperatively by the students and teachers. Only Stewart Chases' critique of society, *Goals for America*, had been selected in advance to serve as the primary text. Students developed a set of expectations of what a good society should provide, later refined to a series of "major wants," or what would have been called "social needs." This was followed by four weeks devoted to the examination of economic/political issues (the longest segment of the project) and then concurrently the study of art, education, human relations (what would now be viewed as multicultural education), science, and politics for five weeks. The program concluded with a two-week period to summarize the "design for America," review and synthesize the various positions of the group, and administer student examinations and evaluations by the cooperating staff.

37.   Brameld, *Design for America*, 105.

38.   Brameld, *Design for America*, 108.

39.   Thomas P. Thomas, "The Difficulties and Successes of Reconstructionist Practice: Theodore Brameld and the Floodwood Project," *Journal of Curriculum and Supervision* 14:3 (Spring 1999): 282.

40.   Brameld, *Design for America,* 114.

41.   Craig Kridel, "The Theory and Practice of Theodore Brameld's 'Defensible Partiality': A Mid-Century 'Resolution' to the Imposition Controversy," Midwest History of Education Society, Chicago, IL (30 October ,1976); Craig Kridel, "Theodore Brameld's Floodwood Project: A Design for America," In *Educational Reconstruction*, ed. Frank A. Stone (Storrs, CT: Varousa Press, 1978): 81–90.

42.   Personal interview with Lewis E. Harris, 1976; Lewis E. Harris and Rae Harris, *Bootstraps: A Chronicle of a Real Community School* (Cable, WI: Harris Publications, 1980). I am pleased to say that *Bootstraps* was written as a consequence of my 1976–77 Floodwood research. Harris so enjoyed discussing his years at Floodwood High School that he embarked on the preparation of this memoir. Although Brameld recognized the high school's more liberal orientation among the different Minnesota school systems, there is evidence that Brameld's experiment was not well received by all members of the community. During the war years, several new and returning businessmen moved into the area, an influx which led to growing criticism of the high school's general education program ("too much general and not enough

education") and charges of subversive activity as a result of Brameld's curriculum project.

43.   Craig Kridel and Robert V. Bullough, Jr., *With Adventurous Company: Stories of the Eight Year Study and Rethinking Schooling in America*, in press.

44.   Personal correspondence, Charles E. Lindblom to Theodore Brameld, (March 27, 1954): 2; Biographical File, New York University Archives, Bobst Library.

45.   Personal interview, Maxine Greene, New York, New York, October 15, 2004.

46.   Wilton Y. Olette, "Red Bank 'Pink' Rap Makes Prof See Red," *NYU Commerce Bulletin* 20:18 (20 February , 1952): 2.

47.   Gene Gilmartin, "11 NYU Profs Called 'Reds' in Mag Article," *Square Daily* 1:13 (22 April , 1953): 1.

48.   "How to Create Utopia," *Time Magazine* 9 (July 1956), 68.

49.   George F. Kneller, "The Angels and Demons of Theodore Brameld," *Educational Theory* 17:1 (January 1967): 74; George F. Kneller, Philosophy and Culture, *Educational Forum* 22 (January 1958): 153–164; Theodore Brameld, "Culture and Philosophy," *Educational Forum*, 22 (January 1958): 165–175; Theodore Brameld, "Reconstructionist Theory: Some Recent Critiques Considered in Perspective," *Educational Theory* 16:4 (October 1966): 333–343; George F. Kneller, "The Angels and Demons of Theodore Brameld," *Educational Theory* 17:1 (January 1967): 73–75.

50.   James McClellan, *Toward an Effective Critique of American Education* (Philadelphia: Lippincott, 1968).

51.   In the late 1970s, another educational philosopher berated George Counts' *Dare the School Build a New Social Order?* on the grounds that since a school is an inanimate object, it could not take action. Such were the odd exchanges when analytical philosophers of education critiqued Progressive and Social Reconstructionist thought.

52.   McClellan, *Toward an Effective Critique of American Education,* 129.

53.   Brameld, *Education for an Emerging Age,* 210214.

54.   Brameld, *Education for an Emerging Age,* 210.

55.   Brameld, *Education for an Emerging Age,* 211.

56.   Theodore Brameld, (ed.) *The Battle for Free Schools.* (Boston: The Beacon Press, 1951).

57.   Brameld, *The Battle for Free Schools,* 77.

58.   Brameld, *The Climactic Decades,* 198.

59.   Brameld, *Ends and Means in Education,* 18.

CHAPTER 5

EDUCATION FOR SOCIAL RECONSTRUCTION IN CRITICAL CONTEXT

William B. Stanley

INTRODUCTION

As the essays in this book attest, Social Reconstructionism or education for social transformation, which developed in the 1920s and 30s, remains an influential school of thought in the current education reform dialogue. At the same time, Reconstructionism has had only a marginal influence on educational policy and practice over the past century. This relative lack of influence is not surprising, given the Reconstructionists' call for public education to play a leading role in the radical transformation of the American political and economic system, a program in direct conflict with the dominant culture's commitment to the ideologies of individualism and free market economic theory. Furthermore, since K–12 schooling has, in general, functioned to reproduce the dominant social order, it would be more plausible to argue (as did orthodox Marxists) that the current economic and political systems would need to undergo radical change *before* fundamental change in education could take place.

Social Reconstruction: People, Politics, Perspectives, pages 89–110

The mainstream rejection of Reconstructionism is one part of the more general conservative resistance to progressive political reform efforts in the twentieth century. Less understood is the critique of Reconstructionism by groups on the Left, including liberal progressive, pragmatist, socialist, Marxist, and existentialist critics. It is this critical reaction to Reconstructionism from both Conservatives and the Left that will be explored here, in the hope that the analysis sheds some light on the extent to which this approach to curriculum theory remains relevant to current debates over education reform.

Toward this end, Reconstructionism is first discussed within the context of the response to modernism in the first half of the twentieth century. In this analysis, modernism is used to refer to both the dramatic emergence of modern industrial society in the late nineteenth century and the intellectual discourse that developed in response to the rapid changes in science, technology, culture, and society. Modernism challenged and disrupted the core assumptions of the dominant Western culture (including curriculum theory) that were in place at the end of the nineteenth century. Reconstructionism was part of the unique American response to these changes, and this section explains how Reconstructionists tried to distinguish themselves from earlier progressive and pragmatist approaches to education and social reform.

Second, Dewey's critique of Reconstructionism is examined. Dewey was the leading American intellectual and educational theorist during the first half of the twentieth century, and his rejection of indoctrination and counter-socialization as central aims of education posed a serious challenge to reconstructionist theory. Third, there is an exploration of the attack on Progressivism by conservative critics who questioned the assumptions of liberal democratic theory and education for democracy in particular. The fourth section covers the critics who emphasized the existential and tragic dimensions of education, the limits on human reason, and the importance of custom and tradition in human praxis. Finally, there is a discussion of how the issues identified by progressive, conservative, and tragic/existentialist critics might be applied to the current application of reconstructionist curriculum theory.

THE CHALLENGE OF MODERNISM AND THE RECONSTRUCTIONIST RESPONSE

It is impossible to understand fully the nature of Reconstructionism without considering this curriculum theory within the context of a more general reaction to modernism in the early twentieth century. In the United States, modernism challenged our core cultural foundations including the synthesis of Western culture derived from classical Greco-Roman tradition, Christianity, and secular thought from the Renaissance through the Enlightenment.

Nietzsche is associated with the modernist claim that "God is dead," but it was Darwin who did more than anyone to promote the eclipse of religion and the emergence of science as the dominant mode of thought in the twentieth century. Published in 1859, Darwin's *Origin of the Species* is probably the single most influential modernist text. This book undermined our central religious traditions and led to the eventual triumph of secular scientific reasoning that described a universe that had evolved absent of design or purpose. Darwin's influence was amplified by the work of Marx, Nietzsche, and Freud. The rising credibility of scientific thought also reinforced the earlier arguments of Adam Smith and other proponents of market economic theory. Indeed, capitalism came to embody a dominant modernist impulse in the twentieth century, one that continues in the present era.

The emerging dominance of scientific thought proved to be a mixed blessing. On the one hand, scientific method seemed to provide a superior approach to solving social problems by increasing human knowledge in the sciences, technology, engineering, medicine, and education. On the other hand, science provided no clear guidance with respect to how scientific knowledge itself should be used nor any insight into the meaning of human existence. Indeed, certain elements of modernism anticipated much of what we have come to call the postmodern condition. In the words of Patrick Diggins, modernism

> is the consciousness of what was once presumed to be present and is now seen as missing. It might be considered as a series of felt absences, the gap between what we know is not and what we desire to be: knowledge without truth, power without authority, society without sprit, self without identity, politics without virtue, existence without purpose, history without meaning.[1]

The modernist challenge to our cultural assumptions left Western societies in search of new ways to overcome skepticism regarding foundations for knowledge and values, the limits of human reason, and the inadequacies of traditional social institutions, like religion, a free press, public schools, and free elections, thought to promote a just, democratic social order.

A series of historical events in the first half of the twentieth century appeared to confirm the worst fears generated by the impact of modernism. Rapid changes in technology, industrialization, mass immigrations, media, and urbanization had transformed American society in fundamental ways by 1919. The horrors of World War I and the subsequent failure of the Versailles treaty left a legacy of bitterness, cynicism, and disillusion in the 1920s and 30s. Scientific developments in quantum theory between 1900 and 1930 appeared to problematize our conceptions of reality itself. The earlier attempts at progressive political reform lost their effectiveness in the 1920s, as the Progressive movement fragmented and the Left divided into warring factions reflecting a mixture of confusion, optimism, and despair. From 1920 to 1932, conservative groups dominated public policy. This was the context in which Reconstructionism first emerged in the work of Harold Rugg and George Counts. With the onset of the Great Depression in 1929, the Reconstructionists moved further Left politically.

There were three general intellectual reactions to modernism in America between 1900 and 1941, which will be called Progressive, Conservative, and Tragic/Existentialist. Like all categories, these are oversimplifications. Certain individuals do not fit neatly within a single category, and differences between individuals within each category were often significant. Still, the categories work reasonably well for the purpose of this discussion.

First, various *Progressives* acknowledged the dramatic challenges of modernism, but believed science provided a method and opportunity to create a new and more just social order. This group represented a wide ideological range including Liberals, progressive educators, Pragmatists, Socialists, Marxists, and the Social Reconstructionists. A second *conservative* group consisted of two different factions including, Foundationalists (e.g., Mortimer Adler and Robert Hutchins) who rejected modernist claims regarding the impossibility of establishing foundations for human knowledge and values, and democratic Realists (e.g., Walter Lippmann) who questioned the relevance and practicality of liberal participatory democracy in modern society. The third group, *Tragic/Existentialists* (e.g., Henry Adams and Reinhold Niebuhr), accepted the main elements of the modernist critique regarding the foundations of knowledge, the limits of human reason, our assumptions regarding progress, and the existential nature of human existence. The Tragic/Existentialists considered both the reactionary assumptions of Foundationalists and the optimism of progressive educators, including Pragmatists like Dewey and the Reconstructionists, to be naïve. While members of this group were often strong supporters of social reform, they did not believe science or reason had the capacity to explain moral purpose and meaning of human existence.

Although progressive educators were generally on the Left politically, the movement reflected a wide range of ideological positions and never reached consensus on the best approach to education reform, splitting into child-centered, social-efficiency/ life-adjustment, and social-meliorist factions. Reconstructists, as proponents of using educational programs for radical social transformation, were social meliorists on the Left wing of the progressive education movement. However, Reconstructionism was never a monolithic movement. There were significant differences between the views of the leading proponents, Rugg, Counts, and Brameld, and each man changed his views over time. Still, a summary of Counts' views during the early 1930s reveals the core elements of a strong form of Reconstructionism and how this approach differed from liberal forms of progressive education.

George Counts' challenge in 1932 to use the schools to build a new social order goes to the heart of Reconstructionism.[2] Counts argued that the Depression confirmed the reconstructionist claim that our society was in a state of crisis and required the creation of a new social order based on democratic social justice and a fundamental redistribution of economic and political power. Since political and economic power is held largely by a powerful elite class, the realization of a truly democratic social order could not happen unless the capitalist economy of the United States was eliminated, "or changed so radically in form and spirit that its identity [would] be completely lost."[3] While Counts' economic views gradually moderated over time and he came to accept the retention of capitalism in *some* form, he continued to believe there was ample evidence to indict capitalism on moral and economic grounds.

Counts acknowledged the accomplishments of progressive education, particularly a focus on the interests of the child as they relate to real-world activities. However, the very term "progress" implies moving forward and this "can have little meaning in the absence of clearly defined purpose."[4] Progressive education's failure to develop a theory of social welfare, "unless it be that of anarchy or extreme individualism," was its core weakness.[5] Progressive educators were generally members of the middle class and seemed "incapable of dealing with the ... great crises of our time."[6] They had become too fond of their material possessions and, in a crisis, would likely "follow the lead of the most powerful and respectable forces in society and at the same time find good reasons for doing so."[7]

Counts was also concerned with the pervasive influence of philosophic relativism in much progressive thinking, which functioned to block the development of a theory of social welfare under the guise of objectivity and academic freedom. He believed that philosophic uncertainty, combined with the instrumentalism of most Progressives and the narrow scientific approach of other educators, had resulted in the general tendency to avoid endorsing programs designed to resolve pressing social problems. Here Counts was responding to those elements of modernist thought that denied the possibility of providing the intellectual foundations to ground a theory of social welfare based on social justice.

Progressive educators must free themselves from philosophic relativism and the undesirable influences of an upper-middle-class culture to permit the development of "a realistic and comprehensive theory of social welfare" and "a compelling and challenging vision of human destiny."[8] The construction of an educational program oriented by a radical theory of social welfare would also entail freeing progressive education from its apparent fear of imposition and indoctrination. Put another way, progressive educators must come to accept "that all education contains a large element of imposition, that in the very nature of the case this is inevitable, that the existence and evolution of society depend upon it, that it is consequently eminently desirable, and that the frank acceptance of this fact by the educator is a major professional obligation."[9] The reconstructionist curriculum would be designed to expose the antidemocratic limitations of individualism, market economic theory, and promote a strong version of participatory democracy and a more collectivist economic system to reduce disparities of income, wealth, and power. As the depression continued, the reconstructionist position moved in a more radical direction, particularly in the work of Brameld. Brameld was strongly influenced by Marxism and raised the possible need to resort to coercion in order to bring about necessary reforms.[10]

DEWEY'S CRITIQUE OF SOCIAL RECONSTRUCTIONISM

Dewey, like Counts, agreed that education, by definition, must have a social orientation. It "is not whether the schools shall or shall not influence the course of future social life, but in what direction they shall do so and how."[11] Beyond that, the way the schools actually "*share* in the building of the social order of the future, depends on the particular social forces and movements with which they ally."[12] Teachers cannot escape the responsibility for assisting in the task of social change, or maintenance, and this requires a particular social orientation. According to Dewey, education "must . . . assume an increasing responsibility for participation in projecting ideas of social change and taking part in their execution in order to be educative," with particular attention to a more just, open, and democratic society.[13]

Considering such sentiments, it is not surprising that many scholars include Dewey within the Reconstructionist movement in the 1930s.[14] Dewey did believe that the schools should assist in the reconstruction of society, but his view of this process differed significantly from the views of Reconstructionists like Counts and Brameld. Rather than indoctrinating students with a particular theory of social welfare, Dewey believed the schools should participate in the general intellectualization of society via a pragmatic method of intelligence, i.e., by providing students with the critical skills necessary for reflective thought applied to the analysis of social problems.[15]

The central aim of education is "to prepare individuals to take part intelligently in the management of conditions under which they will live, to bring them to an understanding of the forces which are moving to equip them with the intellectual and practiced tools by which they can themselves enter into direction of these forces."[16] Dewey's approach to education was designed to cultivate the pragmatic method of intelligence by which students acquired the knowledge and skills that enabled them "to take part in the great work of construction and organization that will have to be done, and to equip them with the attitudes and habits of action that will make their understanding and insight practically effective."[17] He understood human intelligence as a capacity or competence to help clarify and achieve desirable social ends.

Dewey's insistence on a commitment to the method of intelligence was posed as just that, a commitment to a method, and not to any specific social outcome as a result of employing that method. He explicitly rejected the Reconstructionists position that the schools should seek to indoctrinate students to promote a particular theory of social welfare, although he realized that schools could not help transmitting some social values. He pointed to the lack of consensus regarding any single system of social value in our complex modern society. To attempt either to indiscriminately impose such a system, or to follow all the values of the current society, would be to abandon the method of intelligence.[18]

This commitment to intelligence could be conceived as instrumental, empirically grounded, and designed to draw tentative conclusions. To go beyond that point would be indoctrination, which Dewey rejected. While Dewey's curriculum theory was not based on a particular theory of social welfare, it did emphasize the centrality of providing the conditions under which democracy and pragmatic intelligence might survive and be applied. Thus, it is an exaggeration to claim, as some critics have, that Dewey's pragmatic theory had no political valence.[19]

Dewey was quite specific in his response to reconstructionist critics like Counts who attacked his instrumental approach as neutral. He did not believe it was neutral, mechanical, aloof, or "purely intellectual" in its analysis of social conflict. The Pragmatist's application of modern advances in science and technology to improve society did so not through indoctrination but by the "intelligent study of historical and existing forces and conditions" and this method "cannot fail ... to support a new general social orientation."[20] From Dewey's perspective, indoctrination was not only undesirable but unnecessary as well. In due time, the development of pragmatic intelligence would reveal ways to improve the social order. Those supporting indoctrination

rest their adherence to the theory, in part, upon the fact that there is
a great deal of indoctrination now going on in the schools, especially
with reference to narrow nationalism under the name of patriotism,
and with reference to the dominant economic regime. These facts
unfortunately *are* facts. But they do not prove that the right course is
to seize upon the method of indoctrination and reverse its object.[21]

In a paradoxical sense, Dewey did recommend that education impose
the pragmatic approach to the development of intelligence, but he did not
see this recommendation as contradictory. "If the method we have recommended leads teachers and students to better conclusions than those
which we have reached—as it surely will if widely and honestly adopted—so
much the better."[22] For Dewey, any attempt to inculcate preconceived theory of social welfare would ultimately work to subvert his approach to pedagogy and be antithetical to education for democracy.

CONSERVATIVE CRITIQUES OF PROGRESSIVISM

Foundationalists and democratic Realists represented the two major conservative reactions to modernism in the 1920s and 30s. More recently, elements of this conservative tradition have become an important part of the
education reform discourse over the past two decades. In contrast to democratic Realists, Foundationalists were hostile to modernism and argued
that tradition and reason did reveal essential truths to guide the development of human society and conduct.

The Foundationalist Response to Modernism

Two of the most prominent proponents of this view during the 1930s were
Robert Hutchens, president of the University of Chicago, and Mortimer
Adler, a former student of Dewey's, who joined the University of Chicago
faculty as a Thomist philosopher. Both Adler and Hutchens believed
human reason capable of discovering the truths and certainty of natural
law. Hutchens instituted the "great books" curriculum at Chicago and
placed metaphysics, as opposed to science, at the top of the curriculum.
He argued that science was not capable of addressing moral issues. Only
metaphysics could discover universal truths and first principles.

   Hutchens and Adler were also harsh critics of Dewey, particularly Pragmatism's rejection of the human quest for foundations and certain knowledge.
The persistence of Foundationalism is impressive, perhaps reflecting a fundamental human desire for certainty, as Dewey claimed. The foundationalist

arguments posed by Hutchens and Adler persisted in the last half of the twentieth century, and were recently revived by Alan Bloom to become a featured part of the "culture wars," including the debates over educational reform in the 1980s and 90s.[23] Sidney Hook, Dewey's most prominent student, perhaps best summarized the central flaw of Foundationalism in a review of Alan Bloom's *Closing of the American Mind.* Hook argued that the position taken by Bloom and his mentor, Leo Strauss, was unable to get beyond the Greek view that understood the cosmos as also an ethos, and thus concluded that what is moral for humanity is to be found in the cosmic order as opposed to morality that is derived from the reflective choices humans make when confronted by problems of what to do.[24]

Democratic Realism and the Lippmann/Dewey Debate

Jefferson's argument that a well educated citizenry is essential to the survival of a democratic society has become a core cultural assumption. Dewey never lost his faith in the potential of education, in combination with a vigorous free press, to help create the conditions necessary to enable a strong democratic society to emerge in America. On the other hand, there remains no clear consensus regarding the meaning of democracy. Yet the way we define democracy is central to evaluating any argument to use our schools for social transformation (as was apparent in Dewey's critique of Reconstructionism). The conservative critique of progressive education is rooted in a very different view of democracy than is held by either liberal Progressives or the more radical Reconstructionists.

As noted earlier, modernism had called into question liberal assumptions regarding democracy in practice and education for democracy in particular. In the early decades of the twentieth century, writers, called democratic Realists, applied social science analysis to critique prevailing liberal political assumptions regarding democracy.[25] These scholars concluded that most voters behaved irrationally, were motivated by narrow self-interests, and lacked the adequate knowledge and competence to participate in meaningful deliberation regarding public policy. The most influential democratic Realist in the 1920s and 30s was Walter Lippmann, the prominent journalist (and former Socialist, Pragmatist, and progressive intellectual).

Lippmann argued in *Public Opinion,* published in 1922, that industrialization and urbanization had transformed fundamentally the widespread network of small communities that had provided the context for participatory democracy throughout the first century of our national history. This loss of community undermined the capacity of individuals to acquire directly the knowledge to determine their interests and contribute to informed public policy decisions. In addition, the exponential expansion of social and scientific knowledge, and the increasing complexity of modern society, were now largely beyond the access or comprehension of the masses.[26]

According to Lippmann, the governing assumptions supporting liberal democracy, specifically the competence of individual citizens enabled by public education and a free press, could not restore the requisite conditions for popular democracy that modern industrial society had destroyed. In reality, the average person had neither the time nor interest to acquire the knowledge necessary for making complex public-policy decisions. The masses' understanding of reality had been reduced to a cluster of distorted representations (what Lippmann called stereotypes) that bore little resemblance to actual conditions.

Following his experience working for the government during World War I, Lippmann also came to understand how easily the government could employ highly effective propaganda techniques to shape public opinion. As a result, public consent was now generally manufactured from above by government and business interests rather than originating from a collectivity of informed individuals. Lippmann's concept of manufactured consent remains a central focus of analysis in journalism, communications, marketing, and political science.

Lippmann, like Dewey, agreed that a scientific habit of mind could overcome the constraints impeding our understanding of modern society, and believed the recently created social sciences offered the best way to acquire an accurate understanding of modern society and the knowledge required to make complex policy. In other words, only an enlightened elite (disinterested experts), not the masses, had the capacity to make complex public-policy decisions that served the general public interest.

Lippmann's views regarding the inadequacy of liberal democracy to confront the challenges of modern society were more strongly expressed in 1925 with the publication of *The Phantom Public*.[27] He even came to doubt the capacity of elites to acquire the scientific knowledge to resolve our increasingly complex policy problems. However, there was no turning back to the conditions of an earlier era. Only collective government of experts had the potential to meet our needs. While popular consent remained critical in a democratic society, it was important to understand that such consent was now manufactured from above, not generated from below by the collective consciousness of individual citizens. In fact, the minimum level of popular participation possible was desirable in modern democratic societies. Traditional democratic practices and institutions (education, a free press, citizen participation in policy decisions) were no longer effective. In Lippmann's scenario, citizenship and popular government was largely limited to the right to vote to retain or change leaders. The success of government should not be judged by the level of public participation but rather a society's ability to provide a high level of security, goods, and services.

Lippmann's elitist conception of democracy was not acceptable to Dewey. However, Dewey did praise Lippmann's accurate analysis of current social and political conditions, while rejecting his recommended solutions and critique of education's ability to develop the reflective citizenship skills required to participate fully in our modern political process. Dewey's response was presented in reviews of Lippmann's books and in Dewey's own book, *The Public and Its Problems*.[27] Unfortunately, Dewey's critique of Lippmann was both obscure and inconclusive. He raised some strong theoretical objections, but never adequately addressed the practical problems that Lippmann raised regarding the core assumptions of liberal democracy.[28] To the extent that Lipmann's analysis was accurate in the 1920s and 30s, one could argue that his views should be even more persuasive in our contemporary culture, which is saturated by mass media at a level Lippmann could only glimpse in part toward the end of his career.

The Neoconservative Critique of Liberal Democracy

A central tenant of reconstructionist curriculum theory was our current social crises were caused by "cultural lag" or a profound mismatch between antiquated, but still dominant cultural ideas, and the sort of social order required to best serve the public interest in a rapidly changing modern industrial society. The most dysfunctional dominant ideas, from the reconstructionist perspective, were our exaggerated emphasis on individualism, capitalism, and the further assumption that both were essential to the survival of democracy. Dewey, too, rejected the conservative arguments that capitalism was essential to the realization and survival of a democratic society. Indeed, Dewey criticized the capitalist economic system in the 1920s and 30s as responsible for the Depression and as a fundamental impediment to establishing a strong version of deliberative democracy consistent with his education theory.

In direct contrast to the Reconstructionists' position, Conservatives like Frederick Hayek argued that our current social order was a spontaneous and natural result of human evolution and had developed the way it had for good reason.[29] In addition, human society was always far too complex to permit the sort of knowledge one would need for the central planning of our economy as advocated by welfare-state Liberals or Radicals.[30] Any attempt by government to interfere with the natural (evolved) social order would only make things worse.[31]

Hayek also argued that human values, like human intelligence, had evolved over time as the result of the multitude of individual social actions and interactions. Thus, human liberty must always take precedence over general claims to social welfare, inasmuch as individual liberty was a prior condition for the creation of any concept of social welfare. For Hayek, the liberal or progressive emphasis on the need for a conception of "social justice" to drive public policy was among the most powerful threats to individual liberty that had emerged in recent years. From Hayek's perspective, the emphasis on social justice at the heart of social reconstructionist education reform could only work to invert the "original and authentic concept of liberty, in which it is properly attributed only to individual actions."[32]

Milton Friedman, a colleague of Hayek's at the University of Chicago in the 1950s, extended Hayek's ideas in the post–World War II era, claiming that the original concept of Liberalism had been corrupted in the twentieth century and confounded with the actions of a central government to improve the social welfare of its citizens.[33] Such efforts were doomed to fail. Like Hayek, Friedman argued that true liberty requires individual economic freedom. Thus, a free market economy was inherently the best way to maximize individual freedom and the potential of our social institutions, including schooling.

Although he never mentions Lippmann, Richard Posner recently proposed a neoconservative theoretical extension of democratic Realism applied to our even more complex postindustrial society.[34] Posner makes a case for what he calls Type II democracy, as contrasted to the stronger Type I form of strong deliberative democracy reflecting, albeit in different ways, Jefferson, Dewey, the Reconstructionists, and most of the contemporary progressive political and curriculum theorists.[35]

Posner analyzes Dewey's work and, like earlier critics, rejects both his conception of democracy, and education for democracy, as naïve and unworkable. It is clear he would have no sympathy for the reconstructionist approach to education. His conception of Type II democracy is largely shaped by his own "practical" conception of Pragmatism fused with the theory of conservative intellectuals, like Hayek and Schumpeter, as well as the liberal John Stewart Mill, to develop a theory that views deliberative democracy as a quixotic, and even counterproductive, approach to governing modern societies.

In an innovative application of Schumpeter's market economic theory, Posner argues that our democratic political system functions much like a free-market economy. Like Lippmann, Hayek, and Schumpeter, Posner considers modern society far too complex for the mass of humanity to understand. In fact, he asserts that even elite technocratic groups never have the access to the knowledge necessary for a full understanding of social issues. However, the current American political system does provide a workable structure (think in terms of John Stewart Mills' "marketplace of ideas" wherein different views compete for attention and scrutiny) wherein highly complex technical information is sorted in a way that has the best potential to enable Democratic politicians to sell their candidacy to voters much as entrepreneurs do in terms of products or services.

For Posner (again, like Lippmann), the right to vote in free elections is a critical element of democracy, something necessary to build public confidence, legitimate public policy, and ensure politicians must compete for public support. While the average person is unlikely to have the competence to make complex policy decisions, she is qualified to determine, over time, if elected officials are acting in the public interest. In this respect, he does seem to have more faith than Lippmann in the competence of the masses to make good choices regarding their political representatives. However, even if a case could be made that the public often selects candidates unwisely, voting would remain a necessary condition for the success of Posner's model of democracy.

Following the logic of Posner's argument, education for social transformation would be a bad idea, since it is focused on developing an illusionary and unworkable conception of participatory democracy that can only lead to cynicism in the long run. Instead, schools should help students move away from the naïve conception of Type I participatory democracy and secure a better understanding of how our current Type II democracy works, how it might be improved, and why it is the preferred political system.

The consequences of the foundationalist and democratic-realist conservative agenda have had far reaching effects. First, an influential movement to deregulate and privatize public education has gained legitimacy.[36] While Conservatives have always sought to influence the nature of public education, many are now arguing that public schooling is an institution whose time has passed. The call for charter schools, home schooling, and vouchers are all elements of this move toward privatization. Second, the focus on free enterprise as both the cornerstone of democracy and the best way to create educational excellence poses a direct challenge to both the progressive and reconstructionist conceptions of education for democracy. The current standards-based education reform has shifted the focus to studying core-content knowledge and away from the study of social issues and justice.[37]

If one is obligated to start with the assumption that a free-market economy is the precondition for individual liberty and democracy, all attempts to analyze alternative economic and political systems are reduced to an examination of why the alternative systems are inferior.

THE TRAGIC/EXISTENTIALIST VIEW OF EDUCATION

Human progress guided by scientific reasoning was a core assumption of Progressivism and Reconstructionism. Consequently, the element of modernism that problematized the assumption of progress posed a significant challenge to the reconstructionist program. Recall the reconstructionist confidence in science and reason to provide the knowledge required to develop the conception of a new social order to address the major crises we faced in the 1930s. Two exemplars of the tragic/existentialist response to modernism were Henry Adams and Reinhold Niebuhr.

Adams, a respected historian and descendant of a distinguished American family, was preoccupied with the problems posed by modernism. Adams turned to the scientific study of American history for the meaning of human existence threatened by the rise of scientific thought. Instead, after decades of study, he found no fundamental truths or causal patterns in history and concluded that human "experience ceases to educate."[38] American history revealed that liberty was intrinsically linked to power, a series of events defined by their effects as opposed to principles or some overarching purpose. Adams concluded that history was a record of individuals who lived without any clear sense of vision, theory, or the meaning of their actions. As a consequence, their behavior communicated little to the present. Human knowledge was indeterminate and there was no going back to Enlightenment assumptions regarding reason and values.

Historian John Patrick Diggins argues that Adams had concluded that our culture's liberal faith in democratic institutions, like open elections, a free press, and public schools, was unable to guarantee liberty.[39] Diggins traces the origins of Adams skepticism to the roots of the early republic. The founding fathers themselves were well aware of the role of factions, passion, and irrationality in human politics. They had designed a political system of checks and balances to secure liberty because they did not believe human reason or principles were capable of doing so alone.[40]

Theologian Reinhold Niebuhr was among those intellectuals in the 1920s and 30s who gradually lost faith in the capacity of Liberalism, human intelligence, and science to bring about the reforms necessary for a just social order. Niebuhr's own experiences working with the poor in Detroit reinforced his skepticism. Niebuhr had been an advocate of nonviolence, but came to question the efficacy of that policy, given the limits of reason, religion, and education to constrain narrow and predatory self-interest. He came to see conflict as inevitable, something no social order can eliminate. Since some level of conflict and injustice are intrinsic to human existence, they must be confronted with power, which will include coercion and, on occasion, violence.[41]

Modernist science, for all its insights, is incapable of providing the human "nerve and will" to resist social injustice. On the other hand, the utopian faith of the Social Gospel movement in the late nineteenth century and the progressive ideas that had guided American social reform movements in the early twentieth century were both naïve and counterproductive because they resulted in a false sense of progress. Niebuhr was especially skeptical regarding ideals and absolutes. While he did believe absolute ideals could be identified, he denied the possibility of humans acting consistently on such ideals in the real world. No form of government or approach to education was capable of getting people to work together toward the good of all. Dewey's optimistic appeal to disinterested social intelligence as the basis for social reform ignored the harsh realities of social life and also denied the masses' need for morale, which can only be "created by the right dogmas, symbols, and exceptionally potent oversimplifications."[42]

Niebuhr was not a defeatist and remained an activist on behalf of social justice throughout his life. Instead, he espoused what he called "Christian realism," the need to maintain a consciousness of human limits and possibilities as we go about our social reform work. We should continue to act for social justice motivated primarily by hope and love, not science and social engineering. Too often progressive reformers overestimated human finitude, acting on the illusion that they were making progress and blind to their own selfish motivations. Even on those occasions when people are able to rise above self-interest and act with the best intentions, the policies they create generally have unintended negative, and often ironic, consequences. History contains a long record of reform efforts that, in effect, strengthened the status quo.

The legacy of the tragic/existential response to modernism continued throughout the twentieth century and into the present. The work of Christopher Lasch is one recent example of a writer working in this tradition.[43] The Postmodern/Poststructuralist movement in the last decades of the century is another recent arguable challenge to Foundationalism, the limits of human cognition, and scientific knowledge, having much in common with the Tragic/Existentialists. However, the tragic critique cuts too close to the bone for most Americans who, despite episodes of self-doubt, tend to cling to Foundationalism, resist all forms of Relativism, and take progress for granted. It is interesting that many contemporary critics on both the Left and Right, whatever their other differences, refuse to give up claims of privileged access to foundations for epistemological and/or axiological knowledge.

CONCLUSIONS

American society is still adjusting to the effects of modernism. While there is no going back to a pre-modernist society and culture, we continue to struggle over what social order would best serve human interests in the modern era. The Reconstructionists' call to use schools to build a new social order captures one aspect of this struggle. It is clear by now (and was to Brameld, Counts, and Rugg over time) that schools are in no position to create a new social order alone. The real question is this: to what extent can education in conjunction with other critical institutions including a free press, free elections, the family, religion, and various interest groups create the conditions necessary for the survival of a democratic society? Furthermore, does the reconstructionist legacy remain relevant to the current education reform debates? The answer is unclear. Certainly, the various objections to Reconstructionism described above need to be considered by contemporary advocates of the curriculum theory. Consider the following observations.

First, the foundationalist critique of Progressivism and Reconstructionism is the least convincing intellectually, but has remained a powerful, and some would argue growing, cultural and political influence. As the 2000 and 2004 national elections demonstrate, various foundationalist religious, academic, and political groups have had a major impact on the culture, education, elections, judicial appointments, and public policy of the United States. The Foundationalists have generated a good deal of fundamentalist dogmatism (both ideological and religious), which is antithetical to a democratic society. By invoking "God's will" as the basis for policy recommendations, they have moved beyond the bounds of democratic deliberation.

While we can agree there is much to fear from a cultural and political drift toward fundamentalism, it would be unwise to dismiss these foundationalist arguments out of hand. Lasch has documented the elitist arrogance and condescension the Left has frequently displayed in criticism of tradition, religious fundamentalists, and other "uninformed" groups who reject or resist a progressive accommodation to modernism.[44] Let it be clear that this is no brief on behalf of fundamentalism; it is one of the most serious dangers to democracy in the present era. However, as we deliberate over education reform, we need to keep in mind the genuine loss felt by foundationalist groups in the wake of modernism. Let us at least acknowledge that Progressives and Reconstructionists believe that they are representatives of a superior (more enlightened) conception of knowledge and society and are willing to use power and coercion to impose their approach to education.

The reconstructionist call to use the schools to help build a new social order had in mind a secular society, designed by "experts," and based on the best available "scientific" knowledge. They claimed the primary cause of the crises America faced in the 1920s and 30s was "cultural lag," i.e., our unreflective adherence to outmoded traditions and forms of knowledge that sustained an unjust society. Consequently, intellectual enlightenment was a critical component of social reform. There was a good deal of social engineering in the reconstructionist program, and reconstructionist "experts" were convinced they were acting on behalf of the general public, even if that public could not fully appreciate how its best interests were being served. Pushed too far, this sort of elitism on behalf of democracy is, paradoxically, antidemocratic. At the very least, we need to acknowledge that education for democracy will always contain some level of coercion for certain groups.

Second, as unpalatable as they might be to some, the criticisms of liberal democracy by democratic Realists (Lippmann and Posner), free-market Libertarians (Posner), or Tragic/Existentialists (Adams and Niebuhr) are not so easily dismissed. As noted earlier, Dewey was in full agreement with Lippmann's disturbingly negative description of voter knowledge, behavior, and the political process in general, although he rejected Lippmann's elitist remedy for the problems identified. The analysis of voting behavior by political scientists over the past six decades tends to reinforce the description of democracy in practice by both Lippmann and Posner.[45]

What Lippmann accepted as a necessary evil in our complex modern society, Posner sees as a positive good, i.e., the evolution of a pragmatic and more effective form of democracy (his Type II vs. Dewey's Type I) better able to preserve democracy and meet human needs. Even those who support Dewey's view generally acknowledge democracy has not been, and is not now, the natural human condition. It is rather easy to document how infrequently democratic societies (even loosely defined) have existed throughout history. A society has to struggle to create and maintain democratic institutions.[46] To acknowledge this fact, it seems, is not an argument against but rather a compelling reason for including education for democratic citizenship in our K–12 schools (something we should note is not even mentioned in NCLB). On this point, Dewey, Posner, and various Progressives would agree. Democracy doesn't just happen; it must be cultivated and learned. Posner's assertion that schools should teach the arguments for and against Type I and II democracy is also easy to agree with, but his recommendation that we teach Type I as inevitable and superior is unacceptable. On this point, he is far too complacent and even somewhat dogmatic. However, any reconstructionist approach to education reform must address the concerns raised by the democratic Realists and Posner's proposal. And it is important to recall that Dewey never provided a fully satisfactory response to Lippmann's challenge.

Third, there is a deeper intellectual problem at the heart of radical progressive arguments for social transformation. The problem was well described by Dewey in his rejection of education as indoctrination or countersocialization. When Reconstructionists argue that education should shift from socialization to focus on countersocialization aimed at supporting a new social order, they typically are construing "socialization" as the inculcation of the dominant social order's established norms—that is, as a debilitating training for conformity, rather than a habilitating, enabling, and empowering formation of competence to act effectively within a particular society.

While most of the reconstructionist critique of the dominant social order is correct, Dewey's critique of countersocialization as antithetical to democracy is persuasive. The reconstructionist arguments for countersocialization rest on the questionable assumption that they had privileged access to a superior conception of social justice and society. In this sense, Reconstructionism was placing far too much confidence than warranted in a view of "scientific" knowledge derived from the study of history, philosophy, and the social sciences. In this regard, Brameld was strongly influenced by Marxist dialectic, but Counts drew on non-Marxist, American radical traditions to develop support for his approach to indoctrination.[47] In either case, there was an assumption that the reconstructionist expert knew best what was good for society. Some recent attempts to revive a Marxist approach to education reform suffer from an even more extreme version of the same assumption.[48]

Dewey's critique described above will not be repeated except to restate that the reconstructionist commitment to countersocialization works to undermine the very form of democracy they claim to support. It makes more sense intellectually to justify education for democracy as "socialization." In a linguistic context, James Gee notes how development as a member of a language community or a society is fulfilled only at a stage where one is competent to improvise and to participate in fundamental transformations.[49] No longer should we describe as "countersocializing" those educational experiences in which students acquire the abilities to challenge social norms or policies; for these abilities also are not antisocial, but are essential aspects of the educated democratic mind.[50]

Finally, the tragic/existentialist critics have much to teach us, but it is a harsh lesson. Henry Adams and Reinhold Niebuhr criticized the optimism of free-market Conservatives, Liberal/Progressives, Reconstructionists, and Radicals; each of whom shared a belief in the possibility of creating a political program that would result in either indefinite progress and/or a utopian social order. The Reconstructionists, no less than most twenty-first-century Liberals and Conservatives, were optimistic regarding two possibilities: one, that a middle-class (or some comparable) standard of living was a possibility for all Americans (and perhaps most of the world), if only we would adopt the correct political system and public policies; and two, that the new social order could lead to human perfectibility (or at least the creation of the system that maximized human potential). In some respects, this view is similar to Francis Fukuyama's "end of history" thesis, but it is the sort of utopian vision held by the Reconstructionists.

The Tragic/Existentialists raised objections to both of these assumptions. What all of these groups failed to understand were the inherent limits of human reason, technology, and the capacity to satisfy the infinite demand for human wants. In particular, they overestimated the ecological capacity of the planet to support the indefinite growth required to sustain their utopian vision. The Reconstructionists also (in conjunction with many liberal Progressives, Conservatives, and Radicals) underestimated the corrosive cultural and political effects resulting from a blind faith in the inevitability of human progress. The optimistic reaction to modernism viewed traditional modes of thought and parochial attachments not as elements necessary to human existence but as impediments to progress. In contrast, Tragic/Existentialists like Adams and Niebuhr believed the imperfect nature of humanity was a given, and particularistic attachments—as opposed to modernist cosmopolitanism or the classless society—were essential to human society. Consequently, Reconstructionists failed to appreciate both the danger of assuming an ideological superiority grounded in a scientific faith in progress and the importance of particularistic attachments (e.g., family, ethnicity, gender, religion, sexual identity, and nationality) to generate human morale, will, and hope.

The Tragic/Existentialists rejected the inevitability of progress and urged us to accept the inherent limits of human existence and the often tragic nature of life. Education worthy of the name was, by definition, both potentially enlightening and destructive. Education always involved trade-offs and unintended consequences. How are we to measure human progress? We have a rising standard of living, remarkable medical advances, dramatic technological achievements, quantum physics, and the spread of "democracy." We also have increased dramatically our capacity to enact war, genocide, terror, environmental damage, drug abuse, crime, the spread of new diseases like AIDS, and a virtually unlimited capacity to invade privacy and violate human rights. Are these negative effects only temporary setbacks on the road to universal democracy and social progress, or are they evidence of inherent human limitations only exacerbated by developments in science as the Tragic/Existentialists argued?

It is important to struggle with such questions. For the Tragic/Existentialists, a conception of human society based on limits, with hope might represent genuine progress in human thought and education. To assume a level of progress that is not possible is a sure way to produce human despair. We must be careful not to confuse the tragic/existential view with either fatalism or the sort of complacency associated with unreflective Liberalism and Conservativism. Modernism, in its optimistic mode, viewed the tragic/ existentialist critique as an unnecessarily negative way of thinking. But Tragic/Existentialists were anything but complacent. Niebuhr, in particular, remained committed to activism on behalf of social justice. One can also point to the more recent tragic/existentialist social critic, Christopher Lasch, as an example of the hostility to complacency and commitment to social justice represented by this tradition.

The question remains: given all of the criticisms described above, does Social Reconstructionism remain relevant to the current education-reform debates? The answer is a qualified yes, provided that we develop a reconceptualized version of Reconstructionism that addresses the concerns raised by conservative and progressive critics. The Reconstructionists were right to remind us that: one, since social change tends to outpace the capacity of existing social institutions, in order to make necessary adjustments, social criticism is an essential component of education; two, there is some value in utopian thinking (in terms of what might be possible) as part of problem solving; and three, the dominant social order will always try to use education to perpetuate its control.

However, we should be both realistic and relevant in our social criticism, or few students will have much interest in our ideas. We must constantly bear in mind that we are teaching "other people's children." We must resist the progressive tendency to act as if we know what is best for the masses (e.g., the "If only others read the right books, they would understand clearly what must be done" syndrome), while simultaneously preaching about participatory democracy. As humans, we simply do not have access to this kind of definitive knowledge, and to assume we do can quickly become just another form of elitist dogmatism. Although it is difficult, we must try to distinguish between our role as educators and political activists. Dewey was a Socialist in his political life but not in the classroom. What he did recommend was a form of education that would enable citizens in a democratic society to apply human intelligence to the solution of social problems. Dewey, unlike the Reconstructionists and many contemporary progressive educators, believed that it was possible to cultivate the formation of the democratic mind by attending to requirements of competence for social action, without the need to direct instruction toward a specific aspect of social welfare or conception of a preferred social order.

Like Reconstructionism, Dewey's views should also be filtered through the harsh reality of democratic Realism and the tragic/existentialist critique of education. Nevertheless, like Dewey argues, the only valid path to education for social transformation lies in enabling students themselves to develop the competencies for active participation in a democratic culture. We will never know in advance if this approach will work as we hope. What we do know is that competent citizens, not reconstructionist school teachers, are in the best position to preserve a democratic social order and determine the shape of the democratic society to come.

NOTES

1. John Patrick Diggins, *The Promise of Pragmatism: Modernism and the Crisis of Knowledge and Authority* (Chicago: University of Chicago Press, 1994), 8.

2. George S. Counts, *Dare the School Build a New Social Order* (New York: John Day, 1932), 48.

3. Ibid., 47.

4. Ibid., 6.

5. Ibid., 7.

6. Ibid., 6.

7. Ibid., 8.

8. Ibid., 9.

9. Ibid., 12.

10. William B. Stanley, *Curriculum for Utopia: Social Reconstructionism and Critical Pedagogy in the Postmodern Era* (Albany: SUNY Press, 1992) Chapter 2.

11. John Dewey, "Education and social change," *The Social Frontier* 3 no. 26 (1937): 236.

12. John Dewey, "Can Education Share in the Social Reconstruction," *The Social Frontier* 1 no. 1 (1934): 11.

13. John Dewey and John L. Childs, "The social-economic situation and education," *Educational Frontier* ed. William H. Kilpatrick (New York: D. Appleton-Century, 1933), 318–319.

14. See Henry A. Giroux, *Schooling and the Struggle for Public Life: Critical Pedagogy in the Modern Age* (Minneapolis: University of Minnesota, 1988) and *Teachers as Intellectuals: Toward a Critical Pedagogy of Learning, rev.* (South Hadley, MA: Bergin & Garvey, 1988); Ronald W. Evans, *The Social Studies Wars: What Should We Teach the Children* (New York: Teachers College Press, 2004).

15. John Dewey, "The Need for Orientation," *Forum* 93 no. 6 (1935): 334.

16. Dewey and Childs, "The social-economic situation and education," 71.

17. John Dewey, "Education and Social Change," *The Social Frontier* 2 no. 26 (1937): 235.

18. Dewey "Education and Social Change," 236.

19. See Gerald Posner, *Law, Pragmatism, and Democracy* (Cambridge, MA: Harvard University Press, 2003) and John Patrick Diggins, The Promise of Pragmatism: Modernism and the Crisis of Knowledge and Authority (Chicago: University of Chicago Press, 1994), 8.

20. John Dewey, "The Crucial Role of Intelligence," *The Social Frontier* 1 no. 5 (1935): 9.

21. Dewey, "Education and Social Change," 238.

22. Dewey and Childs, "The Socio-Economic Situation in Education," 72.

23. Allan Bloom, *The Closing of the American Mind: How Higher Education Has Failed Democracy and Impoverished the Souls of Today's Students* (New York: Simon and Schuster, 1987).

24. Sidney Hook, "The Closing of the American Mind: An Intellectual Best Seller Revisited," *American Scholar* 58 (1989): 123–35.

25. Robert Westbrook, *John Dewey and American Democracy* (Ithaca, NY: Cornell University Press, 1991).

26. Walter Lippmann, *Public Opinion* (New York: Harcourt Brace, 1922).

27. Walter Lippmann, *The Phantom Public* (New York: Macmillan, 1925).

28. Robert Westbrook, *John Dewey and American Democracy*, 300–318

29. Frederic Hayek, *The Road to Serfdom* (London: Routledge, 1944).

30. Hayek, *The Constitution of Liberty*, (London: Routledge, 1937/1960), 387.

31. Frederic Hayek, *The Constitution of Liberty*, 387.

32. Frederic Hayek, *The Constitution of Liberty*.

33. Milton Friedman, *Capitalism and Freedom* (Chicago: University of Chicago Press, 1963).

34. Richard Posner, *Law, Pragmatism, and Democracy* (Cambridge, MA: Harvard University Press, 2003).

35. See Walter C. Parker, *Teaching Democracy: Unity and Diversity in Public Life* (New York: Teachers College Press, 2003).

36. House, E. R., *Schools for sale: Why free market policies won't improve America's schools* (New York: Teachers College Press, 1998).

37. Ronald W. Evans, The Social Studies Wars: What Should We Teach the Children (New York: Teachers College Press, 2004).

38. Henry Adams, *The Education of Henry Adams* (New York: Modern Library, 1934), 294.

39. John Patrick Diggins, *The Promise of Pragmatism*, 23.

40. John Patrick Diggins, *The Promise of Pragmatism*, 18–19

41. Reinhold Niebuhr, *Moral Man and Immoral Society* (1932; New York: Scribner's, 1960).

42. Reinhold Niebuhr, "After Capitalism – What?" *World Tomorrow*, 1 (March 1933): 203–205.

43. Christopher Lasch, *The True and Only Heaven* (New York: Norton, 1989).

44. Christopher Lasch, *The True and Only Heaven*.

45. Louis Menand, "The Unpolitical Animal" *The New Yorker* (September 20, 2004).

46. Walter C. Parker, *Teaching Democracy* (New York: Teachers College Press, 2003).

47. William B. Stanley, *Curriculum for Utopia*, (1992): Chapter 2.

48. David Hill, Peter McLaren, Michael Cole, and Glenn Rikowski, eds. *Marxism Against Postmodernism in Educational Theory* (New York: Lexington, 2002).

49. James P. Gee, *The Social Mind* (New York: Bergin and Garvey, 1992).

50. James A. Whitson and William B. Stanley, "Re-Minding Education for Democracy," in *Educating the Democratic Mind,* ed. Walter C. Parker (Albany: State University of New York Press, 1996), 309–336.

CHAPTER 6

THE TRIUMPH OF AMERICANISM

The American Legion vs. Harold Rugg

Karen L. Riley

When the American Legion set out to help bring down one of the Progressive Era's most prominent progressive educationists, Harold Rugg, it did so out of a long-standing conviction that any form of anti-Americanism must be met head on and extinguished in the most expedient manner. Legion members, ever alert to anti-American rhetoric, believed that they had discovered a genuine threat disguised as an educator, whose goal was to turn red-blooded American children away from democratic principles and toward a malevolent political and economic system (Communism) that could bring America to her knees. Rugg, they believed, would accomplish this task through his textbook series aimed at public-school children. The heightened patriotism of World War II is the historical context for the American Legion's attack on progressive education. In 1941, as the United States prepared for war, the Legion was busy writing and distributing pamphlets titled *The Complete Rugg Philosophy*, which outlined, Legion officials believed, Rugg's plan to indoctrinate students away from what it termed Americanism and toward Socialism, or even Communism.[1] These pamphlets were not the

Social Reconstruction: People, Politics, Perspectives, pages 111–126
Copyright © 2006 by Information Age Publishing
All rights of reproduction in any form reserved.

only vehicles for Legion writers. *The American Legion Magazine* was also a forum for the conservative ideas of Rugg's detractors. To writers whose articles condemned the Rugg materials, the curriculum that Rugg offered American youth was tantamount to a national security crisis.

Rugg, attacked by the American Legion for spreading un-American ideas through his writings, has yet to be completely understood in terms of his philosophy and where it figures into his textbook writings. His materials were condemned, yet the un-American rhetoric in Rugg materials seems to be lacking. Where did the American Legion get the idea in the first place that Rugg's philosophy leaned in the direction of Stalin's Soviet Union? Where are the clues that will help us to understand under what circumstances the Rugg philosophy developed or emerged? In order to assess the nature of the Legion's attack on Rugg, this paper examines the American Legion's publication, *The American Legion Magazine*, from 1941 until the advent of Sputnik, and its pamphlet series titled *The Complete Rugg Philosophy*. The then prevailing progressive educational climate and the scope of progressive thought illuminates our understanding of Rugg's role within progressive education. Additionally, the origins of the American Legion, and its stated goals and purpose, provide a framework for understanding the intense and systematic attack that the Legion launched against Harold Rugg. These origins help to explain two main questions: one, why Rugg was singled out; and, two, why the Legion was so dedicated to Rugg's downfall.

THE AMERICAN LEGION AS "WATCHDOG"

Formed in 1919 by United States military and ex-military service men who fought in World War I and wished to preserve the spirit of their collective experiences in the "Great War," the American Legion held its first national convention on November 11th.[2] Its stated purpose for proposing such an organization was two-fold—one, the fear of Bolshevism, and two, the discontent of those under arms.[3] From its very founding, the American Legion dedicated itself to the preservation of "Americanism," and the eradication of any stream of thought that might be construed as un-American. Ironically, the founders of the American Legion insisted that the organization be egalitarian in nature (privates were to have equal status with generals), yet "cursed" the very system theoretically founded on the notion of a classless society. In less than two decades, the Legion had evolved into a formidable force, and one capable of waging a figurative war on a set of progressive ideas, that was international in scope and espoused by such luminaries as John Dewey, George Counts, and Harold Rugg. Though Legion officials wasted few words condemning the work of Dewey and his followers, they seemed to focus their attention and efforts on curriculum materials developed and written by Harold Rugg.

While the Legion's attack was aimed at Rugg's textbook series as harbingers of his "sinister" philosophy, it is likely that Legion critics drew their conclusions from sources other than Rugg's textbooks. If one looks at the Rugg textbook series, most of which were developed from pamphlet form in the early 1920s, and later refined and published as hardbacks in the late 20s and early 30s, one would be hard pressed to conclude, on the basis of these materials alone, that Rugg was a closet Communist who sought to sneak his philosophy into schoolrooms across America.[4] What is more likely is that a philosophy of Social Reconstruction, published in 1934 as a committee report, with Harold Rugg as chair, and one which clearly outlined Social Recontstructionists' aims in terms of "collectivizing" the energies of citizens in the quest to solve some of the country's problems, heightened the suspicions of Legion officials who staunchly opposed any anti-American discourse.[5]

Far from being the lone voice for Social Reconstruction, Rugg was one of any number of educators throughout the United States who believed that education should offer more to the American way of life than graduating students with some form of common knowledge, but with little ability to effect necessary change.[6] In fact, a good portion of the 1934 proceedings of the National Education Association's (NEA) annual meeting seems devoted to the notions of unresolved problems and new solutions. Despite the countless numbers of those in education who called for progressive approaches to America's social and economic problems, it was Rugg who bore the brunt of the Legion's assault.

For its part, the American Legion played the role that organizations like it normally play—watchdog.[7] Its ordinary citizen body is ever on the alert to threats against the American way of life. Moreover, the self-imposed mission as "watchdog" was one of the fundamental tenets of its founding. In 1919 at the first meeting of the newly organized American Legion, members passed a resolution providing for

the establishment of a National Americanism Commission of the American Legion to realize in the United States the basic ideal of this Legion of 100% Americanism through the planning, establishment and conduct of a continuous, constructive educational system designed to (1) Combat all anti-American tendencies, activities, and propaganda ... [and] (5) Foster the teaching of Americanism in all Schools.[8]

Hence, the Legion's objectives were clearly delineated: one, to "watch" for, and combat, any behavior that might be construed as un-American or anti-American, and, two, to foster the concept of "Americanism," a new word ushered into the American conscience. The term "Americanism" grew out of American Legion jargon of the early 1920s. It was first defined in the 1923 Legion's Americanism Commission's report as a synthesis of "nationalism and patriotism." The report goes on to state that Americanism also means "the undying devotion and belief in the United States of America."[9]

Little wonder that Legion members viewed social studies and social education, with their emphasis on scrutinizing the Nation's economic and social system for the purpose of "fixing" obvious inequities, as a threat to the development of good citizens. Legionnaires believed that a chronological account of events, particularly wars or conflicts in which the United States was victorious, would be far superior in terms of molding young minds, and disposing students to patriotic notions of citizenship, than any curriculum that taught students how to evaluate current problems and find solutions. Moreover, fault finding with U.S. policies and practices was out of the question. The Legion was prepared to challenge any attempt to cast the U.S. in anything but a favorable light. To this end, an education committee comprised, in part, of Legion writers, Augustin Rudd and Hamilton Hicks, that called itself "Guardians of American Education, Incorporated," and originally formed in May 1940 under the name "American Parents Committee on Education," took the battle over Rugg's textbooks directly to the people—the Englewood Board of Education in New Jersey.[10]

The Board deferred the matter to its Fall meeting. Nevertheless, these actions demonstrate, in part, that Legion members not only waged a journalistic war on Rugg, they also took direct action. Thus, if one were to support the Legion ideal of education, ideas great or small should be broken down into recognizable forms. What is valid is tradition, custom, and ritual. Slogans are truth. Oaths, the highest form of wisdom. Clichés the ultimate method of explanation. What is more, the story of America is one of grand conflicts with glorious endings, told in chronological order, not one of greedy capitalists, corrupt politicians, or poverty ridden cities.

THE AMERICAN LEGION'S ATTACK ON RUGG

In the 1958 October edition of the *Legion* magazine, writer Irene Coreally Kuhn, penned an article titled "Battle Over Books," in which she congratulates Col. Augustin C. Rudd for exposing the evils of Rugg's textbook series and the work of other "Frontier Thinkers," such as George Counts. To Kuhn, the entire Teachers College "bunch," who functioned as satellites around the American philosopher John Dewey—described by Kuhn as a "materialistic, shaggy-haired scholar"—were peddling little more than Communism when they advanced their ideas of a new social order.[11] Only one year later, the American Legion published a celebration article on the organization's forty-year involvement with American public schools. Its author claimed that Rugg and a "small group of education professors at Columbia Teachers College and some other teachers colleges" had spent an "unbelievable" ten years attempting to subvert the public schools.[12]

According to Kuhn, Rudd viewed Rugg's textbook series as blatant propaganda. He used such terms as "clever" and "stealth" in describing the methods employed by Rugg in his writing. According to Rudd, Rugg, "with gentle language and a pedagogic smile," led the child "through the successive stages of indoctrination." By way of example, he pointed to one of Rugg's student workbooks. In one edition, Rugg posed the question, "Is the United States a land of opportunity for all our people?" Why? According to the teacher's guide, the answer the child should give is as follows: "The United States is not a land of opportunity for all our people; for one-fifth of the people do not earn any money at all. There are great differences in the standards of living of the different classes of people. The majority does not have any real security."[13] While these statements may seem to hold obvious truth for many of us today, we must recall with clarity the 1940s and 50s context in which Legion reviewers and sympathizers examined Rugg's work. In Cremin's seminal work on Progressive education, the author said of Rugg, "Certainly if any single career symbolizes the constantly changing image of progressive education during the decades after World War I, it was Harold Rugg's."[14]

One writer characterized Rugg's passion for progressivism in this way: "There were many who saw new and unprecedented opportunities in the rise of new governments which would reach such composite power as had not hitherto been recorded. Thus, 'there lies within our grasp the most humane, the most beautiful, the most majestic civilization ever fashioned by any people.'"[15] That Rugg's work came to be associated by the Legion with the rise of one of the new governments of which Odum spoke is all too obvious. Yet, Rugg consistently included democracy in nearly all of his discussions on the plan for a "New Education." Rugg may have entertained a certain intellectual curiosity when it came to the fundamentals or theory of Communism, but his textbook writings indicate a dedication to a democratic way of life with citizens freed from burdens imposed on them by the whims and fancies of unbridled capitalism. Only when the federal government assumed control of the forces of production and engineered a planned economy could citizens release their creative energies in order to engage in problem solving on a large scale, so thought Rugg.

At the time that Rugg wrote a number of his social science textbooks, in the early 1930s, the world had yet to witness with complete clarity the abuses of the communist state. It was too early to count the millions lost to starvation or brutalized by a draconian secret service. Communism, in its infancy, likely looked as though it might be the great social and economic equalizer. What's more, the American public at this time had not "digested" the Orwellian version of the communist state in *Animal Farm*. Yet the mere thought of a new social order caused many to dream of social upheaval and displacement. That was enough to convince any stout-hearted loyal American to resist in any form the slightest talk of a radical change. Hence, when Rugg's textbook series first appeared and his star began to rise, the opposition to his work took on a fierce and strident tone. As M. W. Apple and L. K. Christian-Smith have so succinctly stated in *Politics of the Textbook*, the real battle over textbooks and official knowledge generally "signifie[s] more profound political, economic, and cultural relations and histories. Conflicts over texts are often proxies for wider questions of power relations. They involve what people hold most dear."[16] This was certainly true of the 1930s and 40s' conservative view of educational Liberalism. Thus, the American Legion, only one organization out of a pantheon of many, took up its figurative sword and prepared to do battle.

As world leaders mobilized for the real war in 1941, American Legion writers began to defame Rugg by characterizing him as an academic dictator, bent on destroying the American way of life and supplanting it with foreign ideas of Socialism, or worse, Communism. Yet, Rugg did not act in isolation. In fact, the Progressive Education Association (PEA), the National Education Association (NEA), and a host of organizations worldwide embraced by both academic and political leaders had been meeting throughout the 1930s and into the 40s on the topic of "schools for the world of tomorrow."[17] The substance of these meetings could be viewed as revolutionary even today. In fact, the utopian visionaries attending these international conferences, when one looks at their proposed agenda, seem decidedly disconnected from political realities, and thereby fanning Legion fires.

In 1934, the World Conference of New Education Fellowship scheduled a meeting to be held in Johannesburg, South Africa, during July 2–27. Ralph J. Totten representing the Legation of the United States of America in Pretoria, South Africa, informed the U.S. Secretary of State of this meeting in a letter. He stated in his letter that the focus of the meeting would concern "social regeneration through education reconstruction." Some of the main lectures would include: "problems of the curriculum; vocational education; vocational tests and guidance; educational and sociological problems of the rural community; training of teachers to meet South Africa's needs; ... education in artistic self-expression; problems in social adjustment; and juvenile delinquency." Those expected to attend read like an international array of who's who of twentieth-century education professors and practitioners: John Dewey; Eustace Percy, former Minister of Education in Great Britain; Frederick Schneider, University of Cologne; Mabel Carney, Columbia University; Edmund Brunner, Columbia University; Cyril

Burt, London; Harold Rugg, Columbia University; Helen Parkhurst, Dalton School; Pierre Bovet, Geneva; and B. Malinowski, London, to name a few.[18]

This international consortium held worldwide meetings throughout the 1930s as the "International World Conference New Education Fellowship." The influence of American educators was all too clear. For example, the theme and rationale of the 1940 conference program were reminiscent of statements crafted in a 1934 NEA committee report credited to Harold Rugg. The theme of the 1940 New Education Fellowship meeting was "Human and Material Resources for the World of Tomorrow." Its rationale began: "Mankind stands at the threshold of a great adventure. He has at his command the material resources to make the good life ... he stands at the threshold of plenty and he looks to education to furnish the means for ushering in an age that is nearer mankind's hearts desires."[19] Rugg's committee wrote similar words some five to six years earlier when it delivered its final report on current social problems and their possible solutions.[20]

Fueled by the excitement of a worldwide effort on the part of educators and political leaders to change the future of the economically disenfranchised, Rugg, as only one of any number of educators worldwide, contributed to the goals of the "New Education" movement through the publication of secondary social science textbooks. With the success of the Rugg materials also came the critics. To ultra conservative groups such as the American Legion, Harold Rugg embodied all that was wrong with the New Education efforts of educational theorists and politicians across the globe: Internationalism, which meant un-Americanism. With their founding mission in mind, Legion writers pointed out to readers the real motives of Rugg and his followers—to turn American schoolchildren away from America's traditional stories of its past and the transmission of American cultural values toward a future filled with problems and how the nation itself helped to create them.

The man who the Legion hired as an expert in the field of education to help rid public-school classrooms of "the Rugg philosophy," was R. Worth Shumaker, graduate of West Virginia Wesleyan University and a former county superintendent from 1935 until his acceptance as chief education analyst for the American Legion.[21] In "No 'New Order' for our Schools," the writer opens with equal amounts of scare tactics and platitudes. Shumaker paints a picture for the reader of Hitler and Mussolini meeting in 1940 in the Austrian Alps for the purpose of forging an alliance to "blackout" democracy throughout the world.[22] The author sought to contrast the actions and motives of these two dictators to those of the United States by picturing America as a land where all can come to the figurative floor to be heard and where everyone's voice counts, while citizens of the Soviet Union or Nazi Germany were subject to the whims of despots.[23] While Legion members may have believed these two views themselves—bad guys versus good guys—countless educators, social workers, and intellectuals knew better. They knew that the voices of immigrants and minorities went largely ignored in conservative political circles. This was one of the aspects of American life progressive reformers had hoped to change.

Shumaker's 1941article, hardly an unbiased view of progressive education, heaped praise upon America's educators, pointing out that "[i]n general, the builders of curricula, the writers of textbooks, and the classroom teachers, have performed their tasks most creditably."[24] The author went on to call the National Education Association (NEA) an organization that was part of a collaboration responsible for "building a great educational system which is the pride of the nation."[25] Interestingly, the NEA, some seven years before, sponsored the Rugg committee report that stood as a blueprint for progressive educational reform, calling for such things as "A New Education," one that would vividly present pressing social and economic issues. Rugg's committee insisted that through every avenue of information and education, the issues must be presented, including such concerns as a "*poverty economy* [italics not added] resulting from an outmoded laissez-faire economic system on the one hand and on the other a *plenty economy* [italics not added] which could result from a designed social system."[26] Amusingly, Shumaker seemed unaware that the NEA had actually sponsored this "detestable" document, authored, in large part, by the Legion's arch enemy, Harold Rugg.

In attempting to convey the Legion's message in a certain homespun fashion, Shumaker capitalized on the use of clichés throughout. In one such attempt, the author likened the United States to an old ship: "The old ship of State may have sprung a few leaks but there has been no scuttling of any part of our great heritage—the leaks have always been closed up and the ship continues seaworthy."[27] In other words, yes, the United States has problems, but it has always been able to fix them without getting rid of its form of government. Shumaker's purpose was clear: to convey the idea that what Rugg and other Frontier thinkers were calling for was an overthrow of the existing system as a way to fix any number of social and political problems. He went on to disparage the field of social studies by revealing its integrated nature as though an integrated treatment of social, political, historical, economic, and geographic issues and content were something undesirable. The Legion favored the traditional treatment of social science subjects as isolated subject areas—history, geography, economics, etc.

Shumaker leaves the reader with little doubt that he and other Legion officials believed that Rugg and other Frontier thinkers were behind a plan to transplant the Soviet Union's model of collectivism to the United States through the agency of the school. In keeping with the Legion's original 1919 mission of rooting out un-American activity, the publicity division of the American Legion issued a special news bulletin on April 5, 1941, which stated, in part:

> Specific information to aid American Legion Posts everywhere in their discussion of textbooks used in the public schools everywhere is to be supplied by the National Americanism Commission of the American Legion.
>
> Following up his article NO NEW ORDER FOR OUR SCHOOLS Assistant National Americanism director R. Worth Shumaker is preparing a series of pamphlets to discuss the textbooks that The Legion considers subversive in text and philosophy. These will be distributed in the near future.
>
> Legion organizations in the field interested in the battle to eliminate subversive teachings in the textbooks supplied for classroom work will have new background material for their studies....
>
> A cover message from the publishers cautions Americans to "examine your child's textbooks. Demand to see the teacher's guides. Find out if 'social science' textbooks have replaced courses in civics, history and geography. Look for subversive material, protest at once to school officials, the board of education, and school associations. Remember most of your teachers are loyal. Support them.[28]

This level of political activity is surprising if one takes into account that the American Legion's constitution reads that the organization "shall be absolutely non-political and shall not be used for the dissemination of partisan principles."[29]

Rugg was also attacked for his call to abolish intercollegiate sports as he believed that they held no academic value. One might recall that many university presidents and faculty, long before Rugg uttered his "sporting" challenge, sought to abolish intercollegiate sports as well, and for the same reason. Other charges brought about by Shumaker against Rugg included Rugg's "lack of emphasis on true American life and too great an emphasis on the unfavorable aspects, failure to give due acknowledgment to the deeds of our great American heroes, questioning private ownership, too favorable emphasis on what has been done in the Soviet Union, the creation of doubt in the minds of pupils and teachers as to the ability of our democracy to function successfully, the dissemination of alien propaganda, statements that the United States Supreme Court favors vested interests."[30] To bolster the Legion's position on Rugg, Shumaker quoted extensively from Rugg's work, most notably his *Great Technology*, which was not a book designed for secondary school consumption, yet offered little criticism of Rugg's actual textbook content for secondary students.

An examination of Rugg's textbook, *Problems of American Culture*, reveals that far from being a vehicle for propaganda, it takes a sort of straightforward approach in dealing with pressing social, political, and economic issues. For example, Rugg posed this question: "Is there a place for better planning in the development of the press?" He added that since the advent of universal elementary education, more and more individuals were reading newspapers, magazines, and books. To Rugg, the greater the ability to reach individuals through the written word, the greater the responsibility for accuracy in reporting. Although not alone when it came to exposing the problems of the press, he was, nevertheless, a prime target of the Hearst papers, itself allied with the American Legion for the purpose of disposing with Rugg and his ideas.[31] But what had he actually told students or young people about the press and its problems in his textbook? In *Problems of American Culture*, Rugg simply posed the question of whether or not there was room for better planning in the development of the press. He challenged youngsters to consider that

> [w]e have noted the important role of advertising and business in determining the content of newspapers and magazines. We have seen the widespread tendency for tabloid picture newspapers and other sensational periodicals to print "news" without too great regard for accuracy. Hence, although reputable publishers are already doing much to improve the character of the press, insistent problems present themselves. Underlying them are difficult questions of propaganda and censorship. Similarly, there emerge the equally important problems of the more fundamental education of our people, of the cultivation of a taste for better literature and of a demand for a more scientific attitude in the press.[32]

Rugg was certainly not the first to speak of things like sensationalism in the press. Recall the allegations leveled at press organs that sensationalized the "Sinking of the Maine," in the Havana harbor some thirty years earlier. The first quarter of the twentieth century, it seemed, had been devoted to exposing this or that falsehood and flashy deal making. Why were Rugg's proposals on journalistic practices treated as something new?

Make no mistake, Rugg certainly advocated change. The type of change that he and others, many others, sought to effect might even be considered radical or drastic. However, these radical changes could be viewed as proportional to the problems that progressive reformers perceived and sought to ameliorate. However, as A. Oliver succinctly reminds us in her discussion of how the "right" functions, "[t]hroughout the United States, national organizations have been formed by conservatives to fight against what counts as 'official knowledge' in schools.[33] This was certainly true of the battles that took place from the 1930s to the 1950s, during which ultra conservatives attempted to destroy the progressive message of Rugg and his followers.

A second article on Rugg appeared in the next issue of the *American Legion Magazine*, May 1941. Hicks, in "Ours to Reason Why," opened with a more scholarly, but no less damning account of Rugg and his proposal for a New Education than Shumaker had in the April issue. However, when one reads past the first several pages, the article begins to break down into a confusion of surreal images of youngsters tricking their parents by leading them into the chaos of a totalitarian state after years of subtle Rugg propaganda in their schools. Hicks actually went further in condemning Rugg than did Shumaker when he likened the Frontier thinker to Adolf Hitler. In fact, Hicks boldly said, "*The Great Technology* is Rugg's *Mein Kampf*."[34] As proof of Rugg's malevolent methods and motives, Hicks pointed out that a Legion post held an essay contest for high schoolers. Students were given a plan to stabilize business based upon both a Soviet and Nazi government model. Students were asked to write an essay without benefit of consulting any texts, dictionaries, or other printed materials. The results of the essay startled Legion members. The students, all of whom had attended a school which utilized the Rugg materials, responded as follows: three recognized the plan as either Communist or Nazi inspired; three others pointed out the pros and cons; and three thought the plan to be excellent. These outcomes likely confirmed what Legion rank and file believed all along, as long as Rugg and his sort were allowed to influence American youth, our country was doomed.

Like Legion articles published in the early 1940s, those produced in the 50s linked Rugg to the most perverse type of subversive activity—teaching the youth of America to find fault with its government. Also, like the articles of the early 40s, the authors likened Rugg to Hitler, Stalin and Mussolini, although Hitler remained the favorite. Unlike the 1941 Shumaker article, in which the author heaped praise upon the NEA, Kuhn's article entitled "Your Child is their Target," alerted the reading public to a different NEA. She was quick to point out that

> [o]ne of the strongest forces today in propagandizing for a socialistic America is the hierarchy of the National Education Association. They have had things pretty much their own way for a long time, too, but the public opposition and nation-wide parents' rebellion which have sprung up in the past two years may force the N.E.A. into a re-examination of itself. It is too soon, though, to say how the organization will eventually react. Some of its performances have been more typical of the tactics of a captured labor union complete with goon squads, than of a respectable national organization of more than a half million

teachers. The N.E.A. has no reason to be proud of those goon squads which have turned up to do a discrediting job on citizens whenever there has been an uprising in a community against "progressive" education.[35]

The mistrust of ordinary citizens such as the Legionnaires and other ultra-conservative groups of their schools, teachers, administrators, along with professional teaching organizations, is palpable in this 1952 article. Nearly twenty years after the 1934 Cleveland meeting of the NEA, when Rugg and his committee took up the challenge of articulating a philosophy of social reconstruction presented as a committee report on America's social and economic problems and their implications, the Legion continued to beat the same drum in its organization's publications. Kuhn, like Shumaker some twenty years before, trotted out all of the data on that decades-old meeting as if it were a current red flag.

While the *American Legion Magazine* published other articles excoriating Rugg and his contemporaries, the few presented here suffice as examples of the type of message and method of delivery employed by one of our largest ex-servicemen's and patriotic organizations. Perhaps far more than magazine articles, the Legion's three-volume series on the philosophy of Harold Rugg was the most damaging of its written publications. In *The Complete Rugg Philosophy*, the Legion laid at the doorstep of one educator the entire blame for what its members collectively believed was a communist plot to subvert the minds of American children. This step-by-step analysis of the "Rugg program" relied on excerpts from Rugg's work juxtaposed with original interpretations by Legion-employed experts of his work. In volume two, writers assert that

> [t]he Legion recognizes the right of freedom of speech. This is a precious heritage which must be preserved. The Legion is firm in its position, however, that this right ceases to be a privilege when controversial issues are presented to children through textbooks which serve as an instrument of propaganda to promote the personal ideas and program of the author.[36]

While Rugg clearly held ideas that America could and should be a better place to live for all of her citizens, he never advocated the kind of collectivism as practiced in Stalin's Soviet Union. Perhaps he used the wrong language—"democratic collectivism"—to introduce his ideas, or perhaps his terminology was correct and the terms were simply perverted by totalitarian-minded Soviet leaders. Whatever the case, Rugg was only one of hundreds, if not thousands, of educators in the United States and worldwide who eagerly sought the promise of Progressivism and the hope for mankind ushered in by a "New Education."

CONCLUSION

What set Rugg apart from other intellectual Reconstructionists of the 1920s and 30s, and thus made him an easy target for patriotic watchdog organizations such as the American Legion, was that his writings and materials actually made their way into the public-school system, the stronghold and incubator of American traditionalists. Additionally, Rugg's talk of collectivism in his 1934 NEA Committee Report sounded eerily to Legion ears like the brutal system and economic policies of Stalin's Soviet Union— never mind that Rugg referred to democracy in a positive light throughout his writings and textbooks for children. No matter that what he and other Reconstructionists envisioned was what they called "democratic collectivism," a term not easily understood even today despite decades of scrutiny by scholars of Social Reconstruction, his opponents remain unconvinced. Rugg's reconstruction of society embraced a dual strategy: one, a planned economy in which the federal government would control the production of goods as well as the financial and transportation infrastructure, which in turn would free the people from the whims of capitalism, and two, allow Americans to release their collective spirit and work together to solve America's problems, especially in the area of social justice.

While Rugg's detractors rarely referred to direct quotations from his textbooks as clues to a far left ideology, they routinely pointed to the NEA's 1934 Cleveland meeting and "Rugg Committee Report" as the tell-tale irrefutable evidence and smoking gun that showed that what Rugg advocated was a revolution of some sort. Others might be fooled by talk of Reconstruction, but not folks who belonged to patriotic groups such as the American Legion. To them, Reconstruction was just another word for revolution and they knew what *that* meant. Always vigilant, patriotic groups like the American Legion kept watch over America's schools, lest those with un-American ideas sneak anti-American rhetoric in through the back door of change. Rugg and his committee certainly gave them something to think about when they delivered their report at the 1934 Cleveland meeting. It was filled with all of the ills and injustices suffered by the underclass and lower working class at the hands of a few at the top of the socioeconomic ladder.

What the report pointed out again and again was that now, and never before had, Americans possessed the technological skills to effect the radical change called for by the Rugg committee and international educational community. It urged members of the NEA to stand united and to put into place far-reaching changes in areas such as curriculum, teacher-education programs, adult education, and a new philosophy of change. Thus, in one report, Rugg and his committee had put to paper what had been discussed at NEA annual meetings years before. For Rugg the individual, his authorship as chairman of the committee may have sealed his financial doom and legacy as Legionnaires and their hired experts took a long look at the Cleveland meeting and saw the red handwriting on the wall. In the end, Rugg never reconciled his new-world-order political beliefs with the social criticism of American life found in his textbook writings to the satisfaction of his opponents, especially the keepers of the spirit of Americanism—the American Legion. For its part, the American Legion held true to its founding principles of promoting "Americanism" by eradicating ideas that its leadership believed smacked of un-American activity. Its self-proclaimed mission to serve as a bulwark for anti-American propaganda needed ideas like Rugg's to serve as a common enemy and "rally the troops." Thus, under the glare of the un-American spotlight and watchful eye of the American Legion, Rugg and his philosophy of Social Reconstruction fell from grace as quickly as his high-school textbooks fell from the shelves of school libraries and classrooms across the American educational landscape.

An earlier version of this chapter was published in *The International Journal of Social Education*, 18, 2 (Winter 2003).

NOTES

1.   What remains of this decades-old contest—ultra-conservatives vs. liberals of any degree—is the belief that school is a place where one goes to learn prescribed information and pass standardized tests demonstrating that the individual knows and understands what a good citizen should know, not a place where one goes to learn how to become a change agent. The pedagogical grip today that politicians and their watchdog agencies like the American Legion exert over the nation's schools is formidable; it was formidable in Rugg's day. In the case of the Legion, its members dedicated themselves from their very inception to the preservation of the American way, as they defined it. Their mission was to "seek out and destroy" un-American elements and activities. To that end, the American Legion was successful in that it brought down one of the most flamboyant and recognized of the Social Reconstructionists, Harold Rugg, who, in the eyes of its members, was a misguided and dangerous man. In the end, the great social reconstructionist plan to educate the nation's youth toward a more socially just and politically active society, where citizens might enjoy a more equitable division of the nation's wealth, fell far short of the envisioned utopia. In the

end, the conservative drumbeat became stronger and louder, signaling the defeat of Rugg and his co-conspirators, and exalting the triumph of Americanism. 1. *Rugg Philosophy Analyzed* II (Indianapolis, Indiana: The American Legion, 1941).

2. W. Gellermann, *The American Legion as Educator,* (New York: Teachers College Press, 1938), 6.

3. Ibid., 10.

4. For a discussion on the Rugg textbook controversy, see N.T. Bagenstos, "Social reconstruction: The controversy over the textbooks of Harold Rugg," Paper presented to the Annual Meeting of the American Educational Research Association at their annual meeting. *ERIC Document Reproduction Services No. (ED 137 190),* 1977; E. Bosenberg and K.S. Poland, "Struggle at the Frontier of Curriculum: The Rugg Textbook Controversy in Binghamton, NY," *Theory and Research in Social Education,* (Fall 2001), 640–670.

5. Committee Report of the NEA, "Our social-Economic Situation and the new Educatiaon," *Journal of Educational Sociology* 7, 9 (May 1934).

6. For an extensive treatment of Rugg other frontier thinkers, see Carbone 1969 and 1971 and Murry Nelson 1977, 1978, 1982.

7. For a discussion on "extreme" patriotism, see B.E. Chmaj in "Paranoid Patriotism," *The Atlantic Monthly* (November 1962), 91–97.

8. *Summary of the Proceedings of the First National Convention of the American Legion* (1919), 39; in Gellerman (1938), 68.

9. *Reports to the Fifth Annual Convention of the American Legion (1923);* in Gellerman (1938), 70.

10. M. Nelson, *Building a Science of Society: The Social Studies and Harold O. Rugg* (Unpublished Ph.D. diss., Stanford University, 1975), 154–155.

11. I. C. Kuhn, "Battle Over Books," *The American Legion Magazine,* (October 1958), 20.

12. R. B. Pitkin, "The American Legion and the Schools," *The American Legion Magazine* (September 1959), 40.

13. Kuhn, "Battle," 38.

14. L. Cremin, *The Transformation of the School* (New York: Vintage Books, 1961), 181.

15. H. W. Odum, "A New Deal Popular Bookshelf: How Much Social Realism, How Much Social Science, How Much Grinding Grist?", *Social Forces* 12 no. 4 (May 1934), 604.

17. Letter from the Legation of the United States of America, Pretoria, Union of South Africa, to The Secretary of State, Washington D.C., August 28, 1933, National Archives, Box 14, 542.AP, 1/1.16. M. W. Apple and L. K. Christian-Smith, eds. "The Politics of the Textbook," *The Politics of the Textbook* (New York: Routledge, 1991), 3.

18. Ibid.

19. Letter from Frederick L. Redefer, Executive Secretary of the Progressive Education Association, to Ben Cherrington, United States Department of State, Washington, D.C., Division of Cultural Relations, October 24, 1939,

Program of the New Education Fellowship meeting attached, National Archives, 811.427 10, Washington-Education/605.

20.   For the contents of the committee's report in its entirety, see, Committee Report of the NEA, "Our social-Economic Situation and the new Education," *Journal of Educational Sociology* 7 no. 9 (May 1934).

21.   O.E. Jones, *Activities of the American Legion in Textbook Analysis and Criticism, 1938–1951,* (Unpublished Ph.D. diss., Norman, Oklahoma, 1957), 87.

22.   R. Worth Shumaker, "No 'New Order' for Our Schools," *The American Legion Magazine* (April 1941), 5.

23.   Ibid.

24.   Ibid.

25.   Ibid.

26.   Committee Report of the NEA (1934), 540.

27.   Shumaker, "No New Order," 6.

28.   *News Bulletin,* National Publicity Division, The American Legion, Indianapolis, Indiana, December 16, 1940; in Jones (Unpublished Ph.D. diss.) *Activities of the American Legion in Textbook,* 86.

29.   Hamilton Fish, Jr., writing in *The Forum* (July 1931), 29; in Gellerman, 42.

30.   Shumaker, "No New Order," 7.

31.   See Gellerman, *The American Legion as Educator,* 82 for a brief analysis of the Hearst relationship to the American Legion.

32.   H.O. Rugg, *Problems of American Culture* (Boston: Ginn and Company, 1931), 604.

33.   A. Oliver, in *Cultural Politics and Education,* ed. M.A. Apple, (New York: Teachers College Press, 1996), 42–43.

34.   H. Hicks, "Ours is to Reason Why," *The American Legion Magazine* (June 1952), 57.

35.   I.C. Kuhn, "Your Child is their Target," *The American Legion Magazine* (June 1952), 52.

36.   *Rugg Philosophy Analyzed* II no. 2.

CHAPTER 7

RECENT SOCIAL TRENDS, SOCIAL RECONSTRUCTIONISM, AND THE AMERICAN HISTORICAL ASSOCIATION, 1929–1941

Joseph Watras

From 1929 until 1941, the American Historical Association's (AHA) Commission on the Social Studies published seventeen books aimed at enhancing the teaching of the social studies. Made up of the foremost historians, political scientists, geographers, and educators, the commission offered guidance to schoolteachers whose task was to form citizens who would have to direct a period of momentous social change. In this effort, the commission presented rational, scientific explorations of social conditions, competent explanations of the nature of the subject matter, and research describing the circumstances under which teachers worked. Supporters found the reports to be well constructed and helpful, and some of the reports, such as Merle Curti's *The Social Ideas of American Educators*, remain important texts today. On the other hand, critics complained that the commission members took an elitist view of education and denigrated the importance of liberal studies.

Social Reconstruction: People, Politics, Perspectives, pages 127–148
Copyright © 2006 by Information Age Publishing
All rights of reproduction in any form reserved.

Such a wide range of praise and criticism seems odd. Unlike textbook controversies that took place in the last half of the twentieth century, the supporters and the critics were intellectuals who shared similar values and orientations. The disparity among the evaluations makes more sense when the work of the commission is not considered a set of curriculum proposals. It is better considered as an extension of the model of social reform made popular during the Progressive Era, advanced by Herbert Hoover, and criticized strongly in subsequent years. Often called social surveys, these efforts were based on the belief that social science experts, who strove to be objective, could provide the information that would lead to the creation of a rational and just social order. At its outset, the model rejected the give and take of traditional politics. During the New Deal, though, its exponents changed their orientation and their research proposals represented another force lobbying for change. Further, the results of the surveys seemed inconclusive because the experts disagreed with each other. This happened because, although advocates of social surveys compared social scientists to engineers, the social scientists could not control the material they studied as easily as engineers could control the manufacturing processes in factories.

There have been many different reactions to the work of the AHA's commission. Three examples illustrate the range of critical appraisals. Some commentators favored the AHA commission's reports. One such author was Michael Whelan, who in 1997, argued that the results of the AHA commission reinforced the best of social studies education throughout the twentieth century. He contended that there was a direct line from the 1893 report of the Committee of Ten to the AHA Commission on the Social Studies and through to modern social studies instruction. He found this influence in two important principles that he believed characterized social studies instruction. First, historical studies should be the primary focus of social studies curriculums. Second, some conception of worthy citizenship should be its chief rationale. According to Whelan, the AHA commission's reports represented enthusiastic acceptance of these principles.[1]

On the other hand, authors preferring academic curriculums contended that the commission's members reinforced improper aims. Among these critics is Diane Ravitch, who in 2000, complained that the AHA's commission was part of a forty-year chain of events that removed the liberalizing influences of history as a course of study from schools by transforming it into the social studies. Ravitch asserted that the chain started in 1893, when the report of the National Education Association's (NEA) Committee of Ten urged all students to study liberal, academic subject matters, such as history, because these courses would improve the students' ability to think. She added that a change took place in 1918 when the NEA's Committee on the Social Studies blended history with subjects such as political science, geography, and sociology to create the school subject called social studies, whose aim was to help students develop good citizenship and adjust to contemporary society. According to Ravitch, the 1934 AHA's Commission on the Social Studies advanced this narrow aim by recommending that teachers indoctrinate students to accept a collective society. She claimed that the commission members believed the historical trends were in favor of collectivism and people who opposed this change were on the wrong side of history.[2]

Other historians complained that the social activism that they found in the reports of the AHA's commission represented problems caused by a large group of educators. In 1969, C.A. Bowers decried what he saw as the tendency of progressive educators to use the schools as political tools. Bowers felt that, during the Great Depression, educators ignored John Dewey's vision of developing the intelligence of individuals. Bowers added that the AHA lent its prestigious support to, what he called, a most bizarre proposal. He contended that by not challenging the use of indoctrination, the association made such methods appear to be acceptable.[3]

Finally, some social studies educators contended that the AHA commission did not offer any direction at all. For example, in 1981, Hazel Whitman Hertzberg noted that yearbooks published by the National Council of the Social Studies (NCSS) and many local curriculum guides commented on the official commission statements as well as the different volumes by different individuals who wrote for the commission. Hertzberg thought that the AHA commission could not encourage reform because the reports lacked a central focus. To her, this problem arose because the members of the commission could not agree with each other. To write the two volumes that the commission produced as a whole, the authors had to qualify statements to the point where Hertzberg felt unable to offer a clear summary. As a result, she added, the commission failed to create a coherent perspective similar to those found in other, earlier commission reports.[4]

Although these critics offered different interpretations of the AHA commission, they tended to consider the AHA report as a specific educational document in a line of related committee reports. While the AHA commission's work was tied to other educational documents, it was more closely associated to Herbert Hoover's President's Research Committee on Social Trends. Many of the controversies that took place among the members of the AHA commission turned on questions about whether the report should address recent social trends or advance educational technologies then becoming popular.

Since the AHA commission met at about the same time that Hoover's commission released its report, the AHA commission borrowed many findings from *Recent Social Trends*. The connections were strengthened by the fact that one member of the AHA commission, Charles E. Merriam, was

the vice-chairperson of the president's committee and that the director of
research for the AHA commission, George Counts, had studied with Merriam
and with Charles H. Judd, who wrote the chapter on education for the
president's committee. As a result, in their conclusions and recommendations, the AHA commission members noted their dependence on the findings of the president's committee.

Although some of the members of the AHA commission criticized the
reports published by Hoover's committee, they disagreed with specific
practices of the President's Research Committee on Social Trends in ways
that they could improve the work of the AHA commission as a social survey
that sought to enable schools to solve social ills. For example, Charles A.
Beard, a leading member of the AHA commission, complained that the
report of Hoover's committee provided a compilation of empirical findings, but lacked a theoretical structure within which these could be understood. Beard noted that without such integration, the report could not
provide a basis for intelligent action.[5]

To correct the flaw he saw in *Recent Social Trends*, Beard sought to construct a theoretical structure for the AHA commission around which the
other members of the commission could present their different findings.
As a result of the work of the AHA commission, many textbooks in educational philosophy describe an educational perspective called Reconstructionism that arose from the Great Depression. Attributing this perspective
to such theorists as Counts, these texts claim that, under a reconstructionist view, schools were to bring about extensive social change. Some of these
texts complain that educators cannot know what changes are needed, and
the authors question the right of the teachers to impose their views on
other students. Despite these criticisms, Beard and his colleagues on the
AHA commission were part of a tradition of social surveys that involved a
wide range of distinguished scholars to plan a set of social improvements.
Like Hoover, they believed that the public would recognize the reasonable
nature of their suggestions.[6]

SOCIAL SCIENCE AND SOCIAL PLANNING

Recent Social Trends and the AHA commission shared many characteristics
with what is called the social survey movement. According to Barry D. Karl,
social surveys had begun in the early years of the nineteenth century. As
early as the 1830s, sanitary engineers conducted survey studies of cities to
suggest systematic reform measures. After the U.S. Civil War, groups such
as the Civil Service Reform League sought to join the emerging social sciences into reform movements. Karl adds that reformers had established
the steps in the process by 1900. First, a core group of interested specialists

identified a problem. Second, these specialists called a conference, involved more people, enlisted popular newspaper and magazine writers to publicize the concerns, and appealed to philanthropists to support the project. Third, the experts would make the survey. Finally, they wrote a final report and expected reasonable politicians to enact the measures they recommended.[7]

During the first years of the Great Depression, the social survey movement reached its peak. Writing in a social science journal in 1933, Shelby M. Harrison, of the Russell Sage Foundation, proudly proclaimed that his foundation listed nearly 3,000 different surveys in its bibliography. He explained that the surveys took definite form in 1907 with a survey done in Pittsburgh where the term "social survey" was applied to the process. Harrison defined the surveys as the application of the scientific method to the study of social problems that had structural relationships to each other and existed within geographical limits. The surveys drew upon the knowledge of many professionals from several disciplines and included such personnel as social workers, physicians, community planners, and journalists. Most important to Harrison, in each survey, various agencies joined together to sponsor them, and citizens volunteered to participate. When the surveys ended, the participants carried out intensive campaigns to inform the public of the results and recommendations, so that reasonable action could follow.[8]

The popularity of the social survey movement was tied to the fortunes of Herbert Hoover. In 1921, Hoover gained national attention using this model of reform. When Hoover served as the U.S. Secretary of Commerce, he constructed three national surveys to enlarge the general understanding of the economy and to reduce unemployment. The final report of the U.S. President's Conference on Unemployment, *Recent Economic Changes in the United States*, was completed in February 1929. Although the report did not predict the coming Depression, it expressed the hope common to the survey movement. This was the need to continue objective fact-finding that would encourage business and political leaders to work together to maintain economic equilibrium. Arguing that the economic machine was complex, the report claimed that surveys enabled people to see the relationships among the parts and the whole. As a result, people could choose more effective relationships between production and consumption, thereby avoiding such problems as wasted resources and unemployment.[9]

In September 1929, seeking to expand the use of such surveys, Hoover met with an advisory group to plan the composition and the work of the Committee on Recent Social Trends. In December, he set up the committee announcing that the information such studies would gather would help everyone see where social stresses occurred and where efforts could be made to deal effectively with those problems. The Rockefeller Foundation provided the financial support for the project. According to one of the committee members, Howard W. Odum, this survey represented the first time that a comprehensive, wide-ranging campaign enlisted many different social scientists to jointly attack the emerging social problems on a national basis.[10]

When opponents complained that Hoover set up too many investigations, he replied that he had not initiated enough. He claimed that the increasing complexity of society and the delicacy of its adjustments required that he use the best scientists to discover the way things worked. While he acknowledged that the U.S. Congress could set up its own investigations, he believed the office of the president had more agencies on which to call. Further, he thought this method was in line with the democratic traditions. Citizens volunteered to work on these commissions, and their unselfish willingness made it more likely that the public would accept the resulting proposals. Thus, Hoover did not see a problem in the fact that he as president had requested these studies. He stayed away from the work of the committees, he did not fund them, and he expected the experts on them to function independently.[11]

In the case of *Recent Social Trends*, the work was remarkable. When the committee finished its work, the manuscript totaled more than 1,560 pages, divided into twenty-nine chapters. In addition to writing the chapters, at least thirteen of the authors wrote lengthy monographs explaining their findings more completely. The committee published these texts separately.

The different contributions explained the changes and described the needed reforms for a wide range of areas of social life. For example, T. J. Woofter, Jr. claimed that there was continued exploitation and prejudice against racial and ethnic groups, yet he expressed the hope that the rise of organizations to help African-Americans, Native-Americans, and other ethnic groups to adjust to modern society could enrich American life.[12] In another chapter, Sophonisba P. Breckinridge noted that increased numbers of women joined the work force, yet she complained that industries refused to take full advantage of the abilities that women offered.[13] In the concluding chapter, Merriam pointed out that many business operations such as those involving currency, loans, and taxation had become intertwined with government practices. As a result, he urged that issues of social planning and social control be confronted in ways that maintained ideals of liberty and justice.[14]

It was this set of essays that informed the deliberations of the AHA commission. In addition, Beard and Merriam had gained fame by claiming that their disciplines could provide valuable information to reduce practical problems. As a result, the AHA commission began its work on hopes similar to those that Hoover expressed.

THE SOCIAL STUDIES AND SOCIAL IMPROVEMENT

Although the AHA did not coin the term "social studies," it is incorrect to think that AHA members had a different set of aims for high school courses than did advocates of the social studies. Writing in a manner similar to that of the social studies educators, historians claimed that the study of history was essential to the creation of a good society. As early as 1892, the historians who gathered together to form the Madison Conference, one of the NEA conferences that formed the Committee of Ten charged with determining the proper instruction of high school subjects, pointed out that such courses as history were essential to the making of a good citizen and that historical understanding reinforced feelings of patriotism in students. Although the members of the Madison Conference noted that some schools offered classes in civil government, they added that students learned best about the machinery of government through practical, local demonstrations or within history courses.[15]

The term, social studies, did not become a popular way to describe a school subject until the NEA's Committee on the Social Studies released its report in 1916. The members of this committee called for combining subjects such as history, geography, political science, and economics that related to the development and organization of human society into programs that enabled the students to cultivate the ideals of good citizenship. Although many commentators point out that the members of the 1916 committee were not academics, this report followed what the members of the Madison Conference had suggested. In fact, in writing the 1916 report, the authors quoted the members of the Madison Conference to show how citizenship could come from academic studies. As in the case of the earlier work, the 1916 report argued that students developed the qualities of citizenship when they learned how human society had evolved. As a result, although the 1916 report acknowledged that citizenship required loyalty to national ideals, the members recommended that the students develop feelings of membership in the world community.[16]

Public attention to good citizenship continued after World War I as a result of the many varied programs to Americanize the immigrants and to build patriotic feelings among native-born Americans. By 1916, a private philanthropic organization, the American National Committee began campaigns for what the vice-chair, Frances A. Kellor, called Americanization. This sentiment was a plank in the platform of U.S. President Woodrow Wilson's Democratic Party, and the following year, Wilson called on school officials to increase the training in community and national life for native-born elementary and high school students.[17]

In a short time, different organizations formed to consider ways to teach the social studies. In 1921, college educators and public school people formed the National Council of Teachers of Social Studies to provide a way to join together the work of the different local, regional, and national organizations. In 1922, The National Society for the Study of Education (NSSE) produced its twenty-second yearbook on the social studies.

Edited by Harold Rugg, the NSSE yearbook noted that many schools offered courses in the patterns suggested by the 1916 NEA report. For example, they introduced such courses as community civics, wherein students discussed how cities develop and how they can be planned. Unfortunately, when Rugg examined texts used in this course, he did not find adequate treatment of contemporary industrial, social, or political problems. As a result, Rugg called for comprehensive revision of the texts that teachers used.[18]

In an attempt to understand the development of citizenship, social scientists began to study different societies to determine how the members indoctrinated the children with a love of country. For example, in the 1920s, Merriam secured financial support from the Laura Spellman Rockefeller Memorial to publish eight monographs explaining how different countries undertook civic education. Entitling the series, *Studies in the Making of Citizens*, Merriam contracted with authors living in the countries, such as Germany, Italy, and the Soviet Union, to explain the broad trends of civic training. Merriam wrote the summary volume for this series, in which he stated a variant of the view that appeared in his chapter in *Recent Social Trends*: people could not understand systems of civic education until they were taken as part of a total social situation. Thus, in his summary work on citizenship education, Merriam tried to trace the patterns of devices that produced political control in the different states.[19]

In line with these concerns, the AHA created its Commission on the Social Studies in an effort to improve citizenship in the United States. Writing the forward to the introductory volume of the AHA commission in 1932, A. C. Krey, a historian interested in medieval Florence who chaired the commission, pointed out that the AHA had long been concerned with the problems of citizenship education. He described the results of *The History Inquiry* published by the AHA in 1924. Krey had served on this committee and had found the curricula of social studies around the country in a state of chaos. According to Krey, the problems arose because the number of pupils in public schools rose dramatically and because the social conditions changed rapidly. Optimistically, he added that the problems could be solved by close cooperation of all organizations concerned with the problem. Krey noted that the AHA council appointed a committee in 1925 to determine if such a study was possible. When the committee decided that such a study could take place, the AHA's council agreed to support a planning committee composed of historians, educators, and political scientists. In 1928, the Carnegie Corporation appropriated the funds to support the commission, and work began in 1929. Since Merriam was prominent in the field of civic education, the AHA asked him to serve on the planning committees that formed the Commission on the Social Studies and as a member of the commission.[20]

The AHA worked in ways that were roughly similar to the steps taken by Hoover's commission on recent social trends. The experts met, drafted a statement of the problem, attracted funding for the study, and informed the public about the process. When the AHA commission sought to write a statement of objectives, historians Beard, Guy Stanton Ford, and Krey met with the political scientist, Merriam, and educators, George Counts, Franklin A. Bobbitt, Boyd H. Bode, and Rugg. The fact that the committee members came from such a range of fields indicated that the AHA members agreed that the problems of cultivating effective citizenship in young people transcended the boundaries of any one discipline. Above all, since the funding came from a private philanthropy, there was no implication that the studies would result in coercive legislation or imposing policies. The information would become available for reasonable people to use in shaping the policies of different schools. The difference between the AHA commission and Hoover's committee on recent social trends was that the statement of objectives was to serve as an organizing theme to which the different authors would direct their findings.

To set out the objectives, staff members analyzed courses of study, read textbooks, and made summaries of pedagogical writings, the commission members held extensive discussions. Beard took these materials and wrote the first volume entitled *A Charter for the Social Sciences in the Schools.* The hope was that other commission members would furnish ways to apply the abstract ideas in the *Charter* to the practical problems of classrooms. In this way, the AHA commission tried to provide the integration that Beard found lacking in *Recent Social Trends.*[21]

Beard divided the *Charter* into six parts. First, considering the requirements of scholarship, he described the attitude of scientific detachment that scholars cultivated. Second, describing the nature of the social disciplines, Beard pointed out the difficulties in achieving a synthesis because the practitioners of each science held different points of view as they gathered the material they studied. Third, depicting the requirements of the social realities, Beard pointed out that society was rapidly changing, that the spread of industrialism caused the need for increased planning and intelligent cooperation, and that the students were to become active participants in the democratic society. Fourth, reviewing what he found to be the climate of American ideas, Beard claimed that the U. S. Constitution set out the progressive ideal promoting the general welfare, enhancing liberty, and promoting justice. He added that this implied social studies instruction should help achieve eight goals. These included a system of national economic planning, expansion of insurance and health systems, and provision of equality of opportunity for all people. Fifth, assessing the framework of laws and established programs, Beard found that teachers should regard regulations and textbooks as suggestions open to amendments rather than restrictions to practice. In this way, the teachers could follow directions while they acted as intellectuals with academic freedom. Sixth, concluding with a statement of what he called the supreme purpose of the social studies, Beard wrote that civic instruction should create rich, many-sided personalities in the students.[22]

Franklin Bobbitt, a member of the commission, considered Beard's objective to create rich and many-sided personalities vague or general. To Bobbitt, it was fruitless to urge teachers to use the social studies to prepare children for citizenship unless the statement listed what the good citizen should be able to do. This was in line with Bobbitt's advocacy of what he called scientific curriculum making, which asked that teachers prepare students to master specific skills deemed valuable for later life. Other members, such as Boyd Bode, disagreed with Bobbitt. They claimed that an overly precise definition of the duties and responsibilities of citizenship would tie the document too closely to present day concerns. For example, according to Henry Johnson, a member of the AHA commission, Beard's objective of creating rich and many-sided personalities was similar to the one made earlier in the twentieth century by Herbartian educators, such as Charles and Frank McMurry, who sought to create in children many-sided interests.[23]

In A Charter, Beard tied his aim for the social studies with a view of industrialism as a conditioning element of society that impinged on the teaching of the social sciences. Because industrialism caused people to leave farms and move to cities, and therefore created new professions, Beard pointed out that young people had to develop the capacity to adapt, rather than depend on any specific skill or ability, to ensure economic security. In addition, Beard noted that industrialism brought what he called "the engineering rationality" to everything, including government and social arrangements. As a result, he predicted that rationality, planning, and intelligent cooperation would have increasing sway in domestic and industrial affairs.[24]

Beard's explanation of such things as the need for government control of the economy did not detract from the popularity of the introductory volume. Reviewers praised Beard's A Charter for the Social Sciences, and readers purchased it.[25] Two years later, when the commission released what was supposed to be the summary volume entitled, Conclusions and Recommendations, educators criticized these same suggestions.

According to Lawrence J. Dennis, the AHA commission had assigned Krey, Beard, and Counts to write the *Conclusions and Recommendations*. When Krey took ill, Counts and Beard drafted the chapters with the result that Counts inserted words such as "collective" and "indoctrinate" that appealed to his reconstructionist temperament. When Dennis reviewed the transcripts of the meetings to discuss the conclusions, these words appeared to him to have caused the most heated debates. Dennis noted that, in revising the text after the meetings, Counts and Beard tried to accommodate the views of the other members, but he added that events moved quickly and they retained the original, activist tone of the report.[26]

CONTROVERSY OVER INDOCTRINATION AND COLLECTIVISM

The strongest criticism directed against *Conclusions and Recommendations* came from educators. Prominent among these critics were Boyd Bode and Franklin Bobbitt who had served on the subcommittee to write the *Charter*. In an editorial to *The Phi Delta Kappan*, Bode complained that the AHA commission's report represented an attempt to possess and exploit the students' minds. According to Bode, the problem came from what Counts and Beard had labeled "frame of reference."[27]

In the *Conclusions*, Counts and Beard had defined frame of reference as a perspective that was based on the results of scholarship and as consisting of generalizations, judgments, interpretations, and affirmations of the commission's members concerning the nature of the social sciences, the conditioning factors of American life, and the choices deemed desirable. As far as the nature of the social sciences, Counts and Beard restated the importance of the scientific method that had appeared in the *Charter*. In the area of conditioning factors of American life, they stated that the age of individualism and laissez-faire government in the economy was closing and a new age of collectivism was emerging. Since Counts and Beard could not point to the way this trend of collectivism would unfold, the choices they deemed desirable included the equitable distribution of wealth, increased cultural opportunities for all people, and the maintenance of democratic principles.[28] To Bode, this frame of reference violated democratic principles. Instead of telling students the age of individualism was over, Bode preferred that students and teachers have the freedom to discover if that was true. Bode claimed such freedom came from a faith in intelligence, and he asserted that if the commission members did not have this faith, democracy was dead.[29]

Bobbitt made similar complaints. Writing in *School and Society*, he complained that the *Conclusions* claimed the economy and the government were moving into an age of collectivism without showing how this was happening or what sort of collectivism would result. To Bobbitt, collectivism implied a state-controlled society similar to those found under Communism or Fascism. Thus, he found it strange that the *Conclusions* repeatedly affirmed a faith in democracy while predicting a coming age of collectivism. He added that the report complicated matters by calling for the students to be indoctrinated into accepting social planning.[30]

Shortly after Bobbitt's comments appeared, Percival W. Hutson, of the University of Pittsburgh, pointed out that Bobbitt's criticisms made sense if a person adopted Thomas Paine's ideal of democracy, that the least government is best. Hutson added that this was not true in twentieth-century America. Even the tax-supported public schools that Bobbitt supported represented a move away from rugged individualism and toward collectivism. To Hutson, collectivism meant that people had to learn to work together in democratic ways to build parks, provide utilities, and conserve resources.[31]

On this point, Hutson was correct. The *Conclusions* did not express undemocratic views because they stated a frame of reference, pointed to a coming collectivism, and called for indoctrination. Beard used the term "frame of reference" when he delivered his presidential address to the AHA in January 1934. In that address, "Written History as an Act of Faith," Beard argued that historians could not be objective because their works were limited by several factors: they looked at incomplete records and they considered those records from the prejudices of their time and place. Beard recognized that observing the relativity of historical writing destroyed the idea of anyone knowing anything, including the idea that things were relative to their time and place. When Beard considered what historians could do, he suggested that they examine their frames of reference, clarify them, enlarge them by attending to other areas of thought, and provide as much consistency as possible to their interpretations of the movements in the world. In this way, Beard recommended that historians should realize that they could not escape these choices nor could they make them securely. He advised them to plunge ahead in an act of faith.[32]

Philosophers found many problems in Beard's pronouncements. For example, although Maurice Mandelbaum agreed that every historical work was limited by sociological and psychological conditions, he disagreed that historians would make their statements any truer if they clarified why they wrote what they wrote. According to Mandelbaum, Beard had committed what he called the genetic fallacy. Telling the origins of a statement did not make it true. In addition, Mandelbaum noted that Beard made unreasonable assumptions about the nature of history. Beard had asserted that historians picked out a fragment of history to study and imposed a reality they possessed in order to connect their work to what happened elsewhere. Mandelbaum claimed that Beard assumed that the stream of history was one consistent thing when he could not give a reason to hold this view.[33]

In response to such criticisms, Beard tried to modify his position without much success. Beard claimed that he was calling for a form of limited relativism because he felt that each historical statement was relative to the writer. The limits came from the fact that there were a limited number of perspectives in the world and the authors developed these perspectives from their social backgrounds. Again, Mandelbaum found fault. This time he could not find evidence that writers' perspectives came from their social backgrounds. Worse, he added, if writers expressed perspectives that they took from their backgrounds, the notion of limited relativism was contaminated with similar prejudices.[34]

Although Beard's recommendation that historians disclose their frames of references did not solve the philosophical problems of subjectivity, it had come from Beard's faith that the give and take of democratic discussion would lead people closer to whatever truth they could understand. Responding to Theodore Clarke Smith's criticism that he was undermining the basis of previous historical studies, Beard claimed that there were two reasons why historians would improve their work if they revealed the cultural patterns that controlled their research. The first was that historians would develop clearer insights about their own interpretations if they had to explain their assumptions. The second was that such discussions could alert observers to the perspectives implicit in a set of ideas. In this regard, Beard compared the title of his own work, *An Economic Interpretation of the Constitution*, to Charles Warren's *The Making of the Constitution*, Beard argued that his title alerted readers to the pattern of his thought and did not hide behind an appearance of objectivity. Thus, readers could look for problems that they might overlook otherwise.[35]

In his work for the AHA commission, Beard advanced his belief that historians and teachers had to have a frame of reference in order to think or teach in reasonable ways. For example, in his volume for the AHA commission, *The Nature of the Social Studies,* Beard pointed out that some teachers tried to help the students understand social problems by presenting objective information about those problems. Beard contended that in order for someone to see some event as a problem or a need, the person had to have a frame of reference that defined the situation as irregular. There were parts of the world, Beard added, where a person lying in a gutter represented neither a problem nor a need.[36]

This point made particular sense to Ernest Horn, a member of the AHA commission who refused to sign the *Conclusions*. Horn began his book for the AHA commission, *Methods of Instruction in the Social Studies*, by quoting approvingly a passage from the *Conclusions* to the effect that teachers had to select their instructional methods with the aim of satisfying the purposes they had selected from their frame of reference. Horn noted that teachers tended to select their instructional aims and their methods without regard to a consistent frame of reference. As a result, there was no consistency in their courses. To cure this difficulty, Horn recommended that teachers read the AHA commission's *Charter* and the *Conclusions*.[37]

On the matter of indoctrination, Horn found people's fears to be unreasonable. For Horn, the slogan, "Teach children how to think but not what to think," was absurd because it put knowledge and thinking in opposition to each other. If a teacher only tried to teach students to think, the lessons would not have any content. As a result, Horn found that some indoctrination had to be present. It appeared among history teachers when they omitted information or presented descriptions that led to a particular conclusion. He believed that the best antidote to shallow thinking was what he called intellectualization. The students could learn this process by examining controversial issues and formulating contrary hypotheses. In addition, they could seek evidence to disprove different points.[38]

Other volumes that followed *Conclusions* expressed the view that social scientists had to express a frame of reference, that the age of individualism was over, and that schools must indoctrinate. For example, when Merriam, who refused to sign the *Conclusions*, wrote his volume for the AHA commission, he began by noting that social science should direct social education so that curriculum reforms would come from understandings of social changes. Claiming that technology, the rise of modern corporations, the increase of labor unions, and the growth of governmental agencies made social life increasingly coordinated, he warned these changes could produce increased benefits or threaten personal freedoms. To increase the benefits and to counter the possible dangers, he recommended that civic education encourage students to adopt an attachment to the principles of democracy. To him, this meant a distrust of irresponsible elites, a disposition in favor of mass control of institutions, a desire for the equitable distribution of wealth, and a belief in the continued advancement of human happiness. Although he acknowledged that this implied some indoctrination, he warned against substituting loyalty for intelligent thought. While Merriam would not describe how the curriculum could be formed, he did conclude that civic education should help people accept the plans that expert social planners recommended to improve society.[39]

In 1926, Bessie Louis Pierce published *Public Opinion and the Teaching of History* for Merriam's series on civic education. In her volume for the AHA commission, she took materials from that research. She showed how indoctrination prevailed in such different associations as patriotic organizations, military groups, peace advocates, fraternities groups, religious sects, business and labor unions, and narrow special interest activists such as prohibition supporters. Although Pierce had found these groups expressed a wide variety of aims, they shared the conviction that schools should train the youth to hold the organizations' beliefs. In line with the conclusions that

Merriam had expressed in his original series on the making of citizens, Pierce noted that such a feeling was a natural human condition.[40]

The most radical member of the commission may have been George Counts, but when he explained what he meant by collectivism and indoctrination, he showed they did not diminish democratic aspirations. In the volume that Counts wrote for the AHA commission, *The Social Foundations of Education,* he argued that the social sciences were to be organized in schools within the frame of reference provided by the ideal of democratic collectivism. This implied that those subjects served seven functions. They showed the lives and fortunes of ordinary people through the ages. They demonstrated the evolution of the arts and culture. The social sciences that traced the development of the ideal of democracy, showed the growth of industrialism, explored the conflicts and contradictions in contemporary society, and provided students the means to critically appraise their present-day life in terms of the democratic ideal. Finally, the school should introduce students to the suggestions for social reform put forward by the pertinent theorists. To accomplish these ends, Counts called for a sort of spiral curriculum that would lead the child from concerns with family, to the neighborhood, to the community, into the state, and finally to the nation and the world. For Counts, everything in this spiral was directed toward improving, enriching, and refining the common life of the people.[41]

The members of the AHA commission recognized the problems teachers faced if they chose to present material that contradicted the interests of powerful people in their communities. As a result, they asked Howard K. Beale to write *A History of Freedom of Teaching in American Schools.* In this work, Beale noted that powerful elites had always controlled the ways teachers taught. In surveying the opinions of teachers, though, Beale found that the extent of such pressure varied in different types of communities and in different parts of the country. Administrators in small towns in the South restricted teachers more than did school leaders in large cities in the Northeast. Beale added that the financial problems from the Great Depression had removed protections that tenure laws had provided, and the growing collectivism resulting from industrialism gave birth to various social movements such as those of Huey Long, which encouraged people to further restrict the freedom of thought among teachers and students. Despite these problems, Beale remained optimistic. The Depression had caused people to think seriously about social change: many schools used Rugg's textbooks that took a radical view of fundamental issues, officials in the U.S. Office of Education urged teachers to discuss controversial issues in classes, and the NEA approved vigorous resolutions demanding academic freedom for classroom teachers.[42]

Recognizing that school administrators had to protect the freedom of teachers, the AHA commission asked Jesse H. Newlon, director of Lincoln

School and professor at Teachers College, to write a volume entitled *Educational Administration as Social Policy*. In this volume, Newlon explained the ideas that he had developed as superintendent of the Denver, Colorado Schools and had brought him to national attention. This was the view that teachers had to work together to develop democratic programs of instruction.[43]

In his volume for the AHA commission, Newlon called for administrators to think of themselves as social scientists whose tasks were to ensure that teachers had opportunities for extensive participation in policy making and to encourage the teachers to direct their decisions in directions that advanced the public interest. To prepare for such a role, Newlon advocated that administrators have extensive training in subjects of history, anthropology, economics, politics, and philosophy. While Newlon acknowledged that administrators had to be aware of technical administrative concerns such as school publicity and building programs, he warned that many programs of educational administration concentrated excessively on these technical areas that could be learned quickly on the job. For Newlon, the most important qualification for school administrators was a broad social frame of reference from which they could make intelligent decisions that would enhance the democratic ethos in the school and in the community.[44]

The AHA had designed its Commission on the Social Studies so that experts in different fields would write volumes analyzing parts of the complex problem from the perspectives of their disciplines. Although the hope was that this would provide a complete view, the analyses and the recommendations the experts made conflicted with each other frequently. This was particularly true in the matter of curriculum suggestions. For example, Horn disagreed with Newlon's claim that school administrators could profit from studies of academic subjects and did not need training in technical matters. Horn wanted the administrators to concentrate on the technical aspects, such as building programs and public relations that Newlon thought they should learn on the job.[45]

Even theorists who thought alike could disagree about curriculum orientations. For example, in chapter nine of his book, *The Nature of the Social Sciences*, Beard listed the knowledge and information students should acquire in the various social studies. This twenty-page outline contained facts and concepts in geography, economics, sociology, political science, and history that followed Beard's view that academic disciplines tended to remain apart from each other because they had their own centers of interest and that the disciplines provided the means to understand contemporary situations. Although Counts agreed with Beard on most things, he was more concerned that they hold certain ideals than he was that students acquire information. He seemed to believe that the students could master information as they engaged in activities that related life to school. When William C. Bagley wrote his description of the qualifications of the social studies teacher for the AHA commission, he recommended that prospective teachers complete college training and that their studies include the knowledge and information Beard had listed. In making this comment, Bagley added that the Soviet Union had tried to build curriculums of the activity model that Counts liked. Bagley added that after twelve years, Soviet officials declared the educational effort to have been a failure.[46]

Other experts held that the commission's recommendations were not reasonable. For example, although the superintendent of schools in Washington, DC, Frank Ballou, served as the secretary for the AHA commission, he refused to sign the *Conclusions*, complaining that the report did not give teachers concrete directions that they could follow. He claimed that the *Conclusions* offered glittering generalities and misrepresented the practical scientific efforts educators had developed to improve teaching.[47]

THE FATE OF RECENT SOCIAL TRENDS AND OF THE AHA COMMISSION

According David Kennedy, the report, *Recent Social Trends*, had little impact in its own time. Hoover lost his office before he could use the report, and Franklin D. Roosevelt refused to accept it. For Kennedy, the report served historians by providing an incomparably rich source of information about the years before the Great Depression. Kennedy felt that portraits of a people engulfed in sweeping social, economic, and political changes arose from its pages. Despite the fact that the report had little influence in political matters, Kennedy asserted that the project represented Hoover's commitment to mastering the social transformations occurring in his time. Kennedy expressed admiration for Hoover's hope to initiate national social reform based on the findings of social science in ways that would lead to the construction of a rational society and the elimination of such social problems as poverty.[48]

According to Barry Karl, the ideal behind Hoover's Committee on Recent Social Trends was similar to the notion of rational social control that John Dewey described in the *Public and its Problems*. In Karl's view, the progressive elements that contributed to this perspective feared that politics threatened intelligent debate. Karl added that social scientists hoped that community members would recognize the needs that the studies addressed, they would examine the results of the reports, and they would decide on the policies to follow. Karl concluded that this model declined in popularity with the end of Hoover's administration. Roosevelt and the officials in charge of the New Deal had campaigned against Hoover's policies. As a result, they had to repudiate Hoover's locally initiated and democratically debated system in favor of nationally imposed solutions. The result was that social scientists worked to justify programs that government officials had begun. Thus, the aim of social science in the New Deal was to manipulate the public and their representatives into supporting the proposed reforms.[49]

Some historians look back at the AHA commission to conclude that its reports marked the end of historians' involvement with secondary school curriculums. For example, in 1988, Peter Novick complained that the AHA Commission on the Social Studies made no specific curricular recommendations, but he contended that the report urged teachers to adopt an activist and reformist program that was suitable for a new age of collectivism. Novick added that this perspective annoyed many historians, and as a result, the AHA never accepted the commission's report. He added that most historians ignored it and separated themselves from social studies education.[50]

Other historians argued that the AHA commission provided important direction to teachers and administrators in secondary schools. For example, Howard Rai Boozer quoted Conyers Read, the executive secretary of the AHA, claiming in 1937 that the work of the Commission on the Social Studies was the most important contribution in the literature on social studies instruction in secondary schools. Citing textbooks and yearbooks by such organizations as the NEA's Department of Superintendence, Boozer claimed that the commission's seventeen volumes exerted a considerable effect.[51]

Despite the contradictions, both accounts may be true because it may be that the members of the Commission on the Social Studies did not seek to have the AHA accept the report, nor did they think that more historians had to become curriculum planners. For example, in his volume for the commission, Beard expressed the hope common to Hoover's committees. This was that the AHA commission could create a scheme of objectives and a program of social studies that it would submit to the public. The commission trusted that people would act intelligently.[52]

Of course, the members of the commission continued to write reports and make suggestions. For example, in 1937, Beard wrote the preliminary report of the function of education in American democracy for the NEA's Educational Policies Commission (EPC). Although members of the EPC revised Beard's draft, it retains the structure found in his *Charter for the Social Studies*. The volume begins with an explanation of the way industrialism transformed society, an age of individualism ended, and social planning became necessary. Within this framework, schools have to teach students to be intelligent and democratic citizens, the academic subjects are the best vehicles for such instruction, and teachers have to be free from imposition to use those disciplines to examine controversial issues.[53]

The longest-lasting aspect of the AHA commission was not its place in the social survey movement. Instead, the greatest influence came from the work of Leon Marshall and his daughter, Rachel Marshall Goetz. In their volume, *Curriculum Making in the Social Studies: A Social Process Approach,* Marshall and Goetz claimed that a list of five categories or processes, that they believed were found in all societies, provided a simple means to organize social studies curricula. These included adjusting to the external world, continuing biologically, guiding human motivation, developing social organization, securing cultural continuance, and molding personality. According to the authors, this scheme had several advantages. If students learned these sets of processes, they could group information about social living in meaningful units. They could build on their own experiences, and they would be prepared to take part in engineering improvements in their own society.[54]

To explain how the students learned to take part in social engineering, Marshall and Goetz offered examples of how the process approach enabled students to consider contemporary difficulties in objective manners. Under the category, "Adjusting to the External World," the authors listed economic activities. They noted that, using the process approach, students realized that every society had to find some way to determine what the members would produce, to decide how to apportion resources, and to work out ways of sharing the products. In this way, students understood that the ways each society chose to apportion resources, for example, had to coincide with the values accepted by the people in the society. According to Marshall and Goetz, such lessons showed the students that changing economic systems was not simple but required reforms carried out with broad understandings.[55]

Although historians in the 1930s complained that Marshall and Goetz's social process model turned history into sociology, it remains a significant curriculum idea. Most statements about the ways that social studies should be framed base their proposals on the system that Marshall and Goetz proposed. This includes such diverse reports as the standards of the National Council of the Social Studies, or the 1988 report of the Bradley Commission on History in Schools, *Building a History Curriculum: Guidelines for Teaching History in the Schools.*[56]

The source of the popularity of Marshall's and Goetz's approach arises from the fact that it allows teachers to consider controversial issues and critics cannot complain that the teachers are portraying society in a poor light or threatening any vested interests. Teachers can claim that the social process approach illuminates the common features of all societies. Thus, the model provided the AHA commission and subsequent commissions with a way for teachers to avoid political controversies and remain true to the progressive ideal of reforming society.

NOTES

1. Michael Whelan, "Social Studies for Social Reform: Charles Beard's Vision of History and Social Studies Education," *Theory and Research in Social Education* 25 no. 3 (Summer 1997): 309–312.

2. Diane Ravitch, *Left Back: A Century of Battles over School Reform* (New York: Touchstone, 2000), 48–49, 127–128, 228–229.

3. C.A. Bowers, *The Progressive Educator and the Depression* (New York: Random House, 1969), 34–35.

4. Hazel Whitman Hertzberg, *Social Studies Reform, 1880-1980* (Boulder, CO: Social Science Consortium, 1981), 50–53.

5. Charles A. Beard, "Limitations to the Application of Social Science Implied in Recent Social Trends," *Social Forces* 11 no. 4 (May 1933), 505–510.

6. An example of a once-popular text that includes reconstructionism among the important philosophies of education is Howard A. Ozmon and Samuel M. Craver, *Philosophical Foundations of Education* (Columbus, OH: Merrill Publishing Co., 1990).

7. Barry D. Karl, "Presidential Planning and Social Science Research: Mr. Hoover's Experts," *Perspectives in American History* 3 (1969): 347–350.

8. Shelby M. Harrison, "Trends in the Study of Local Areas: Social Surveys," *Social Forces* 11 no. 3 (May 1933), 513–516.

9. Conference on Unemployment, *Recent Economic Changes in the United States* (New York: McGraw-Hill, 1929), Volume I, xx–xxii.

10. Howard W. Odum, "Notes on Recent Trends in the Application of the Social Sciences," *Social Forces* 11 no. 4 (May 1933): 480–481.

11. Ray Lyman Wilbur and Arthur Mastick Hyde, *The Hoover Policies* (New York: Charles Scribner's Sons, 1937), 41–43.

12. T. J. Woofter, "The Status of Racial and Ethnic Groups" in President's Research Committee on Social Trends, *Recent Social Trends in the United States* (New York: McGraw-Hill, 1933), 600–601.

13. Sophonisba P. Breckinridge, "Activities of Women outside the Home" in President's Research Committee on Social Trends, *Recent Social Trends in the United States* (New York: McGraw-Hill, 1933), 750.

14. Charles E. Merriam, "Government and Society" in President's Research Committee on Social Trends, *Recent Social Trends in the United States* (New York: McGraw-Hill, 1933), 1541.

15. National Education Association, *Report of the Committee of Ten on Secondary School Studies with the Reports of the Conferences Arranged by the Committee* (Cincinnati: American Book Co., 1894), 169, 179–181.

16. National Education Association. Committee on the Social Studies, *The Social Studies in Secondary Education* Department of Interior Bulletin No. 7 (Washington, D.C.: GPO, 1916), 9.

17. For a more complete description of the Americanization movement and its effect on schools, readers should consult the following sources: John F. McClymer, "The Federal Government and the Americanization Movement, 1915–1924," *Prologue* 10 no. 1 (Spring 1978): 23–42, and Edward A. Krug,

Shaping of the American High School, 1880-1920 Vol. I (Madison: University of Wisconsin Press, 1972), 410–411, 420.

18. Harold O. Rugg, "Do the Social Studies Prepare Pupils Adequately for Life Activities" in *The Social Studies in the Elementary and Secondary School*, ed. Harold O. Rugg (Bloomington: Public School Publishing Co., 1923), 6–11.

19. Charles E. Merriam, *The Making of Citizens* (1931; reprint, New York: Teachers College Press, 1966), 9, 43, 59.

20. A. C. Krey, preface to *A Charter for the Social Studies*, by Charles A. Beard (New York: Charles Scribner's Sons, 1932), vii–ix.

21. Krey, preface, ix–xii.

22. American Historical Association. Commission on the Social Studies in the Schools, *A Charter for the Social Studies* (New York: Charles Scribner's Sons, 1932).

23. Henry Johnson, *Teaching of History in Elementary and Secondary Schools with Applications to Applied Studies* (New York: Macmillan Co., 1940), 114–115. References to the comments of Bobbitt and Bode appear in Lawrence J. Dennis, *George Counts and Charles A. Beard: Collaborators for Change* (Albany: SUNY Press, 1989), 42–43, 53.

24. AHA, *A Charter for the Social Studies*, 33–34.

25. Dennis, *George Counts and Charles A. Beard*, 57–59.

26. Dennis, *George Counts and Charles A. Beard*, 83–87.

27. Boyd Bode, "Editorial Comment" *The Phi Delta Kappan* 17 no. 1 (November 1934): 1, 7.

28. American Historical Association. Commission on the Social Studies in the Schools, *Conclusions and Recommendations of the Commission* (New York: Charles Scribner's Sons, 1934).

29. Bode, "Editorial Comment," 1, 7.

30. Franklin Bobbitt, "Questionable Recommendations of the Commission on the Social Studies," *School and Society* 40 no. 1025 (18 August 1934): 201–208.

31. Percival W. Hutson, "Collectivism and Democracy," *School and Society* 40 no. 1029 (15 September 1934): 354–355.

32. Charles A. Beard, "Written History as an Act of Faith," *The American Historical Review* 39 no. 2 (January 1934): 219–231.

33. Maurice Mandelbaum, *The Problem of Historical Knowledge: An Answer to Relativism* (New York: Harper Torchbooks, 1938), 19–20, 28, 90–91.

34. Mandelbaum, *The Problem of Historical Knowledge*, 179–180.

35. Charles A. Beard, "That Noble Dream," *American Historical Review* 41 no.1 (October 1935): 84, 87.

36. Charles A. Beard, *The Nature of the Social Sciences* (New York: Charles Scribner's Sons, 1934), 183–184.

37. Ernest Horn, Methods of Instruction in the Social Studies (New York: Charles Scribner's Sons, 1937), 2–4.

38. Horn, *Methods of Instruction*, 89–95, 104–107.

39. Charles E. Merriam, *Civic Education in the United States* (New York: Charles Scribner's Sons, 1934), ix–xvii, 33–38, 115–117, 181–186.

40.   Bessie Louis Pierce, *Citizen's Organizations and the Civic Training of Youth* (New York: Charles Scribner's Sons, 1933), ix–xiii, 3, 314–317.

41.   George Counts, *The Social Foundations of Education* (New York: Charles Scribner's Sons, 1934), 532–550.

42.   Howard K. Beale, *A History of Freedom of Teaching in American Schools* (1941; reprint, New York: Octagon Books, 1978), 237–276.

43.   Lawrence A. Cremin, *The Transformation of the School: Progressivism in American Education, 1876-1957* (New York: Alfred A. Knopf, 1964), 299–302.

44.   Jesse H. Newlon, *Educational Administration as Social Policy* (New York: Charles Scribner's Sons, 1934), 253–270.

45.   Horn, *Methods of Instruction*, 35–36.

46.   William C. Bagley and Thomas Alexander, *The Teacher of the Social Studies* (New York: Charles Scribner's Sons, 1937), 66–71.

47.   Frank W. Ballou, "Statement Concerning the Report of the Commission on the Investigation of History and the Other Social Studies of the American Historical Association," *School and Society* 39 no. 1014 (2 June 1934): 701–702.

48.   David Kennedy, *Freedom from Fear: The American People in Depression and War, 1929-1945* (New York: Oxford University Press, 1999), 12–13.

50.   Peter Novick, *That Noble Dream: The "Objectivity Question" and the American Historical Profession* (New York: Cambridge University Press, 1988), 190.49. Karl, "Presidential Planning," 363, 407–409.

51.   Howard Rai Boozer, *The American Historical Association and the Schools, 1884-1956* (Ph.D. diss., Washington University, 1960), 261.

52.   Beard, *The Nature of the Social Sciences*, 184–187.

53.   Educational Policies Commission, *The Unique Function of Education in American Democracy* (Washington, D.C.: National Education Association, 1937).

54.   Leon C. Marshall and Rachael Marshall Goetz, *Curriculum-Making in the Social Studies: A Social Process Approach* (New York: Charles Scribner's Sons, 1936), 11–22.

55.   Ibid., 78–79.

56.   Bradley Commission, *Building a History Curriculum* (NP: Educational Excellence Network, 1988): 10–11.

CHAPTER 8

SOCIAL RECONSTRUCTIONISM AND EDUCATIONAL POLICY

The Educational Policies Commission, 1936–1941

Wayne J. Urban

Interest in Social Reconstructionism has waxed and waned over the decades since its heyday in the late 1930s and early 40s. From the mid-60s to the present, Social Reconstructionismwas a salient, and controversial, topic in the first decade or so and only of occasional interest to educational historians since that time. In the late 60s and 70s, scholars in history, and philosophy of education, paid substantial attention to Social Reconstructionism and its leading advocates, especially George S. Counts.

One notable work by C. A. Bowers, published in 1969, was thorough in its analysis of Social Reconstructionism and critical in its conclusions about that phenomenon.[1] Bowers was worried about the authoritarian aspects of Counts' endorsement of the phenomenon of indoctrination in the classroom, a worry that also had animated many of Counts' educationally progressive contemporaries, such as Boyd Bode. Bowers dealt at length with

Social Reconstruction: People, Politics, Perspectives, pages 149–166
Copyright © 2006 by Information Age Publishing

149

the debate over indoctrination in the late 1930s and its airing in the pages of the leading social reconstructionist journal, *The Social Frontier.* Bowers' criticism of Counts and Reconstructionism did not go unanswered. Gerald Gutek explicated Counts' educational theory in a largely appreciative volume that, while not directed explicitly at the Bowers argument, provided those who admired Counts' position with ample reasons to continue their admiration.[2] Others, including this wrter, have published appreciations of Counts' radicalism.[3]

While those in the fields of curriculum theory and other curriculum studies, several of whom are represented in this volume, did not lose their appreciation of Counts and his ideas, and of the rest of the educational Progressive movement, after the 1970s, it still seems fair to say that Counts, the Social Reconstructionists, and other educational Progressives diminished in visibility in the professional educational world of the 80s and 90s. Though an edited volume of Counts' work was published in 1980 with a title that insisted on the contemporary relevance of the man and his ideas,[4] the rest of that decade and the following decade found no significant books or monographs devoted to Counts and other reconstructionist educators and thinkers.

This inattention has carried over into the twenty-first century, and it seems fair to conclude that the contributions to this volume are intended to redress an unjust neglect of Social Reconstructionism and other versions of progressive education in contemporary scholarship. This chapter, rather than stress the intellectual arguments of Reconstructionists, their sometime progressive allies, or their opponents, will deal with an attempt to place the social radicalism of Reconstructionists in the forefront of professional educational discourse and advocacy. That attempt took place over the first five years of the existence of a prestigious group of educators, the Educational Policies Commission (EPC). Those years, 1936 to 1941, coincided with the end of the Great Depression and the onset of World War II. The argument of this chapter is that two of the five major documents published by the EPC during that period, the first and the last, reflected the point of view of radical Social Reconstructionism, though with a decidedly different emphasis. The first document took a distinctly domestic focus and mounted a spirited defense of public education as necessary for the needed reconstruction of American society in the midst of depressed conditions. The last document, adopted in the midst of an oncoming World War, had a decidedly more international focus that took attention away from needed domestic changes and focused instead on the role of the school in creating a new international perspective. The other three documents published, one of which will be considered in some detail, while not avowedly Reconstructionist, did not directly contradict the Reconstructionism of the first and the last EPC documents of the period. Rather, they tried, in varying degrees, to apply it to more directly institutional educational concerns. That application, however, always carried with it the danger that Social Radicalism would be overwhelmed as a focus, if not contradicted by more practical educational concerns. The difference in emphasis between the first social reconstructionist EPC document and the last, combined with the practical emphasis of the other three documents to thwart the socially radical reformist vision that animated the first document and the EPC that published it. Before considering the documents in detail, however, a look at the birth of the Educational Policies Commission is in order.

THE EDUCATIONAL POLICIES COMMISSION: BIRTH

The body which proposed creation of the Educational Policies Commission was the Joint Committee on the Emergency in Education, which had been established in February of 1933 by the National Education Association and its Department of Superintendence.[5] The Joint Commission on the Emergency's tasks were to highlight the financial crisis created for the public schools by the Great Depression that had begun in 1929, and to signal a way out of that financial crisis, if possible.[6] According to the Secretary of the Joint Commission, its major purpose was "to help the schools to sustain morale and to meet the most catastrophic effects of the depression."[7]

More specifically, the members of the Joint Commission were worried about the increasing effectiveness of taxpayer groups in local school districts who were using the Depression as a wedge to force tax reductions that had draconian effects on school budgets. The Joint Commission produced a small book on "Essentials of Taxation" in the hope that "better public understanding of the basic principles of public finance would produce more informed decisions on school support by the electorate." They felt that the schools relied too much on local property tax and needed other state taxes to redress the inequities of the property tax and, further, that "Federal funds were needed to shore up support for schools in those areas where combined state and local efforts were inadequate."[8]

Thus, the major goal of the Joint Commission was the establishment of a more economically equitable school-finance system. This was to be achieved by the addition of a substantial federal investment in education and by increasing the importance of the state as a taxing entity for public schools and thereby decreasing the reliance on local property taxation for school support. Local taxation, which depended on the wealth of the locality that was being taxed for the amount it raised, was for the Joint Commission a guarantee of poorly valued rural property and, thus, poorly funded rural schools in almost every state. State funding, because of stark differences in wealth among the states, would guarantee inequitable funding among the states unless it was supplemented by federal funds to redress the inequities.[9] By 1935, the Joint Commission had widely publicized its school-finance recommendations. While those recommendations certainly constituted a commitment to substantive, and progressive, school-finance reform, they said nothing about any other aspects of education or the relationship between the school and society. Thus, one might argue that the fiscal equity reform proposed by the Joint Commission was a necessary, but not a sufficient, condition for more extensive educational reforms in the interest of the full democratization of the public schools in the midst of the Depression.

However, one year before its demise in 1935, the Joint Commission had been charged by its parent organizations to add to its purview, "an appraisal of the present educational program and long-term planning for such changes as may be required to enable our schools to meet as effectively as possible the challenge presented to them by the changing social, industrial, and economic order."[10] The Joint Commission deflected this larger charge, contenting itself with reporting that it had pursued: "(a) vigorous and continuous support of the principle of equal educational opportunity, and (b) planning for the fundamental improvement of those conditions in the schools which lie back of the difficulties experienced in recent years."[11] The Joint Commission recommended its own dissolution, but ended its recommendation with a final proposal that sought to provide for the program appraisal and planning that it had been charged with. According to the Joint Commission's 1935 report:

> There should be created jointly by the Executive Committee of the National Education Association and of the Department of Superintendence an Educational Policies Commission. This commission should be made responsible for the development and execution of a long-term program for the National Education Association. This program should bring a new type of thinking and higher statesmanship into the process of adapting educational institutions to the ever-changing needs of our dynamic democracy. The Educational Policies Commission should provide for the *continuous self-appraisal* by the teaching profession *of the American educational system. It should develop a constructive program whereby the changes which should be brought about in the purposes, organization, and procedures of our educational institutions may be speedily accomplished.*[12]

The Joint Commission added that it had already recommended the creation of the EPC to the NEA and Department of Superintendence Executive

Committees and that it deemed the establishment of the EPC a matter of "utmost importance."[13]

In response to this proposal, in December of 1935, the Educational Policies Commission was appointed by the executive committees of the sponsoring entities, the National Education Association and the NEA Department of Superintendence. Its first organizational meeting was held in January of 1936 and its task was defined as "evolving well-considered and effective plans and policies." The EPC, in a statement that exhibited impatience with previous educational research and reform activity, noted that there were substantial amounts of data relevant to effective plans and policies already extant. It concluded: "The Commission proposes not to repeat these studies and investigations but rather to utilize them in evaluating proposed procedures toward educational progress and improvement." Indicating that the task at hand was acting on available data as much as, or more than, it was creating new data, the EPC added:

> Thousands of pages of reports, studies, pronouncements, and recommendations, and conclusions of inestimable value in the intelligent administration of public education have been forgotten or otherwise ignored during the past decade of economic and social confusion. The best work of our wisest educational leadership in America stands dust-covered in government archives or on the shelves of research bureaus, while the children of America suffer for that educational opportunity which those pronouncements would, if applied, provide for them.[14]

The EPC then specified several current critical issues which it intended to address, including school finance, educational agencies that had been established outside of schools to serve youth, and, in an obvious nod to the priorities of educational Reconstructionism in the age of the Depression, the relationship of education to the Social Reconstruction that would follow the end of the Depression. In this last regard, the report noted that "the next five years should be a period of great significance in the rebuilding of the structure of public education; of reestablishing, in the minds of citizens, those great purposes to which public education was originally dedicated; of recreating public enthusiasm for the American ideal, not only in education, but in regard to all matters pertaining to social progress."[15] Here the EPC was emphasizing Social Reconstruction as a priority that arguably could take precedence over either fiscal equity or school improvement as a goal. Another discussion of the EPC founding also notes that the group clearly intended to relate "educational problems to their economic, social, and political settings," meaning that an important educational policy always was a policy with important social implications. This too suggests that social reconstruction, as much as, or more than, emphasis on educational equity or school improvement, was at the forefront of the EPC's concern.[16]

The major output of the Educational Policies Commission in its first five years of existence was a series of five reports, prepared for consideration of the Commission prior to publication. In the next part of the paper is a discussion, in some detail, of three of these reports, and their authorship, their argument, and what they say about the Educational Policies Commission in terms of the relative weight of its three stated priorities of educational equity, school improvement, and Social-Educational Reconstruction. It finally concluded that Social Reconstructionism was clearly the most important of the three priorities in this period.

The EPC considered each of its early reports a collective Commission effort, since the members devoted a substantial amount of time to the consideration of drafts of the reports. This, however, was far from the whole story. Each of the three reports to be considered here, and most of the other EPC reports, had a single prominent author, whose work was acknowledged officially in the early pages of each volume. Thus, each of the three EPC reports discussed here was largely the product of a single author. The individual authorship of the reports in each case reveals much about the report itself, as well as its compatibility, or incompatibility, with the three objectives of the early EPC, finance reform, educational improvement, and social reconstruction.

THREE EARLY EPC REPORTS

All three of the EPC reports considered in this section were officially planned, researched, and published by the group in its first five years of existence. These three, and two others that will be discussed briefly,[17] represent the major early output of the early EPC. Two of the three reports covered, those by Charles Beard and George Counts, represented the liberal to radical social reconstruction agenda of the EPC. They were the first and the last of the five reports in this era, and they formed a set of reconstructionist bookends within which the other three reports were published. The Beard and Counts reports were the products of two well-known American scholars, one a historian and the other an educational theorist, both of whom had decidedly liberal to radical social orientations and priorities in their work that pointed the EPC orientation firmly in the direction of Social Reconstruction. Further, Beard and Counts were in frequent contact with each other in these years, communicating about the prospects and problems of social, political, and educational life in the late 1930s.[18] The noted historian, Beard, was acknowledged as the originator of *The*

Unique Function of Education in American Democracy[19] and Counts, social scientist, social thinker, and social and political activist on the Teachers College faculty, and a member of the Commission, was acknowledged as the originator of *The Education of Free Men in American Democracy.*[20] Unlike Beard, who was drafted by an EPC looking for a noted scholar to prepare its first report, Counts was actually a member of the EPC when he wrote his report.

The third report to be discussed in some depth, on education and economics, was written by John K. Norton, a professor of educational administration at Teachers College, Columbia University who had been the head of the Committee on the National Emergency in Education, the group that had proposed the establishment of the EPC.[21] Norton was also a member of the EPC. Norton's report spoke more directly to the educational equity and school improvement agendas of the EPC, and concentrated on the economic reforms that it considered necessary to that improvement. It neglected wider issues of social and educational reconstruction such as those which animated Beard's and Counts' reports. The reports will be reviewed in the order in which they were published, Beard, Norton, and Counts respectively, and show how they represented first a venture into radical Social Reconstruction, then a qualification of that venture that weakened it, but did not repudiate it, and finally a return to an avowedly radical reconstructionist stance that, ironically, resulted in its weakening, if not its abandonment.

The Unique Function of Education in American Democracy

The Beard report, *The Unique Function of Education in American Democracy,* was the first major document to be published by the EPC. As already mentioned, each EPC report was technically the product of the EPC, but each was also written by a smaller group, or one author, and then vetted at an EPC meeting before final publication. In the early pages of the *Unique Function* report, the Commission acknowledged Beard as "the man best qualified for the task [of outlining education's democratic function] by scholarship, social insight, and devotion to democratic institutions."[22] Since Counts was an EPC member and a close collaborator with Beard on several projects, it should not be surprising that Counts had an important role in the selection of Beard to do the first report. Beard was sought after by the EPC as an author because of his reputation as a scholar and an interpreter of the past who was firm in his democratic commitments as a guiding force for his interpretations.

While the *Unique Function* report looked back, immediately, to the Depression as its setting, it looked much further back historically, for its inspiration. The early chapters described the political significance of education for the

Revolutionary-Era generation of American political leaders, the founding fathers, and then showed how that significance was extended by their successors in the Jacksonian era and the Civil War and post–Civil War periods. The point of all of this was at least threefold: to establish the intimate relationship between education and American democracy, to prepare the reader for the discussion in the later chapters of the substantial changes that had taken place in American society since World War I, which threatened that democracy, and to show that the activism of the New Deal–Roosevelt administration in support of democracy had historic antecedents that made it an appropriate response to the changes in conditions. Those changes were such that, since World War I, and more particularly given the cataclysm of the depression, "The Assurance of Democratic Society [is] No Longer Taken for Granted."[23] Education, for Beard in this report, was now charged with the social task of consciously building the foundations of American democracy in a period when that democracy was imperiled. Several educational particulars were cited in this document as the blocks of this building effort, including citizenship education, education for employment, and adult education. Further it identified the public schools as the unique agency in American history charged with the building, and now the rebuilding, of American democracy.

For the public schools to achieve this radical purpose desired by Beard, they had to be politically autonomous. Autonomy was necessary for education to provide a countervailing power to the undemocratic influences arrayed against democracy in American life. While Beard was somewhat cryptic in identifying these powers in the *Unique Function* report, readers of his other works[24] in this period know that he was aligned with other liberal scholars and activists against the powerful private business interests that had fought the New Deal program and opposed all serious attempts to grapple with the Depression of the 1930s. Further, much of Beard's text in *The Unique Function* was devoted to establishing historically the interest of the national government in democracy and democratic education, thereby signaling the report's agreement with the New Deal and its implacable opposition to the reactionary forces that opposed it, often in the name of localism or individualism. Beard pointedly favored the centralization being exhibited in the creation of various New Deal agencies to meet the crisis of the Depression, noting, for example, that a demand had arisen for "more centralized control over all divisions of administration,"[25] While he did not address direct federal educational activity such as that of the Civilian Conservation Corps and the National Youth Administration, he left no doubt in his readers' minds that he was a supporter of such activity.

The Secretary of the EPC, William Carr, in his discussion of the *Unique Function*, made its arguments more palatable to its educator readers who might not approve of the political radicalism and embrace of the New Deal of Charles A. Beard. Carr began his treatment of *The Unique Function* with an identification of the concept of "academic freedom" as a synonym for the autonomy that Beard identified as central to the contemporary enterprise of rebuilding democracy. The school-related purpose of academic freedom was, for Carr, that "public authority should not interfere with the efforts of teachers to be impartial and realistic in the classroom."[26] Such interference often came from state laws requiring schools to cater to special interests or mandating that teachers take oaths of allegiance to state government. These attempts needed to be resisted by educators whose first allegiance was to the American democratic tradition and to the defense of that tradition from the most recent attacks against it. A passing attention to educational administration was made in *The Unique Function,* and highlighted by Carr, when he stressed that defense of educational autonomy also included resistance to attempts to make school administration a part of local government.[27] This was still one more instance of inappropriate interference with the schools, which needed to be administered by educators attuned to their "unique function" of perpetuating, and updating, American democracy.

It is important to note, however, that Carr never discussed the New Deal positively, as Beard did, nor did he laud the national government's educational efforts in earlier eras, as Beard also had done. Beard's affinity for a strong national governmental role, including education in its purview, was not shared by the movers and shakers in the NEA and its school administrator group, who represented local school systems and their interests, and who dominated the EPC. Yet Beard's prominence meant that the school administrators in the EPC were loath to publicize their political disagreements with the prestigious author of their first report.

Education and Economic Well Being in American Democracy

Thus one is not surprised to see a different focus, one more in line with local school interests in the next report to be discussed here: *Education and Economic Well-Being in American Democracy.* This report was published one year after the Beard report. It was the longest of any of the first five reports of the EPC and its 227 pages of text were supported by nearly 200 scholarly works referenced, a substantially greater array of references than in any of the other reports. Further, these references were to works by economists, statisticians, and other social scientists, as well as by educational researchers. The "Foreword" to the volume noted that the Commission had "called into conference at Chicago a group of economists and sociologists" to discuss the work, and added that one scholar had prepared a "special memorandum on economic literacy" and another, the economist Harold F.

Clark, had prepared "an extensive memorandum ... especially for the Commission ... which served as the basis for certain chapters in this volume."[28] What the foreword did not say was that neither Clark, nor any other economist involved, could be relied on to produce a volume that would say what the EPC wanted it to say.[29]

To obtain a suitable statement, the EPC turned to one of its members, John K. Norton, professor of educational administration at Teachers College, former head of the Research Division of the National Education Association, a noted authority in the field of school finance, and the head of the Joint Commission on the Emergency in Education, which had recommended creation of the EPC. Norton was acknowledged in the preface as the person who was chiefly responsible for "the writing of this report."[30] In addition to sustained attention to the issues of equitable school financing, which had been raised by the Joint Commission on the Emergency, the economic well-being volume considered the issue of how to achieve the maximum economic productivity of the United States. It was here that the EPC had departed from the economists who had been called in as consultants. None of them were able to see the primacy of the public school in achieving economic productivity, the position that the EPC was to take.[31]

Norton's report noted that the enhancement of the public-school enterprise was essential to national economic improvement. Especially important were the extension of vocational education to all who could take advantage of it and the consideration of vocational concerns as important in all aspects of the educational system, including general and liberal education. Norton also paid attention to the amount and kind of education that needed to be provided for people to enter callings for which there was, and would be, a demand, and advocated the extension of expenditures on education as the way to increase both opportunity and productivity to maximum levels. Such extensions were to be based on occupational surveys that identified the areas of needed productivity increase which, in turn, would be addressed by education in the fields relevant to such increase. Thus, while Beard might be said to have made a case for the revivification of public schools as democratic agents of social reform, Norton made the case for the extension of the reach of the public school through curricular expansion without considering the democratic, or undemocratic, ramifications of such expansion.

The Norton report's call for an enormous increase in educational expenditures, which in turn would facilitate substantial increases in productivity, was accompanied by an estimate of just what such an increase might cost. The report came up with a sum of almost four billion dollars as the amount of the desired increase in necessary educational spending, and proceeded to argue that such an increase was not beyond the realm of possibility and one that was justified in terms of the goal of increasing economic productivity.[32] The report was not devoid of practical suggestions for improving education and educational administration, nor were references to the challenges of a post-Depression economy to the cause of increased educational and economic opportunity missing, but by far the bulk of its pages was devoted to empirically establishing, and supporting financially, the cause of increased educational programming geared to the goal of achieving maximum economic opportunity.

While the amount of four billion dollars represented an enormous investment to be undertaken in the pubic-education enterprise, the report was basically silent on the political or social changes that might be required to undertake such a commitment. Those changes, and the social and political significance of public education which had preoccupied Charles A. Beard in his *Unique Function* report, were to come to the foreground again in the report of George Counts, published in 1941 as World War II loomed ominously on the horizon.

The Education of Free Men in American Democracy

Turning to the Counts volume, we find that the threat to American democratic education had taken on a distinctly new character in the four years since the publication of the Beard report. Counts replaced the primacy of the threat of the domestic foes of democracy discussed in the first EPC volume with the international danger posed by the political regimes of the Soviet Union, Italy, and Germany in the late 1930s. These despotic regimes had gained the allegiance of much of their citizenry, largely through astute appeals to the cultivation of a blind, national solidarity. A truly democratic nation, in the midst of this type of propagandistic cultivation of the loyalty of the citizens of nations implacably opposed to democracy, had to make a new commitment to an invigorated democratic tradition that would instill the "loyalties of free men" in its own citizenry. To accomplish this end, education must take on a "moral character" in which the schools recognized that "Democracy is a vast and complex cultural achievement in the sphere of human relations and social values."[33] This achievement was crucial to the survival of American democracy, and that survival was dependent on its educational institutions.

Counts noted specifically that the schools needed to "moderate the egoistic tendencies and strengthen the social and cooperative impulses of the rising generation." This meant an enormously important role for the teacher. Specifically, "the teacher-pupil role is the vital element in all education" and "it is imperative that this relationship be marked not only by complete integrity and honesty but also by a spirit of mutual confidence, respect, and even affection." Counts added that teachers who understood the requirements of this new challenge "should keep themselves in the stream of history, refuse to become a class apart, identify themselves fully with the life of the community, and relate the educational program to the interests of all the people." Relating the school program to all of the people sounded a theme that was similar to one Beard had identified four years earlier, the need to keep the school independent of the domestic foes of democracy. In words that could have been written in the earlier report, Counts noted that "Every American community seethes with 'pressure groups' which, speaking in the name of the common good, strive to promote partisan interests and doctrines."[34]

But, as already noted, the novelty of the Counts volume was the identification of the foreign phenomenon of totalitarian despotism as the new impediment to democracy. This threat came from formidable foreign opponents and required reinvigoration of American democratic education in the public schools if it was to be combated effectively. In spite of Counts' own commitment to liberal politics and social reconstruction, his analysis in *Education for Free Men* located the solution to the problems primarily internal to the public schools, in the teacher student relationship and other issues of curriculum and pedagogy, and not in the responsibility of the public school for the reinvigoration of democracy in the larger society. Thus his avowed internationalism and radicalism could easily be harnessed to the agenda of educators possessing no radical social or political views, but committed to the centrality of their institution in waging an international conflict. Also, given that World War II began while the Counts volume was being written, and that the United States would enter that conflict in the same year in which it was published, 1941, the Counts report proved to be the first step in the Educational Policies Commission's commitment to the utmost importance of international affairs for the proper conduct of American education. That commitment would grow during the war years, and intensify with the creation of the United Nations and development of that body's educational activities and organizations. However, this is a story for another essay.[35] What is important to remember here is that the commitment to international affairs took away, substantially, the attention to domestic social and political changes that had been advocated in the Beard report.

DISCUSSION

Both the Beard and the Counts reports were attempts to outline the critical importance to American democracy of the nation's schools. They might be termed as exercises in civic education, but they are better described as statements of the civic role that schools might play than as prescriptions of *how* that role might be played. In that sense, they harnessed the social reconstructionist emphasis of their authors to the designs of the Educational Policies Commission. Those designs were clearly spelled out in the Norton report which downplayed Social Reconstruction in the interests of establishing equity in school finance and increasing educational expenditures. The clash between Beard's reliance on an increased role for the federal government in educational finance and control, and the EPC's devotion to more federal money with little federal involvement in any policy making or regulatory effort was left unmentioned.

Federal financial support, but no other federal involvement, was a major theme of one of the two early EPC reports not discussed in this paper, George Strayer's report, *The Structure and Administration of American Democracy*. That report, however, was the shortest and the least substantial of the first five EPC reports and reflected only the working concerns of local public-school administrators. Norton's report, while it ranged more widely than Strayer into the world of economics and economic theory, went back to school administration and finance in its conclusions about how much money was needed and its neglect of the political and social factors that necessarily were involved in raising those funds.

The other report not yet discussed, written by EPC Secretary, William G. Carr, was entitled *The Purposes of Education in American Democracy*. While a lengthy and substantive effort, this report dealt at greater length with concerns relevant to practicing educators than did the Beard or the Counts volume, and thereby largely ignored the social and political changes that were related to reconstructionist goals. Most of Carr's pages were devoted to explicating four necessary objectives of education in a democracy: education for self-realization, education for economic efficiency, education for civic responsibility, and education for human relations. These four emphases were considered almost solely in terms of classroom concerns. Forays into topics such as educational administration were infrequent and, when launched, were devoted to topics such as freeing the schools from unwarranted intrusion, such as that which came when school superintendents were elected.[36]

Counts' report, while much more in tune with the language and the argumentation in Beard's, ironically narrowed the horizons for Social Reconstruction in and out of the schools by locating the major source for that reconstruction inside of the school walls, in areas such as the student-teacher relationship. Further, Counts' emphasis on the totalitarianism in the school systems of Germany, Italy, and the Soviet Union gave the green light to educators who thought that domestic democratic reform might be accomplished within the schools through civic education, without looking critically at the relationships between those schools and their communities, and the national polity and society within which the school-community relationship was nested. Internationalism in this case, facilitated pedagogical concerns and hampered contextual analysis of pedagogical realities. Thus the educators of the EPC survived the Beard report and its call for a meaningful educational role in social and political reform, restated their own preference for school finance reform that would yield more money for schools in the Norton report, and triumphed decisively over Beard's radicalism in their ability to turn the Counts emphasis on the foreign threat to American education into a pedagogical issue.

CONCLUSION

In the midst of the first decade of the twenty-first century, we are witnesses to an attack on the public school that seems unprecedented. The public schools are under siege now from a White House intent on imposing a standardized testing regime that threatens to rob the pedagogical process of any flexibility; from the most powerful leaders and perhaps even a majority of the members of one political party in Congress who support the White House agenda; from religious groups in the USA that are gaining increasing visibility and political power, and seek to homeschool their children because of the secularization of the public school; from educational-policy analysts who see public schools merely as one of many educational agencies competing for dollars, and refuse to grant the schools and education any status other than that of another pig at the trough; and from well-meaning reformers pushing a voucher system who say they want it to lead to the improvement, not the abolition, of the public school. The severity and diversity of these attacks demand a vigorous response from those, like Charles A. Beard and the Educational Policies Commission that published his report, committed to the public school as an agency of democratic social change, reform, and renewal.

The political, social, and economic Conservatism of most of those attacking the public schools indicates that the institution is still associated, at least in their minds, with a commitment to policies such as political equity, economic opportunity, and social amelioration that offend their commitment to individualism, the maintenance of the status quo, and a roll-back of policies and priorities that allowed much of the last century, particularly the years between the Depression and the Reagan administration, to be characterized as a time of democratic social reform. Reviving the commitment of the public schools, those who support them, and those who work in them to social and political priorities such as equity, opportunity, and social amelioration is a formidable task. Critical attention to the efforts of reformers in the 1930s can help facilitate contemporary reformers in their quest for democratization and their repudiation of the right-wing agenda that seems intent on destroying the public schools. We need an historical understanding of the public school system as an integral, rather as a crucial, part of a democratic society. Charles Beard had such an understanding and the Educational Policies Commission, at least for a time, seemed to embrace that understanding and that commitment to democracy. The times cry out for a new Beard, a new interpreter of the promise of the public schools in pursuit of democracy.

That promise and pursuit should be embraced without getting bogged down in issues such as educational objectives and the pedagogical means to achieving them. These were the issues that the EPC embraced and that carried the EPC away from its Beardian commitment to democracy. In fact, in 1940, as the Counts report was being published, the EPC received outside funding to conduct a study of civic education in the schools that helped turn attention away from the social, political, and economic context that surrounded them. And the years after 1940 saw the EPC embrace firmly pedagogical reform that lacked any clear commitment to meaningful democracy in publications such as *Education for All American Youth* (1944) and *Education for All American Children* (1949). These two reports, devoted to the high school and the elementary school respectively, sought curricular additions such as vocational education, the institution of school guidance services, and more child-centered forms of pedagogy without devoting meaningful attention to the social, political, and economic conditions that surrounded the schools.

And the effort to achieve the United Nations, and an educational agency within it, took much of the EPC's time, attention, and effort in the mid-to-late 1940s. The pursuit of an international educational agency and the subsequent involvement in the dispute over the Soviet Union and Communism that facilitated the Cold War, and the efforts to support it on the part of educational groups like the EPC, intensified the internationalism begun by George Counts. All of this international activity hampered, if it did not contradict, a commitment to domestic democracy.

Contemporary reality is every bit as complex, if not more so, than the reality that faced the EPC and turned its attention away from its initial objective. Only coherent analyses of our current scene, domestic and international, that keep their eye on the goal of democratic renewal and the essential role of public education in achieving that objective can help both to defend the public school and to rebuild American democracy.

NOTES

1.   C. A. Bowers, *The Progressive Educator and the Depression: The Radical Years* (New York: Random House, 1969).

2.   Gerald Lee Gutek, *The Educational Theory of George S. Counts* (Columbus: Ohio State University Press, 1970). 1. C. A. Bowers, *The Progressive Educator and the Depression: The Radical Years* (New York: Random House, 1969).

3.   Wayne J. Urban and Ronald Goodenow, "George S. Counts: A Critical Appreciation," *Educational Forum* 41 (January, 1977).

4.   Lawrence Dennis and William Edward Eaton, eds., *George S. Counts: Educator for a New Age* (Carbondale, IL: Southern Illinois University Press, 1980).

5.   The Department of Superintendence, which later became known as the American Association of School Administrators, was a powerful network of school administrators that functioned under the NEA umbrella, but wielded an overwhelming amount of influence in NEA affairs.

6.   On the Joint Commission on the Emergency. . . , see Edgar B.Wesley, *NEA: The First Hundred Years* (New York: Harper, 1957), 301–02, and Wayne Urban, *Gender, Race, and the National Education Association: Professionalism and Its Limitations* (New York: Routledge/Falmer, 2000), 52.

7.   William G. Carr, *The Continuing Education of William Carr* (Washington, D.C.: The National Education Association, 1978), 48.

8.   Ibid., 50– 51. At the same time, the federal government was responding to the depression by creating quasi-educational relief agencies such as the Civilian Conservation Corps (CCC) and the National Youth Administration (NYA) that threatened school enrollments and school system budgets.

9.   In many ways, the Joint Commission adumbrated the equity movement in school finance that was pursued by many rural and urban public school systems beginning in the 1970s and that is still being pursued in some states.

10.   *Journal of Addresses and Proceedings of the National Education Association* 73 (1935): 166; hereafter cited as *NEA Proceedings.*

11.   *NEA Proceedings* 73 (1935): 166–67.

12.   Ibid., 167, my emphasis.

13.   Ibid.

14.   *NEA Proceedings* (1936): 463–64

15.   Ibid.

16.   Carr, *The Continuing Education of William Carr* 58.

17.   These two reports were *The Structure and Administration of American Education* (1938) and *The Purposes of Education in American Democracy* (1938). Both of these reports were much more school improvement oriented than any of the other three.

18.   On this collaboration, see *George Counts and Charles A. Beard, Collaborators for Change,* ed., Lawrence J. Dennis (Albany: State University of New York Press, 1989).

19.   Educational Policies Commission of the National Education Association and the Department of Superintendence, *The Unique Function of Education*

in American Democracy (Washington, D.C.: The Commission, 1937); Beard acknowledged on *Acknowledgment* page, no page number, as preparer of the first draft of the report.

20. Educational Policies Commission of the National Education Association and the American Association of School Administrators, *The Education of Free Men in American Democracy* (Washington, D.C.: The Commission, 1941); Counts was acknowledged on the *Acknowledgment* page as the major preparer of the volume.[The Department of Superintendence underwent a name change to the American Association of School Administrators shortly after the publication of the Unique Function report in 1937].

21. Educational Policies Commission of the National Education Association and the American Association of School Administrators, *Education and Economic Well-Being in American Democracy* (Washington, D.C.: The Commission, 1938).

22. *Acknowledgment,* [no page number], *The Unique Function of Education in American Democracy.*

23. Ibid., 90.

24. For example, see Beard, *An Economic Interpretation of the Constitution of the United States* (New York: Macmillan, 1913) or Beard, *The Economic Basis of Politics* (New York: A. A: Knopf, 1923).

25. Beard, *The Unique Function of Education in a Democracy,* 104.

26. Carr, *The Education of William Carr,* 59.

27. Ibid., 60.

28. Educational Policies Commission of the National Education Association and the American Association of School Administrators, *Education and Economic Well-Being in American Democracy* (Washington, D.C.: The Commission, 1938), Foreword, no page number.

29. Box 931 of the Educational Policies Commission Papers at the NEA Archives in Washington, D.C. contains the Proceedings of the September 1936 meeting between the EPC and the economists. Economists and other social scientists attending included Harold G. Moulton, President of the Brookings Institution; Robert M. Haig, Professor of Political Economy at Columbia University, and Howard Odum, Professor of Sociology at the University of North Carolina.

30. *Education and Economic Well-Being in American Democracy Acknowledgment,* no page number.

31. *Proceedings* of the Educational Policies Commission meeting of September 9, 1936, Box 931, EPC Papers, NEA Archives, Washington, D.C.

32. The cost estimate of just under four billion is found on p. 184 of *Education and Economic Well-Being in America.*

33. *The Education of Free Men in American Democracy,* 48, 50.

34. Ibid., 62, 93, 96, 97.

35. For an initial effort on this topic, see my 2003 History of Education Society Paper, International Education and an International Teachers' Organization:

William G. Carr, UNESCO, and the World Confederation of the Organized Teaching Profession.

36.   Educational Policies Commission of the National Education Association and the American Association of School Administrators, *The Purposes of Education in American Democracy* (Washington, D.C.: National Education Association, 1938) *passim* and 137. Carr did not address the apparent tension between a defense of democracy in education and his attack on the ostensibly democratic practice of electing school superintendents.

CHAPTER 9

CURRICULUM DESIGN AND HAROLD RUGG

Implementing Social Reconstructionism

Barbara Slater Stern

Harold Rugg's article, *Curriculum Design in the Social Sciences: What I Believe . . . After Twenty Years, 1919–1939*, represents his Social Reconstructionist philosophical approach to K–12 education in general and social studies in particular. Rugg sets this article against the background of three major problems: the declaration of war against Germany by the western democracies (the U.S. excluded in 1939), the Great Depression,[1] and the Progressive movement of the 1920s with its potential to use science and technology to solve the nation's problems. Thus, Rugg's Social Reconstructionism can be seen as an offshoot of the Progressive movement that expands Progressivism to include a mission to solve the problems of society through school curriculum. Rugg explains this belief in "Young Americans Working to Solve the American Problem," the subtitle of the second section of this social studies curriculum discussion.

Rugg defines the American Problem as he sees it: "To bring forth on this continent—in some form of co-operative commonwealth—the civilization of abundance, democratic behavior, and the integrity of expression

Social Reconstruction: People, Politics, Perspectives, pages 167–188
Copyright © 2006 by Information Age Publishing

and of appreciation which is now potentially available."[2] He does not believe that schools can accomplish this task alone but he does believe that the "new school" should be committed, as a leader in our society, to the graduation of "youth who do understand American life as it is actually lived, who are deeply concerned to help build a decent civilization on our continent and are convinced it can be done."[3] In terms of curriculum design, this goal is accomplished by defining fifteen social science factors that students must master in order to understand the American Problem. The question that immediately comes to mind is: why these fifteen factors?

According to Nelson, the Rugg curriculum-writing team identified 888 social studies generalizations that were then broken into sixty-nine groups to be utilized in preparing the Rugg materials.[4] The process was begun by writing letters to individuals Rugg and his team identified as being the leading experts in their fields (in general, the Frontier Thinkers Rugg so admired). The letters solicited the names of the most important books in each field. The books were then collected and read to distill the most frequently appearing concepts and generalizations. A Rugg student and colleague, Neal Billings, compiled the information in [5] *A Determination of the Generalizations Basic to the Social Studies Curriculum.* These generalizations were sorted under the fifteen factors for social studies curriculum.

In keeping with the Progressive faith in scientific method and his engineering background, Rugg claimed this to be a scientific approach to analyzing what content should comprise students' knowledge base but he does not account for his bias in selecting the experts, nor does he use the advice of people outside his team in crosschecking the text analyses, etc. Therefore, the Rugg social studies program reflects a social reconstructionist view of what it is important to know and understand despite the fact that Rugg claims it to be a completely scientific, and therefore unbiased, approach to curriculum content.

Among the fifteen factors isolated are the following:

1. economic factors related to the ability to produce, distribute, and consume goods and services

2. unregulated power over communication, government, and wealth by a minority unwilling to make changes in the social system to create more equity

3. the failure of schools to teach people literacy and democracy (including the pretense that social classes do not exist in America)

4. the apathy of the people to suffering coupled with the tendency of politicians and leaders to be make only superficial changes in the system

5. the influence and power of interest groups

6. the dangers of propaganda and of demagogues using mass media to convince people into following them in an unthinking manner

7. the failure to understand the interdependence of society and to seek solutions that take that complexity into account

8. the "menace of lack of time."[6]

Rugg advises curriculum designers to place these factors in the forefront of their minds as they design their program of study.

The next section of the Rugg curriculum design article contains a chart outlining a grades 3–12 curriculum: an interdisciplinary, integrated curriculum in which all subjects are studied through the social sciences. Following the chart detailing the curriculum Rugg has placed a section entitled "Ten Principles of Design." Each of these principles is then explicated in order to demonstrate how a curriculum should be designed and implemented.

These principles begin with the concept that an overall program must be designed, something we now refer to as "scope and sequence." Second, Rugg states that this design must arise from the current culture of the people as opposed to "some other classic entrenched curriculum."[7] Third, each unit of study would be centered on a human "problem," institution, or social system that is complex and interdependent rather than based in a single subject. Fourth, this curriculum must challenge students' maximum growth in their knowledge encouraging both interest and self-discipline or hard work [a call for rigor]. Fifth, the program balances current interests of children with what is necessary to be studied later in school and in adult life. This creates "Schools of Living," similar to Deweyan ideas, which is number six. The seventh principle focuses on depth, the "mastery of essentials rather than superficial acquaintance with it all."[8] This necessitates (eight) a flexible grade placement in terms of cognitive developmental maturity rather than by age placement (multi-age grades). Ninth, the focus of curriculum on problem solving using dramatic episodes to set the problem aiming for generalizations with repeated occurrence to reinforce concepts and patterns. Lastly number ten: while using more historical data than generally found in traditional history courses, the concentration of the study will be on the facts and concepts that produced contemporary conditions and problems (again depth over breadth).

The rest of this article concentrates on the "why" and the "how" of his curriculum design. In an idea surely springing from the Progressive approach to education, Rugg explains what he calls the "organic" (interdisciplinary) approach to learning as being more valid than the "mechanistic" or single-subject approach. In this sense, one can understand why his entire course of study is entitled "Man and His Changing Society."[9] Rugg states that this differs from traditional studies in three ways: "They [integrated social sciences] build a vast body of concepts and attitudes that formal courses ignore; they start from the social and personal needs and experiences of the students; because young people must assemble the data to answer their own questions, [and] the study cuts ruthlessly across conventional subject boundaries . . . to make available all meanings essential for understanding."[10]

While this is a progressive child-centered approach, Rugg differentiates his curriculum by stating: "Curriculum-design is a product of the balancing of doing what I need to do today (Progressive) with getting ready to do things I shall have to do tomorrow" (Social Reconstructionist).[11] He follows with a discussion of the school as an instrument of social study and his belief in active learning for societal reconstruction. Students must not only learn about government, but also must take part in governing for the study to be effective.[12] Rugg goes on to discuss the role of controversial issues and of history, specifically, in the social studies curriculum.

As already mentioned, Rugg was heavily influenced by the "Frontier Thinkers" and used economic interpretations of history and geography in his program rather than the traditional political approach to these subjects. A review of the curriculum outlined in this article includes an emphasis on world history and world problems at a time when America was in a neo-isolationist period as demonstrated by our failure to join the League of Nations following World War I. Additionally, Rugg focuses on groups in America traditionally ignored in social studies textbooks of the time period: immigrants, minorities, and women.

Rugg and his colleagues designed and marketed a series of social studies textbooks that purport to implement the philosophy described above. The "First Course" (elementary school level) contains eight volumes entitled: *The Book of the Earth* (I); *Nature Peoples* (II); *Communities of Men* (III); *Peoples and Countries* (IV); *The Building of America* (V); *Man at Work: His Industries* (VI); *Man at Work: His Arts and Crafts* (VII); and *Mankind Throughout the Ages* (VIII). The six volumes in the "Second Course" (junior high and secondary school level) were later revised into two groups. The first group included *Our Country and Our People* (I); *Changing Countries and Changing Peoples* (II); *The Conquest of America* (III); *America's March Toward Democracy* (IV). The second group, titled *Community and National Life* included volume V, *Citizenship and Civic Affairs* (Book One), and volume VI, *America Rebuilds* (Book Two). At the height of the texts' popularity, more than five million students were using the Rugg social studies materials revealing an attempt at forging a new national social studies curriculum.

This chapter analyzes one Rugg textbook from the second group of the second course *Community and National Life.* Book One, Volume V, *Citizenship and Civic Affairs,*[13] as well as multiple writings by and about Rugg's social studies materials, in order to determine whether Rugg was actually able to design and implement the curricular change he called for in his 1939 article. The methodology consisted of designing two instruments for the text analysis. One chart (Appendix 2) is based on the fifteen social studies factors students need (according to Rugg) to master, and the second chart (Appendix 1) is based the ten principles of curriculum design called for in the article. The chosen material was then analyzed using these instruments. The question at hand is how successful was Rugg in transferring his curriculum design beliefs to classroom materials that would enhance teacher implementation of Rugg's ideas?

This volume was selected for several reasons. First, this text is designed for a civics/government course, a course of study that has become increasingly fact-laden, boring and meaningless to many secondary students who do not understand the role the government will play in their lives after they complete the course. Second, government can be seen as a course that focuses inherently on controversial issues and problems. Considering the criticism of the Rugg textbook series in the late 1930s and 40s[14] this volume seemed particularly pertinent to the charges leveled against Rugg. Given both the conservative nature of schools then and now, and also the Progressive/Reconstructionist changes called for in this article, the question under consideration is whether Rugg was actually able to do as he said? In other words, is there consistency between what Rugg said was ideal and the materials created to implement this ideal? Third, especially in light of the fact that the books became a commercial venture for Rugg and Ginn and Company publishing as they moved from their original pamphlet form to hardcover textbooks designed for wide distribution, were the revised editions faithful to the Rugg vision?

Several authors have analyzed the Rugg textbooks over the years in terms of content, notably[15] Bosenberg and Poland,[16] Muchinske,[17] Nelson,[18] Riley and Stern, and[19] Sabine, et al. Most of these authors were primarily interested in the political attacks against the Rugg textbooks and in explaining their subsequent removal from the schools, or the unfairness of the charges leveled against Rugg and his writing team. These authors generally begin by explicating Rugg's philosophy on curriculum design. Nelson[20] cites the process by which Rugg approaches curriculum design as stemming from his background as an engineer. Rugg believed in approaching a problem scientifically, in planning and executing the solutions in an organized fashion based on the gathering of evidence and the testing of that evidence. The point is made by Nelson that the Rugg textbook series represents the earliest comprehensive curriculum design "developed and utilized on a nationwide basis in social studies"[21] This fact alone makes the study of the Rugg materials important for curriculum theorists and social studies specialists.

In reviewing the literature it became clear that the chart (Appendix 1), established to determine whether or not Rugg actually put his curriculum design plan into effect, concurs with earlier scholars who believe Rugg was successful in achieving his ten principles of design. The success of the chart for the social studies factors that students need to master (Appendix 2) is more problematic. This relates to the difficulty of defining what is meant by real knowledge in any given discipline included under the umbrella of the social sciences.

Rugg was educated as an engineer, not as a social scientist and certainly not as an historian, geographer, economist or political scientist. Neither is he a specialist in any of the academic disciplines he is trying to merge. This may be less problematic at the elementary school and especially the junior high school levels (where due to the newness of the educational level there was a dearth of materials available and therefore a ready-made market to develop), but as the materials moved toward the high school level and wide commercial acceptance they became more open to academic challenge from experts in the subject fields who believed their individual disciplines were being slighted.

How much of the battle over the actual disciplinary content of the Rugg materials would have played out if his approach had been less incendiary is hard to know but the chart focused on social studies (Appendix 2) reveals less content knowledge, especially in history, than Rugg believed was contained in these books. Also, not only is there less historical knowledge, but there is different knowledge than was generally included in the time period and for a good while thereafter.

In exploring these charts in depth one may find that the chart analyzing the Ten Principles of Design (Appendix 1) focuses on the preface to the book as that is where Rugg explains his concept of how the text fits into the fully implemented social science program, as well as how the textbook was created. By using quotations from the preface addressing the design concerns and then looking for evidence to back up these claims in the execution of the chapters, it is clear that Rugg was successful in most of his design claims. For example, the program was clearly designed as a whole integrated social science entity and the titles of the books in the series along with Rugg's explanation of their scope and sequence (preface vi–vii) detail that fact as well as that the theme for design was to explain how America and the world it shares came to be as they are and what problems need to be looked at to ensure a better future.

Principle four—"It is designed on rapidly rising growth curves to bring about maximum development each year"—is more problematic at this point. This text falls at the end of the second course and it does not always present a comprehensive picture of the topics to allow all students to understand the issues. It should be noted that the text had an accompanying workbook and that each chapter provided a bibliography for in-depth research that Rugg believed students and teachers should be undertaking together. Assuming the availability of both the workbook and the initiative to pursue this outside information, teachers should be able to round out the necessary content materials to enable the understanding of the body of the text allowing that instructional time could be allocated for the research required.

The next three factors are clearly covered in the design of this text. Certainly the focus on social problems and the push in each chapter for substantive discussions where students would need to form opinions about these problems and their possible solutions points towards both "doing now" and getting ready for tomorrow. Further, in Rugg's time period, when recitation of facts was the *modus operandi*, this textbook with its emphasis on the multiple perspectives of differing opinions (generally by social class) on problems and its discussion was revolutionary. And in terms of "rigorous principle of selection" Rugg's choice of topics was extraordinary for a high school textbook. Rugg focuses on gangs, the influence of political bosses, changing roles of women in society, the increase in divorce rates, and the history of education.

What is *not* there is all the material that students currently have on each federal agency and its role. The reader comes away from this text with a conceptual understanding of how government works in ways that affect the individual citizen's life but without the details that students are generally expected to master. The information in this book is useful in seeing how the system really works, as opposed to its structure on paper. This enabled students to become active citizens and understand which problems, such as political corruption, need solving.

Principal nine is fully realized in the text. At the start of most chapters vignettes, or dramatic episodes, center on controversial issues or social problems. The summaries in each chapter help students with generalizations and the recurrence of concepts, especially the focus on different aspects of economic problems and their resulting social differences, are repeated throughout the book.

The most questionable of the Rugg design principles is his claim, in principle ten, that there is more historical data, rather than less, in his approach. While statistical data that was rarely seen in earlier textbooks (due to the fact that earlier texts take a political rather than economic and social approach to history) is present, there is clearly a surfeit of historical factual material in this text. Because this is a government and not a history book, the lack of historical data may not be a major criticism. However, as Rugg is a social scientist, the mention of historical importance without facts backing up his claims is dismaying. In many cases, the reader is left wondering about omissions. For example, the discussion of the addition of the Bill of Rights to the U.S. Constitution is particularly poorly done because it neglects to mention the *Federalist Papers* or the refusal of some states to ratify without promises of the addition of the Bill of Rights. The discussion of the failures and successes of the Articles of Confederation is similarly glib and lacking in enough factual material to promote true understanding of the issues. The resources consulted on the rest of the textbook series reveal a similar concern with a paucity of history in a subject area where the consensus—both then and now—is that history is the centerpiece of any social studies curriculum.

In summary, nine of the ten design features present (with the exception, at this point, of principle ten) the inclusion of more historical data than in earlier texts. What is true of principle ten is the addition of statistical and sociological data in the form of graphs and pictures that would not have been included in traditional textbooks. This integrated approach to social sciences does include then the type of data that has become common in any good history textbook today.

The analysis of the social studies concepts necessary for student understanding (Appendix 2) reveals that Rugg does discuss all the concepts he believes are important, albeit some in more depth than others. Factor one, the capacity of the American economic system to produce goods and services, is illustrated in pictures and graphs as well as text, as the American lifestyle and the results of industrialization since 1890 are discussed in the first chapter of the book.

Factor two, the lag in distribution, is more implied than directly stated as it is illustrated by depicting in words and in pictures the gaps in lifestyle among the social classes. Rugg attributes this gap to several factors stemming from individual greed and "undue control over wealth, communications, and government by a minority" who do not favor social change (as it would disempower them to some extent). Rugg, as an engineer, was a believer in the ability of science coupled with good planning and solid efficient management as a solution to these problems. This planning and uncorrupt, efficient management would be established by a nationwide commitment to intelligence (factor five) and education (factor six).

In other words, Rugg believed that if you could convince people that there were distinct social class differences that could not be overcome simply by individual effort (factor four), and if mass education really focused on the authentic conditions in America, or the American Problem (factor seven), and if we could control the influence of the media and big business—especially the power of advertising (all part of factors three and thirteen)—then American citizens would rise up and demand change! The problem, however, is the apathy of the public (factor nine), part of which Rugg attributes to alienation brought about by big city culture and anonymity , which he illustrates by demonstrating the way citizens try to avoid jury duty. This may be why Rugg devotes so much of the beginning of the textbook to explaining the role of communities in making America successful as he seems to believe that democracy is most secure when people participate at the community level and understand their local government and how it functions.

Rugg is more than simply idealistic or one sided. He points out both the positives and the negatives of small towns and of neighborhoods where people—while they may be supportive and friendly of "those on the inside"—are often not welcoming or openly prejudiced toward newcomers or "those on the outside." Additionally, when discussing positions on controversial issues, Rugg explains differing attitudes towards these issues among the different social classes without condemning any particular point of view. His sections on divorce and the changing role of women (due to labor-saving inventions) sound more like those since the 1990s than those of the 40s. He advocates a larger role for men in the home as women move out of the house and into the volunteer or work force. At times it may be hard to believe that this book was written in 1931. And, to his credit, the statistical data was updated before the printing of the 1940 revised edition.

Yet there are serious flaws with some concepts in the text. For example, factor seven—"the failure of mass education really to practise [sic] democratic method by building a program of study"—is problematic not only by the general topics Rugg chooses to discuss, but also because of the lack of depth in explaining several of the problems. In a section on economic issues the difference between the deficit and interest (on the issue of national spending and the national debt) are not defined. Neither are the differences between regressive and progressive taxes defined. And, while Rugg clearly champions the income tax law as a triumph of the will of the people over special interests (factor eleven), he doesn't explain why this is so and therefore, the point is lost. Thus, while the book does do a really nice job pointing out "conditions and problems of life as it is actually lived," e.g. the numbers of bathrooms and bedrooms, type of landscaping, education and employment of different social classes, much data is missing. And again, there is a real dearth of historical fact beyond graphs and tables to back up assertions.

If, as Rugg believes, that education will be the answer to solving society's problems, then more depth is required on the topics chosen. His discussion of factor eight, susceptibility to propaganda and demagogues, is confined to concerns about the role of advertising in influencing the media, yellow journalism, and more briefly, the dangers of Fascist dictators in Europe. Rugg touches on factor fifteen, the lack of time, in only two places in the text and one of them questions how people will use their leisure time now that we are so industrialized and automated. This should lead to more, not less time, although later in the text[22] a lawyer complains he is too busy to have time to read—a pastime Rugg believes is necessary for an educated population. He does an even better job with factor fourteen, the complex interdependence of society, including several references to America's place in the world of nations, not just within her own continent or locality.

In summary, Rugg does cover the fifteen social studies factors he believes are necessary for social studies students to understand in order to become active participating citizens and solve America's problems in the future albeit somewhat unevenly. In some cases the underlying reasons for or definitions of major concepts and events could use significantly more explication.

This analysis of the Rugg curriculum design and implementation is significant because curriculum alignment has been a perpetual problem regardless of philosophical approach. Today, in many states, the adoption of curriculum standards calls for the creation of appropriate textbooks and teaching materials to implement the standards. Publishers provide school districts with charts displaying the correlation of the textbook content with the state standards. However, these are mostly fact- and date-based traditional standards. In schools looking toward reform with inquiry and/or problem-based learning approaches, the Rugg materials provide a model for this approach. Thus, this textbook analysis provides an example of bridging theory into practice and a model of how to create and implement philosophically coherent and meaningful curricula.

The design of the curriculum and the depth of understanding of the concepts covered under each of the fifteen factors hinges on how the factors were determined from the outset. The analysis of the government book does not contain the factual depth that it needs perhaps for the reason that Rugg was not even aware of what was missing.

On the other hand, it is important to state that compared to a modern government book, this 1940 textbook is more interesting to read and covers more topics that would be of importance to a secondary school student than anything available for the mass market today. One "dramatic episode" early in the book described how traffic would be unable to move freely without laws and the agreement of the people to surrender some rights to allow society to function. At first glance, I thought "how stupid this example is!" Then I watched the evening news and there was a story on the horrors of the traffic in Baghdad as there is an absence of government and laws in wake of the overthrow of Saddam Hussein and the lack of the 20,000 police who used to enforce those laws. I was astounded at how contemporary the Rugg example I had mocked had suddenly become.

I returned to the text with a new respect for the vignettes that had seemed so dated. The idea of focusing on numbers of bedrooms and bathrooms to explain social class was an issue I felt that teenagers would easily relate to and certainly has not been in any social studies textbook I have ever worked with. Thus, when analyzing Rugg materials, it is important to keep a balance between the ideal of what historians, economists, political scientists, or geographers want students to know and what students realistically need to understand to become active citizens maintaining and expanding democracy in our country. The Rugg textbook, *Citizenship and Civic Affairs*, still has something to teach us about the "American Problem."

Thus, in answer to the original question of whether Rugg did in fact create a curriculum design and practical materials that would enable its implementation, the answer is basically, yes. It is most important to remember that the Rugg program emphasized knowledge necessary to understand today and prepare for a better tomorrow in a country and world threatened by problems. This is a different approach than the one that holds the purpose of school as simply to pass on or conserve the great accomplishments and knowledge from the past to the present generation. It should be reemphasized that Rugg firmly believed in democratic government and the American Constitution—he simply believed Americans were losing their democracy due to economic and political forces they did not understand. The Rugg curriculum would supply that understanding.

While criticisms of his materials lacking depth in specific disciplines are valid, it is my belief that students going through the Rugg scope and sequence, then or now (data updated of course), would come out with a more grounded conceptual understanding of the social sciences in general and even of the specific disciplines, than traditional programs with their emphasis on facts over meaning and their lack of bridging the world of school with the world outside the school gates can ever achieve.

Appendix 1.   Ten Principles of Design

Design Principles	Evidence from Rugg Textbooks
1. The program is designed	Preface viii: A Unified Course in Social Science
2. It is designed directly from the culture of the people	Preface vi: Explanation that the First and Second Course are an integrated study of civilization
3. Each unit of study is centered on a human "problem," institution, or social system	Preface vii: "It [the text] serves the special purpose of introducing the economic, political and social problems of American culture"

Appendix 1.   Ten Principles of Design

4. It is designed on rapidly rising growth curves to bring about maximum development each year	Preface vi: "A carefully graduated and steadily maturing plan." Topics discussed throughout the book certainly push students to deal with issues on a mature level. Some topics may not contain the needed background to enable full comprehension.
5. The design balances "doing now" with getting ready for tomorrow	Preface ix: "The chief goal of the social studies is active and intelligent participation in American civilization. . . . *Young people grow in understanding only by particpating actively in the study of society around them*" [italics original]. There is less actual doing than Rugg appears to believe there is, but there is considerable discussion as opposed to recitation.
6. It makes school the chief instrument for social study	Preface v: "It is of the utmost importance that schools bend every effort to introduce our young people to the chief conditions and problems which will confront them as citizens of the world." The book does center all chapters on these problems. Particularly economic and social stratification in America, the preference for democracy over dictatorship as a form of government.
7. It is designed on a rigorous principle of selection	Preface vii: Topics were chosen by "specialists on the frontier of thought who see society from a height, who detect its trends and the long-time movement of its affairs." Clearly emphasis throughout the text was on the topics that created the problems Rugg believes America needs to solve.

Appendix 1.   Ten Principles of Design

8. It is designed on a flexible program of grade-placement, in terms of maturity of meanings, concepts, generalizations, and attitudes	The preface suggests grade level for students in the series by both the order of the books and the separation into First and Second Courses. This volume would fall around 9th or 10th grade but the issues involved and their presentation are generally taught in the old "PAD" course or in 12th grade government today. The book really combines civics (generally 8th or 9th grade) and government (generally 12th grade).
9. To guarantee maximum understanding it builds around problems and controversial issues, training in problem solving and generalization; it employs dramatic episode and generalization alternately and develops understanding by the designed recurrence of concepts	Many chapters open with a "scenario" to engage students. These scenarios often involve controversial issues such as illegal immigration and its effect on wages. A recurring theme is the difference in lifestyle among social classes in America. This is illustrated in vary chapters by vignettes describing the homes (physical), interests, activities, jobs, educational levels, etc. of different social classes throughout the book. And this is done in easily understandable terms, e.g. the number of bedrooms and bathrooms in dwellings occupied by each social class.

Appendix 1.   Ten Principles of Design

10. While employing more historical data, rather than less, it concentrates study upon the identical factors and trends that produced contemporary conditions and problems	Preface viii: "This has *not* caused a reduction in the amount of history or of geography included in the course. Rather it has produced a sharp increase in the amount of these subjects in the curriculum and, in addition, has added to the curriculum a wealth of new material." There is a significantly lower amount of history in the book for two reasons: one is the glossing over of facts to concentrate on concepts, the other is the increase in other social science information, particularly integrated sociology and economics in the text. Nonetheless, while the conceptual framework is quite strong, the factual underpinnings are somewhat glossed over except where graphic data (tables and photos) are presented for analysis.

Appendix 2.   Fifteen Social Studies Factors Necessary
for Students to Understand

Social Studies Knowledge	*Evidence from the Textbook*
1. The giant capacity of the American economic system to produce goods and services	The first chapter focuses on how a new Industrial Revolution has been changing American ways of living since 1890. Sections focus on mass production and robots to increase production.
2. The lag of the ability to distribute goods and services behind the capacity to produce them	The text discusses the distribution of electric power and the time it took to electrify most of the country. The distribution difficulties in this text are focused on the inherent inequities in unrestrained capitalism and a lack of governmental planning.

Appendix 2.   Fifteen Social Studies Factors Necessary
for Students to Understand

3. The undue control over wealth, communication, and government by a minority who believe in relatively uncontrolled individualism and who oppose social change	The book is concerned about special interests, lobbyists and influence of the elite over the mass of American working people. It is clear that Rugg believes that entrenched power and, in many cases, political corruption have led to opposition to social change that would lessen the gap between the rich and the poor. Discussion of the Hearst newspapers spreading control of the media through mergers and his attack on yellow journalism exemplifies this (as well as explaining Hearst's role in the campaign against Rugg).
4. The nationwide commitment to democracy as maximum individual development leading to a belief that society is devoid of social classes	The Rugg belief in democracy as the best form of government is patently clear throughout the text even as the text consistently points to gaps among the lifestyles and beliefs of the different social classes. Thus, the book focuses on social class to disabuse students of the belief that social class does not exist in America. The sections on growth education, private and public, do point to maximizing individual development as a means to reduce class difference, but Rugg does point out the difficulty poor people have in attaining higher education.
5. The nationwide conviction that free play of intelligence among people should determine social policy	Rugg believes that people are basically good and the reader picks this up in repeated discussion of the desire of the people to force Congress to pass the Income Tax law. Additionally Rugg discusses the American Sprit and the influence of the muckrakers as illustrations of the goodness of American intention once citizens have the facts.

Appendix 2.   Fifteen Social Studies Factors Necessary
for Students to Understand

6. The achievement of a structure of universal elementary education and making people literate	Rugg cites the founders of the country and traces the history of education in America in more depth than one would find in most Foundations of American Education classes at the university level. Clearly he believes in education as vital in free society and he illustrates this by pointing to the difference in school curriculum in Nazi Germany and Fascist Italy, from that of the United States.
7. The failure of mass education really to practise [sic] democratic method by building a program of study and discussion of the conditions and problems of life as it is actually lived today	Here is where Rugg's spiral discussions of social class really come to light. He focuses on neighborhoods and prejudice based on income; he describes the numbers of bedrooms and bathrooms in dwellings based on income. These discussions would still not be found at this depth (if at all) in current American civics/government textbooks.
8. The lack of real understanding of the American Problem by the people and their corresponding susceptibility to the propaganda of demagogues	Rugg spends a considerable amount of time describing the roles of participants in city governance. He explains how local party bosses come to power and influence in ways that demonstrate that Rugg believes people award this power to corrupt influence because they do not know or understand how to deal with these issues. By focusing on local politics, describing alternatives like city commissions, city planning, and city managers Rugg is attempting to change the lack of understanding and control citizens exhibit.

Appendix 2.   Fifteen Social Studies Factors Necessary
                for Students to Understand

9. The widespread apathy of the people to matters of public concern and the inertia of potential leaders of an informed thinking citizenry	Although alluded to in several parts of the book, the target starting on page 416 is a section titled: "One of the Greatest Difficulties: The Indifference of Most People." Rugg then uses the example of jury-dodging (getting out of jury duty) to illustrate. At other earlier points in the text, he also speaks of apathy in voting, lack of attention to the poor or to national issues, etc.
10. The powerful appeal of symptoms of mass suffering (caused by unemployment, poverty, disease) and the tendency of political leaders to be content with treating them superficially instead of eliminating the causes	The descriptions of housing and education, the plight of illegal immigrants and the reality of the Great Depression are highlighted repeatedly in the book. Rugg clearly believes that passing laws, such as graduated income tax which he lauds as a reform of the people for the people, is an exception. Overall Rugg believes that planning (his engineering background shining through here) and city management will be the solution but that political leaders are preventing this from occurring. The discussions of crime in America, on pages 394–400, exemplify this concept.
11. The fact that government in our democracy is carried on by the interplay of "interest groups." Policy making in the long run will represent the will of the people	Rugg does believe in democracy and he does discuss interest groups and lobbying in the sections on how laws are made by Congress. He illustrates for students a basic understanding of the committee system and the jockeying of interests in adding amendments and riders to bills. These discussions are much less detailed than the average American government textbook would contain today.

Appendix 2.   Fifteen Social Studies Factors Necessary
for Students to Understand

12. The success of creative minds in inventing and building powerful and worldwide systems of instantaneous communication of ideas and moods among the people	On page 47, Rugg focuses on immigrants who became scientists and created alternating current, which improved long-distance telephone calls. He mentions General Electric and the spread of power and communications, as well as discussing the impact of these changes in modern society. One can only imagine what this book would contain if it were being written in today's age of telecommunications and computers.
13. The danger that people will believe the propaganda of the demagogues of the press, radio and platform who offer the easy way of unthinkingly following, rather than endure the hard, democratic way of study, thought, discussion, and group decision and action	Rugg is concerned with the power of advertising and the business of the media (press and radio). He is concerned with bias in the news due to these influences that will inhibit Americans from making good choices. Thus the book emphasizes reading multiple sources, discussing, and listening to multiple perspectives to improve democracy. The media and modern life are corrupting to the extent that neighbors see each other less and the town meeting is not attended frequently as the size of a town increases—this leads to less hard, democratic decision making and more impersonal, boss-run politics, which Rugg sees as dangerous to democracy.

Appendix 2.   Fifteen Social Studies Factors Necessary
              for Students to Understand

14. The complex interdependence of society	A constant theme throughout the text is the danger posed by the modernization and urbanization of America. The sections on problems of cities and the changing American family illustrate this point. Rugg compares the original New England town with the modern city and seeks to have students wrestle with how to solve the problems wrought by industrialization.
15. The menace of lack of time	This problem is discussed only tangentially in the early part of the book when Rugg questions how Americans will use the leisure time created by labor saving devices created by industrialization. He also bemoans the lack of reading by most Americans and attributes this, on page 494, to lack of time. Thus, this point is not clearly made in the text. Although, given today's modernization, students would have no trouble relating to this concept.

NOTES

1.   "Poverty in the land of plenty." Harold Ordway Rugg, "Curriculum-design in the social sciences: What I believe" *The Future of the Social Studies,* ed. James A. Michener, Anonymous (Cambridge, Massachusetts: National Council for the Social Studies Curriculum Series, 1939), 140.
2.   Ibid., 141.
3.   Ibid., 141.
4.   Murry R. Neslon, "Rugg on Rugg: His theories and his curriculum," *Curriculum Inquiry* 8 no. 2 (1978): 129.
5.   Neal Billings, 1sted. (York, PA: Maple Press, 1929), 289.
6.   Rugg, *Curriculum-design in the social sciences: What I believe . . . .,* 142.
7.   Ibid., 148.
8.   Ibid., 148.

9.   Ibid., 149.

10.   Ibid., 15.

11.   Ibid., 152.

12.   Ibid., 152.

13.   Harold Ordway Rugg, *Citizenship and civic affairs* (Boston, New York: Ginn and Co., 1940), 610, liv.

14.   Karen L. Riley and Barbara Slater Stern, "'A Bootlegged Curriculum:' The American Legion versus Harold Rugg" (2002): 473; 336; 47; 163

15.   Ellen Boesenberg and Karen Susi Poland, "Struggle at the frontier of curriculum: the Rugg textbook controversy in Binghamton, NY," *Theory and Research in Social Education* 29 no. 4 (2001): 640–671.

16.   David Muschinske, "American Life, the Social Studies and Harold Rugg," *Social Studies* 65 no. 6 (1974): 246–249.

17.   Murry R. Nelson, "The development of the Rugg social studies Materials." *Theory and Research in Social Education* 5 no. 3 (1977): 64–83; Murry R. Nelson and H. Wells Singleton, "Governmental Surveillance of Three Progressive Educators," (March 1978); Murry R. Nelson, "The Rugg brothers in social education" *Journal of Thought* 17 no. 3 (1982): 69–82.

18.   Riley and Stern, *"A Bootlegged Curriculum:" The American Legion versus Harold Rugg*

19.   George Holland Sabine, Wesley Clair Mitchell, and American Committee for Democracy and Intellectual Freedom. Committee on Textbooks, *The text books of Harold Rugg, an analysis,* (New York: American Committee for Democracy and Intellectual Freedom, 1942), 28.

20.   Donald W. Oliver and Fred M. Newmann, "Taking a Stand: A Guide to Clear Discussion of Public Issues. Public Issues Series/Harvard Social Studies Project," (1967).

21.   Neslon, *Rugg on Rugg: His theories and his curriculum*, 124.

22.   Rugg, *Citizenship and civic affairs*, 494.

REFERENCES

Billings, Neal. *A Determination of Generalizations Basic to the Social Studies Curriculum.* Baltimore: Warwick and York, Inc. (1929), 289.

Boesenberg, Ellen, and Karen Susi Poland. "Struggle at the Frontier of Curriculum: The Rugg Textbook Controversy in Binghamton, NY." *Theory and Research in Social Education* 29, no. 4 (2001): 640–671.

Muschinske, David. "American Life, the Social Studies and Harold Rugg." *Social Studies* 65, no. 6 (1974): 246–249.

Nelson, Murry R. "The Development of the Rugg Social Studies Materials." *Theory and Research in Social Education* 5, no. 3 (1977): 64–83.

Nelson, Murry R. "The Rugg Brothers in Social Education." *Journal of Thought* 17, no. 3 (1982): 69-82.

Nelson, Murry R., and H. Wells Singleton. "Governmental Surveillance of Three Progressive Educators." (March 1978).

Neslon, Murry R. "Rugg on Rugg: His Theories and His Curriculum." *Curriculum Inquiry* 8, no. 2 (1978): 119–132.

Oliver, Donald W., and Fred M. Newmann. "Taking a Stand: A Guide to Clear Discussion of Public Issues. Public Issues Series/Harvard Social Studies Project." (1967).

Riley, Karen L., and Barbara Slater Stern. *"'A Bootlegged Curriculum:' The American Legion Versus Harold Rugg." International Journal of Social Education* 17, no. 2 (2002).

Rugg, Harold Ordway. "Curriculum-Design in the Social Sciences: What I Believe," in *The Future of the Social Studies.* Edited by James A. Michener. Cambridge, MA: National Council for the Social Studies Curriculum Series, 1939, 140–158.

Rugg, Harold Ordway. *Citizenship and Civic Affairs.* Boston, New York: Ginn and Co, 1940.

Sabine, George Holland, Wesley Clair Mitchell, and American Committee for Democracy and Intellectual Freedom. Committee on Textbooks. *The Text Books of Harold Rugg, an Analysis.* New York: American Committee for Democracy and Intellectual Freedom, 1942.

CHAPTER 10

IN SEARCH OF CURRICULUM THEORY

The Reconstructionists

Marcella L. Kysilka and Susan Brown

INTRODUCTION

During the early twentieth century, American educators were struggling to determine the school's role in educating society's children. Their discussions focused on social factors affecting the change in American society:

1. the rapid industrial growth;

2. waves of immigrants entering the U.S. from a wide range of countries;

3. America's participation in World War I and the aftermath of the war;

4. and, finally, the Great Depression starting in 1929.

Some educators were beginning to realize that schools needed to rethink their role in preparing children and youth for participation in America's "democratic" society. The dominant subject-centered curriculum of the traditionalists was providing little opportunity for children and youth to explore and question ideas, policies, and practices which ultimately would

Social Reconstruction: People, Politics, Perspectives, pages 189–210
Copyright © 2006 by Information Age Publishing
All rights of reproduction in any form reserved.

affect their lives as adults. At the same time, the typical curriculum had little to say about students' individual interests and needs, and how children would develop to become self-fulfilled individuals in the complex contemporary society.

Educators such as George Counts and Harold Rugg were concerned about the lack of relevance of the typical school curriculum to the real world. Social problems were all around them, but the subject-centered curriculum dealt not with these national and world issues, but with topics such as the Great Books of the Western civilization. According to Counts,[1] the public schools did not adequately prepare the students for the new social order because of its middle class orientation and its support of the capitalistic status quo. In the eyes of these educators, reform of the curriculum was necessary for leading the way to societal reform.

During this same period, the growth of progressive education, with its emphasis on the individual child and the need for a child-centered curriculum, became evident. For advocates such as John Dewey, children needed to be seen as unique individuals and active learners, but also as social beings. Thus, curriculum should provide learning experiences that promote students developing initiative, social awareness and responsibility. Furthermore, students needed to develop the skills that would allow them to participate in and preserve the democratic processes essential to the survival of the country. The curriculum of the school then needed to be focused on the learners as active participants in their learning, the needs of society, and the necessary skills and knowledge for students to fulfill their obligation to advance the principles of democracy.

According to Schubert[2] during this period three distinct approaches to curriculum development could be seen: one, traditionalists of the liberal arts, focusing on subject matter; two, social behaviorists, focusing on the society; and three, experientialists, focusing on the child. In 1924, in an attempt to address these three different perspectives of curriculum theory, the National Society for the Study of Education (NSSE) sponsored a yearbook committee charged with the task of developing a general statement of working principles of curriculum making. Harold Rugg was appointed Chairman of this group of diverse thinkers on education. The result of the committee's work was entitled *The Foundations and Techniques of Curriculum Construction, NSSE 26th Yearbook, Part I.*

In the foreword of the 26th NSSE yearbook, Rugg stated that many different approaches to curriculum making had evolved over a period of fifty years, that American society had become horrendously complex, and that there existed "a gap between school and society and between curriculum and child growth."[3] Because of these conditions, he indicated a need to build a synthesis of ideas that incorporated three important factors in education: the child, American civilization, and the school. He was deeply concerned that no group or agency in the U.S. was looking at these three factors as they interacted with each other and believed that the time was right to do so. Rugg wrote:

> Although the task is difficult, there is great need for a new synthesis, a comprehensive orientation of the relation between the school curriculum and the content of life on the American continent today. With three systematic movements for curriculum-making well under way and with an accumulating capital of experience to build upon, it is now possible to evaluate the current needs and to obtain a new vision of the direction in which the educational machine should be guided.[4]

He recognized that the task would require a cooperative endeavor of many persons with different perspectives and ideas on learning, education, schooling, child development, measurement, school administration, educational experimentation, economics, politics, culture, and international affairs. He thought that the broadest perspective would produce a better statement for the reconstruction of the school. Recognizing that an all-inclusive group would be impossible to convene and to prove functional, he invited a group of persons with a "pronounced interest in the general public school situation. The members of the committee are all professional students of the curriculum and have sought constantly to maintain a broad perspective of American life and of growing childhood."[5] This committee consisted of William Bagley, Franklin Bobbitt, Frederick Bonser, Werrett Charters, George Counts, Stuart Courtis, Ernest Horn, Charles Judd, Frederick Kelly, William Kilpatrick, George Works, and Chairman Rugg.

The committee worked together for nearly two and a half years. Their process consisted of a series of round tables that lasted one to two days with six to ten members present at each meeting. In addition, other meetings were held with two to four members. Members also wrote and shared their ideas with each other. Eight members of the group undertook the task of preparing individual statements of the issues and problems of curriculum making as they understood them.[6] These ideas were discussed over a prolonged period of time and revealed that the majority of the concerns were subject-centered curriculum issues. Knowing that the list was not inclusive of other perspectives, the committee continued their work to include child-centered and activities curriculum ideas into their discussions. Their deliberations resulted in a List of Fundamental Questions on Curriculum-Making given below:[7]

EIGHTEEN FUNDAMENTAL QUESTIONS ON CURRICULUM-MAKING

Used as the Basis for the Preparation of the General Statement: Foundations of Curriculum-Making

1. What period of life does schooling primarily contemplate as its end?

2. How can the curriculum prepare for effective participation in adult life?

3. Are the curriculum-makers of the schools obliged to formulate a point of view concerning the merits or deficiencies of American civilization?

4. Should the school be regarded as a conscious agency for social improvement?

   a. Should the school be planned on the assumption that it is to fit children to "live in" the current social order or to rise above and lift it after them? Are children merely to be "adjusted" to the institutions of current society or are they to be so educated that they will be impelled to modify it? Are they to accept it or to question it?

5. How shall the content of the curriculum be conceived and stated?

6. What is the place and function of subject matter in the educative process?

   a. Subject matter is primarily matter-set-out-to-be-learned. It is the conscious and specific end of school activity (educative response) and the learning activity is exactly and precisely means to this end.

   b. Subject matter and learnings are properly both subsequent and subordinate to some normal life activity or experience (the educative process) already under way from other considerations. Subject matter is called for when, and because, this life activity has been balked for lack of a certain way of behaving. This needed way of behaving, as it is sought, found, and acquired, is that we properly call subject matter. Its function is to enable the balked activity to proceed.

7. What portion of education should be classified as "general" and what portion as "specialized" or "vocational" or purely "optional?" To what extent is general education to run parallel with vocational education

and to what extent is the latter to follow on the completion of the former?

8. Is the curriculum to be made in advance?

9. To what extent is the 'organization' of the subject matter a matter of pupil-thinking and construction of, or planning by, the professional curriculum-maker as a result of experimentation?

10. From the point of view of the educator, when has 'learning' taken place?

11. To what extent should traits be learned in their 'natural' setting (i.e., in a 'life-situation')?

12. To what degree should the curriculum provide for individual differences?

13. To what degree is the concept of "minimal essentials" to be used in curriculum-construction?

14. What should be the form of organization of the curriculum? Shall it be one of the following or will you adopt others?

   a. A flexibly graded series of suggestive activities with reference to subject matter which may be used in connection with the activities? Or

   1. A rigidly graded series of activities with subject matter included with each respective activity? Or

   2. A graded sequence of subject matter with suggestion for activities to which the subject matter is related? Or

   3. A statement of achievements expected for each grade, a list of suggestive activities, and an outline of related subject matter, through the use of which the grade object may be achieved? Or

   b. A statement of grade objectivities in terms of subject matter and textual and reference materials which will provide this subject matter without any specific reference to activities?

15. What, if any, use shall be made of the spontaneous interests of children?

16. For the determination of what types of material (activities, reading, discussion problems and topics, group projects, etc.) should the curriculum-maker analyze the activities in which adults actually engage?

   a. For skills and factual material?

   b. For group activities?

   c. For problems and issues of contemporary life?

17. How far shall methods of learning be standardized? For example, is it probable that current principles of learning will favor the use of

'practice' devices? For individuals? For groups? How is drill to be provided?

a. By assignment, under penalty, of specially chosen drill material?

b. By such personal practice as the felt connections call for?

18. Administrative questions of curriculum-making

a. For what time units shall the curriculum be organized?

b. For what geographic units shall the curriculum be made?

1. *In the United States*

2. Individual states

3. A county

4. *An individual school*

c. Shall a curriculum be made especially for rural schools?

d. What is the optimal form in which to publish the course of study?

The committee as a whole then deliberated on the "Eighteen Fundamental Questions on Curriculum-Making" that had been generated. This group work was important to Rugg in order to get a consensus about their final product. The General Statement that finally evolved from the committee consisted of twelve parts with the following headings:

General Statement

1. Introductory: The Next Practical Steps in Curriculum-Making

2. Curriculum-Construction in the Light of Both Study of Child Growth and the Effective Social Life

3. Curriculum-Making and the Scientific Study of Society

4. The School as a Conscious Agency for Social Improvement

5. The Curriculum and Social Integration

6. Changing Conceptions of Learning and of the Subject Material of the Curriculum

7. The Teacher's Need for an Outline of Desirable Experiences Planned in Advance

8. The Place of the School Subjects in Instruction

9. Continuous and Comprehensive Curriculum-Study

10. Measuring the Outcomes of Instruction

11. The Role of Teacher-Training Institutions in the Reconstruction of the Curriculum

12. Problems of Administrative Adjustment in Curriculum-Making

Rugg indicated that arriving at these twelve statements was far from an easy task. The most difficulty the committee had was lack of a common vocabulary, which led to misunderstandings and frustrations. Through the round tables, the members of the committee established a vocabulary that was understood by all. The second problem the committee faced was the lack of synthesis of ideas. Members automatically divided into camps, defending and attacking ideas. The major debate occurred between the child-growth advocates and the preparation-for-life proponents. After considerable debate, the committee recognized that both points of view were valid and important.

All committee members agreed that teachers needed curriculum guidelines that should be done in the form of an outline to provide teachers with the freedom to modify them to meet the special needs of his or her classroom. The final revelation for the committee members resided in the reality that what they were creating was a "platform of practical forward steps in curriculum-making…to fit the difficult administrative conditions of public education, namely, large classes, wide individual differences, heavy teaching programs, inadequate facilities, [and] lack of well-trained teachers"[8]. These statements were not perceived to be policy or mandates.

Although the committee members agreed on the general statement and its components given above, they each had the opportunity to share their personal perspectives on the statement's components in subsequent chapters of the yearbook. George Works of Cornell University and Frederick Kelly of the University of Minnesota chose not to respond to the general statement. W.W. Charters of the University of Chicago, responded by indicating that he " [had] nothing to add by way of elaboration. . . . I am in substantial agreement. . . . The validity of specific points on which I may differ from my colleagues may well wait until it is settled by scientific techniques."[9]

The remaining nine committee members each wrote a response to the statement indicating their support while highlighting issues they were particularly biased towards. For example, Bagley emphasized the need to consider a core curriculum because of the highly mobile society to ensure a "nucleus of a common culture for children of the nation."[10] Bobbitt addressed his concern that the statement overlooked the importance of curriculum making for the individual. His belief was that "education should be administered with a view to giving individuals of whatever age the greatest possible amount of individual freedom, so long as this freedom is accompanied by sense of responsibility."[11]

Counts' reaction was the acknowledgement of school as a social institution, but he raised concern about the interpretation of curriculum making designed around students' interests. Specifically, he stated, "Nothing should be included in the curriculum merely because it is of interest to children; but whatever is included should be brought into the closest possible relation with their interests."[12] He was also concerned about the increasing support of scientific method in curriculum making and warned, "The fundamental goals of education cannot be determined by scientific method. They are the product of a process of evaluation which, while dependent on the results of science, cannot be identified with those results."[13]

William Kilpatrick of Teachers College, Columbia University indicated that he was extreme in his viewpoints, "deviating the most from the present practices [of curriculum making]."[14] He agreed to the general statement because he was participatory in the process and believed that "[the statement] will improve upon what now generally prevails and that we shall then be in position to go on faster and farther to the better things that lie still beyond."[15] He proceeded to launch into a thorough discussion of what he perceived to be the curriculum making process.

Rugg, along with his colleagues, substantially supported the general statement of curriculum making. However, he recognized that the general statement was a compromise of ideas and identified crucial issues important to him. These issues positioned him as a proponent of overarching reform of education.

Rugg chose to comment on what he saw as six problems in the general statement, outlining the following:

(1) The school curriculum needed a radical reconstruction, not a refinement of existing subjects.

In the general version of the report, the committee indicated that what was needed in curriculum was only a refinement and revision of existing subjects and activities. Rugg, however, argued that refinement and revision were not sufficient to bridge the rift between the existing curriculum and the existing society. He stated:

> The content of the school must be constructed out of the very materials of the American life – not from academic relics of Victorian precedents. The curriculum must bring children to close grip with the roar and steely clang of industry, with the great integrated structure of American business, and must prepare them in sympathy and tolerance to confront the underlying forces of political and economic life. Young America must awake to the newly emerging culture of industrialism and she must become articulate.[16]

He advocated that useless information be discarded and argued for the incorporation of major social issues. He believed that students should be taught through cooperative methods and should develop global ideas to maximize their understanding of the role of American society in the world.

For him, the "encyclopedic treatment of content" was not sufficient to develop the deep understanding needed by the students.

(2) Reconstruction needed to be based on comprehensive and scientific study of society with an emphasis on adult society and the interests and doings of children.

At the time of this report there were two opposing positions related to curriculum construction: that which was geared toward preparation for adult life and that which focused on the interests and natural activities of children. To Rugg, there was no either/or decision between the two. The choice had to be based on data from the society as well as from the psychology of child development. He commented, "The data from adult life will go far to determine what is of permanent value; the data from child life will go far to determine what is appropriate for education in each stage of the child's development."[17]

(3) The first steps in reconstruction needed to be a new synthesis of knowledge and the redepartmentalization of activities and materials of the school.

Rugg perceived the American curriculum as being piecemeal and the subjects as being narrow academic compartments of knowledge. To understand life, students cannot operate with disconnected pieces of information, but need to see the larger picture. He wrote: "Only one criterion should be permitted to dominate the organization of the materials of instruction: learning, not subject-matter sequence or authentication."[18] This new knowledge, according to Rugg, will be based on natural relationships inherent in actual adult society and on the ability of the school to structure activities that have a real-life reality to the learner.

(4) The printed word needed to be emphasized, particularly in light of the growing popularity of the child-activity curriculum.

Rugg saw the ability to generalize, draw inferences, and make conclusions as necessary mental equipment to survive in the modern world. He was concerned that the child-centered curriculum as applied in many schools lacked substance and was devoid of the richness of the stories that could be found in all disciplines.

> The bare facts of the curriculum—dead prosaic sorts of things—will be woven into vital accounts of the interplay of human beings upon each other. Concepts (for example, Nationalism, Democracy, Interdependence, the Standard of Living, Imperialism)—cues to understanding—acquire rich meanings only through the study of cases, episodes, and concrete situations.[19]

(5) Curriculum needed to be planned in outline form in advance and could not be made on the spot.The bare facts of the curriculum—dead prosaic sorts of things—will be woven into vital accounts of the interplay of human beings upon each other. Concepts (for example, Nationalism, Democracy, Interdependence, the Standard of Living, Imperialism)—cues to understanding—acquire rich meanings only through the study of cases, episodes, and concrete situations.[19]

Rugg was concerned about "administrative handicaps" that he defined as mass education, the wide range of individual differences in the classrooms, and teachers who were not well prepared in both child learning and the great issues of society. He wrote:

> For the most effective use of school time an in order to guarantee maximal growth, the constructive social and creative activities as well as the correlative skills should be charted, written down, both in broad outline and in some detail. . . This does not mean, of course, that a rigid scheme of subject matter will be given to the teacher to be learned verbatim by the pupils.[20]

He perceived these courses of study to be guides from which the teachers could choose activities to meet the needs and abilities of their students. The teachers could be assured that these suggested activities would be appropriately developed since the activities would have been scientifically designed by a wide range of specialists. The choices of the teachers would produce the needed outcomes for their students.

(6) Tasks of curriculum making are difficult and can be carried out effectively only by professionally equipped specialists.

Rugg felt strongly that curriculum making had to be a collaborative effort. His perception of curriculum designers was that no one individual person could possibly have all the expertise necessary to develop the curriculum for all children at all levels in all subjects. He wanted curriculum to be a product of a collaborative effort of several specialists, including teachers, school administrators, psychologists, sociologists, professors, and others. The curriculum planners must be persons of

> broad background, rich experience, and special training in the human and physical sciences . . . must also have a critical understanding both of childhood and of society . . .and must become a student[s] of learning . . . must solve a host of puzzling problems of great placement and organization . . . the General Statement, there-

fore, in my judgment should have made more emphatic the doctrine that curriculum-making demands the cooperation of several specialists. This generalization has hardly been grasped at all as yet.[21]

In summary, Rugg supported the NSSE general statement. His strong belief that curriculum making needed to force the schools to prepare the students for an ever-changing society went beyond the general thinking of the committee. In his mind, students needed skills and understandings very different from what had been traditionally offered by the curriculum of the schools. The skills and understandings that Rugg supported would be determined by a thorough scientific study of the complexity of the American society and its place in the world.

Rugg's vision was obviously influenced by his personal experiences. He was not trained as an educator nor had he taught except at the university prior to going to the Lincoln School of Teachers College in 1920. In fact, Rugg was trained initially in engineering, and later in psychology and statistics. His advocacy of the scientific approach to curriculum planning and child-centeredness grew out of his background in these three disciplines. Rugg stated: "As an engineer, habituated to meeting situations as problems and to design before building, I tended naturally to regard curriculum instruction as a technological process, not an act of sentiment or evangelical faith."[22]

During his tenure as the educational psychologist for Lincoln School, Rugg honed his ideas about curriculum making. There he had the resources to put his ideas into practice. Given that he perceived curriculum making as a task based upon research and multiple perspectives, he established a team of researchers and formulated procedures for conducting the necessary research. His researchers were to

1. find the problems and issues of modern social life;
2. find the particular questions that had to be answered in order to consider all the various angles of the problems;
3. select typical episodes that illustrate the more important points to be made, collect the facts in narrative, descriptive, graphic, pictorial, or statistical form that were needed to discuss the questions and problems;
4. clarify and fix the essential matters, to discover the basic generalizations that guide our thinking about society.[23] These procedures formulated the pattern of curriculum making that Rugg followed throughout his career as a curriculum theorist.

CLARIFYING ISSUES AND CONCERNS
OF THE RECONSTRUCTIONISTS

The reconstructionists brought a fresh vision to the field of curriculum. According to Kenneth Benne,[24]

> The distinctiveness of the Social Reconstructionists in education was their advocacy of a central role for programs and policies of educational institutions in achieving the deepening and extension of democratic values into the economic and social (ethnic, racial, and social class) relationships through participative planning.

Yet they faced difficulties in disseminating and implementing their vision. From outside the Reconstructionist camp, the advocacy for a reconstructed society did not set well with many educators, who viewed the position as too radical for the times and perhaps too close to Marxist ideology. In spite of opposition, Counts, Beard, Rugg, and others pursued in their push to reconstruct the school curriculum to become more aligned with the changing complex society.

Counts[25] believed that a reorganization of society was needed and that the schools could play an active role in such an endeavor. He challenged teachers to involve students in a curriculum designed to build a more just and equitable society. In order for students to do so, however, students needed to engage in critical analysis of society, searching for inequities and injustices, and exploring and proposing potential solutions to the problems. The difficulty with this approach to education was succinctly stated by Benne: "What will we do with unreconstructed adults while we use the education of the 'rising generation' as a major instrument in the refashioning of society?"[26] Within the Reconstructionist camp, differences in viewpoints also presented stumbling blocks. Although the broad goal of most Reconstructionists was to help students develop the necessary skills to function appropriately in a society that was becoming more diverse, intricate, and political, varying perspectives within the field often interfered with a clear dissemination of their ideas. Even variations in the use of vocabulary were not fully resolved by the leaders. For instance, Rugg and his colleagues struggled with clarity and consensus of language in writing the 26th NSSE Yearbook.

One example of the issues debated within the Reconstructionist camp was the meaning of indoctrination. The Reconstructionists were vehemently opposed to the notion of political indoctrination. Theodore Brameld pointed out, however, that "indoctrination of various kinds flourishes in the readily observed composition of moral codes, religious creeds, social folklore, and especially of attitudes and programs identified with the traditional ideology."[27] Brameld was adamant about the Social Reconstruction needed to facilitate the emergence of a new culture in light of growing poverty, crime, racial conflict, unemployment, wastefulness, and political unrest.[28] However, he recognized that such a change could not occur without some indoctrination of ideas and processes. The meaning of the term was never fully resolved and its use continued to cause controversy within and outside the Reconstructionist camp.

Another issue of debate within the Reconstructionist camp was the importance of and role of the individual. Although few would argue that the individual as learner was paramount in rethinking the curriculum, the focus of too much attention on students' individual interests as advocated by child-centered curricularists was impractical. Rather, curriculum and instruction were supposed to emphasize the social nature of the individual and the way in which that individual participates in society. Counts states:

> The choice is not between individualism and collectivism . . . [but] between two forms of collectivism: the one essentially democratic, the other feudal in spirit; the one devoted to the interest of the people, the other to the interests of the privileged class.[29]

Brameld believed that the school was the place for an individual to develop "as a social being and as a skilled planner of the society reality."[30] He iterated the necessity for the individual to recognize that his or her personal needs can only be satisfied through social consensus.[31]

Taking students' individual needs and desires into account in curriculum planning was fraught with ambiguities and conflicts. For example, should needs be defined as essential survival skills or as personal desires? If personal needs are to have an influence on curriculum decision making, Bode indicates that planners must distinguish between "good" and "bad" desires and between conflicting desires. Procedures must be in place to resolve and negotiate which needs should be addressed in the curriculum.[32] For example: Are basic needs the same for all people? Does culture play a role in personal needs? What if personal needs are in conflict with societal needs?

Rugg,[33] on the other hand, did not see any conflict between children's interests and abilities and the study of society. He recognized that both played a part in determining what ultimately was included in the curriculum and instruction of the school. He stated: "An orientation . . . which will encompass child interest and adult society will produce a sound foundation for the school curriculum."[34] He addressed the children's needs and interests very broadly, thus avoiding the issues raised by Bode.

Another issue that was a point of discussion among the Reconstructionists was the subject matter debate. Reconstructionists as a whole rejected the Traditionalists' emphasis on a single-subjects curriculum design. The disjointed study of subject matter was, in their eyes, ineffective in providing the learners with the necessary knowledge and skills to function in a rapidly changing society. Rugg[35] stated the issue clearly:

> The subjects are narrow academic compartments of knowledge. Representing bodies of technical facts and principles; they have been assembled for school use by specialists in subject matter. Their sponsors . . . are experts in research, documentation, and authentication. . . . If one views American life as a whole, and in the light of the composition of the curriculum of our great school system, one conclusion presses insistently: We must invent a new synthesis of knowledge and make it the basis of the entire school curriculum. The conventional barriers between existing subjects must be ignored in curriculum.

According to the Reconstructionists, the emphasis for the selection and organization of the materials for instruction should be on the learner, not the subject matter. This distinction was also important to the advocates of the child-centered curriculum and its variations. Their child-centered design placed strong emphasis on the student. Subject matter was introduced and integrated as students engaged in lessons focused on their experiences or identified social problems, and teachers and students together engaged in dialogue to ultimately determine what was worth learning. The perceived lack of structure to the child-centered curriculum, however, raised criticism from the Reconstructionists as well as from the Traditionalist camp. Yet the focus of how curriculum ought to be taught was very similar between the child-centered advocates and the Reconstructionists: the traditional subject-centered curriculum was inappropriate, inadequate, and indefensible considering the changing society.

THE DESIGN OF THE CURRICULUM

Given all the discussion related to what the curriculum should be and how it should be implemented in schools, it is difficult to specifically identify a set Reconstructionist curriculum. Reconstructionists' fundamental beliefs indicate that curriculum is based upon the present to influence the direction of the future. The design of the curriculum then must be organic rather than static. Also, according to Rugg,[36] the curriculum must be "designed directly from the culture" defined in "three phases—the external, physical civilization; the social institutions; and the underlying psychology." Rugg further stated:

To say with emphasis that the curriculum must be made directly from the culture of the people does not mean that the curriculum-designer is to base his program on adult life. It must be said with equal emphasis that the doings of 40,000,000 young Americans constitute an extremely vital part of the culture. In fact, from the standpoint of the organization of the educational enterprise, they are the most important part. It is the problems which the children and youths confront at any particular time and the interest which grip them, that must constitute the nuclear activities of the curriculum. These problems and interest emerge, of course, from a wider social context that has been adult-created and will continue to be adult-dominated. But the curriculum design must not fail to keep its perspective of the true role of children's and youths' problems and interests in such an adult-controlled world.[37]

Recognizing that the school itself is a small part of the total environment of the young child, Reconstructionists advocated for out-of-school as well as in-school experiences, and discouraged the "study about aspects of living to the exclusion of participation in actual situations."[38] Therefore, any statement of a Reconstructionist theory of curriculum can only be provided by a set of guidelines that

- adjust to social conditions of the times;
- engage learners in their learning;
- involve a continuous process of planning, not a "specified fixed course of study" or a "day-by-day opportunistic improvising of what to do"[39];
- address the "basic problems of actual cooperative living—health, leisure, work, conservation of material resources, effectiveness of human resources, and the like"[40];
- do not demote teachers to mere technicians.

Thus the reconstructionists reject both the Traditionalist theory of curriculum and the inappropriate implementation of the child-centered curriculum.

In 1939, Harold Rugg assembled yet another group of educators to write *Democracy and the Curriculum: The Life and Program of the American School*. The educators' ideas were certainly progressive and sympathetic to the views of the Reconstructionists. The writers included George Axtelle, Hollis Caswell, George Counts, Paul Hanna, Pickens Harris, L. Thomas Hopkins, William Kilpatrick, J. Paul Leonard, and Caroline Zachry. The book was written based upon the aims to

- aid in the understanding of democracy;

- emphasize how social intelligence has not kept pace with the problems of contemporary society;
- understand that a democratic government is based upon the consent of the people, which can only occur when the people are properly educated and recognize their role in a democratic society.

Hollis Caswell wrote the chapter on "The Design of the Curriculum." He starts by explaining the use of the word design to describe the curriculum planning process. Design was chosen because "it bridges the gap between theory and practice, for in evaluation of plans lies the intellectual testing of action by principle and idea."[41] Finding an appropriate dynamic design for curriculum construction is highly complex and without such a design, there is an inevitable gap between theory and practice. According to Caswell, theory and practice remain aloof from each other because most educators, philosophers, sociologists and psychologists theorize without first hand knowledge of actual school conditions and school practitioners have little time to reflect and theorize.[42]

Because the traditional curriculum was, according to Caswell and his colleagues, devoid of curriculum design the committee established several recommendations that if followed would create a better curriculum for American schools. Curriculum design

1. should be based upon continuous planning;
2. must take into account the stage of growth of each individual;
3. must be a function of the entire environment of the child inclusive of out-of-school activities and real activities, such as problem solving;
4. should be the reflection of "an ideal democratic community," so that students can learn first hand the skills and activities necessary to preserve democracy;
5. should provide an understanding of the problems of contemporary living and encourage students to participate in the solution to those problems, e.g., crime, labor management disputes, old age, homemaking, community planning, etc., through cooperative group action;
6. must provide both creative and recreational opportunities, particularly as leisure time is increasing. Extracurricular activities in school should not be a matter of choice or privileges, but an integral part of the school program;
7. must provide preparation for work, not for a specific job or occupation: "All phases of the curriculum should provide a variety of activities which permit the individual to discover special interests and aptitudes;"[43]

8. must provide the opportunity for students to learn through a variety of methods and techniques;

9. is dependent upon teachers' thinking. Teachers' understanding as to the purpose of the school, the nature of education and learning and the restrictions under which they work will ultimately determine how a curriculum design is implemented.

Although these guidelines may not be specific enough for some individuals to engage in curriculum planning or design, they are very reflective of the philosophy of the Reconstructionists. Curriculum design is based upon these principles; it is fluid, yet structured. Most importantly, curriculum design is a "function of the past and the future as much as the present, and all efforts must be made to bring the present into this perspective."[44]

The Reconstructionists' search for a common curriculum theory resulted in this set of usable guidelines. There was no attempt at establishing a specific curriculum based upon the guidelines as such an activity would have been counter to the beliefs and practices of the Reconstructionists.

APPLICATION TO CONTEMPORARY TIME

An examination of all the ideas, arguments, suggestion, and recommendations made by the Reconstructionists to change public education, simply reveal how little progress public education has made in rethinking how to educate today's children. Many of the concerns and arguments raised by the early Reconstructionists are alive and well in contemporary society. The population is increasingly diverse. Economic strains are evidenced by the closing of small business enterprises, the merging of multibillion-dollar businesses, and the increase in personal bankruptcy actions. The social ills of society are reflected in the rising crime rates in both small towns and large cities, the lack of medical care for huge numbers of today's middle class, lack of affordable housing for millions of Americans, and the growing divide between the haves and the have-nots. A large segment of the populace is unaware of their responsibilities in preserving our democracy—just look at the voting records over time. The curriculum of the schools is still piecemeal, disconnected, and inappropriate for today's problems. The likelihood of reforming or reconstructing public school curriculum in 2006 and beyond is negligible unless the public rethinks the purpose of American schools in light of the changing society.

The looming growth of poverty, crime, urban blight, unemployment, technology which dehumanizes much of the social interactions of a large segment of the population, social injustices, and the involvement of the United States in a global war is reflective of many of the issues raised by the reconstructionists. Today's Reconstructionist voices, e.g., Michael Apple, are rarely heard above the cry for more control and restrictions in our schools in the name of quality education. Our schools are more controlled by state and federal government, by politicians who simply do not understand what schooling and education are all about. The schools are a far cry from what the Reconstructionists envisioned. They remain ineffective in preparing young citizens to solve the social problems they are confronting or will confront in the future. The public schools are disconnected to the reality of life experienced by most students enrolled in them, particularly in the inner cities. With the current emphasis and popularity of "reality TV," doesn't it seem ironic that our educational system cannot engage in "reality education"?

NOTES

1. George Counts, *Dare the School Build a New Social Order?* (Carbondale, IL: Southern Illinois University Press, 1932).

2. William Schubert, *Curriculum: Perspective, Paradigm, and Possibility.* (New York: Macmillan Publishing Company, 1986).

3. Harold Rugg, ed. *The Twenty-Sixth Yearbook of the National Society for the Study of Education: The Foundations and Techniques of Curriculum Construction.* (Bloomington, IL: Public School Publishing Company, 1926), vii.

4. Ibid., viii.

5. Ibid., ix.

6. Ibid., 4.

7. Ibid., 9-10.

8. Ibid., 6.

9. Werrett W. Charters, statement in Harold O. Rugg ed., *The Twenty-Sixth Yearbook of the National Society for the Study of Education:Part II. The Foundations and Techniques of Curriculum Making* (Bloomington, IL: Public School Publishing Company, 1926), 71.

10. William Bagley, supplemental statement in Harold O. Rugg, ed., *The Twenty-Sixth Yearbook of the National Society for the Study of Education: Part II. The Foundations and Technique of Curriculum Making* (Bloomington, IL: Public School Publishing Company, 1926), 33.

11. Franklin Bobbitt, "The Orientation of the Curriculum Maker," in Harold O. Rugg, ed., *The Twenty-Sixth Yearbook of the National Society for the Study of Education: Part II. The Foundations and Technique of Curriculum Making* (Bloomington IL: Public School Publishing Company, 1926), 71.

12. George Counts, "Some Notes on the Foundations of Curriculum Making." In Harold O. Rugg, ed., *The Twenty-Sixth Yearbook of the National Society for the Study of Education: Part II. The Foundations and Technique of Curriculum Making* (Bloomington, IL: Public School Publishing Company, 1926), 80.

13.   Ibid., 90.

14.   William Kilpatrick, State of Position, Harold O. Rugg, ed., *The Twenty-Sixth Yearbook of the National Society for the Study of Education: Part II. The Foundations and Technique of Curriculum Making* (Bloomington, IL: Public School Publishing Company, 1926), 119.

15.   Ibid., 120.

16.   Harold Rugg, (ed.), *The Twenty-Sixth Yearbook of the National Society for the Study of Education: The Foundations and Techniques of Curriculum Construction.* (Bloomington, IL: Public School Publishing Company, 1926), 149.

17.   Ibid., 151.

18.   Ibid., 155.

19.   Ibid., 157.

20.   Ibid., 159-160.

21.   Ibid., 162.

22.   Elmer Winters, "Man and His Changing Society: The Textbooks of Harold Rugg," *History of Education Quarterly,* 7 no. 4 (Winter 1967): 503; Harold Rugg, *That Men May Understand: An American in the Long Armistice* (New York, NY: Doubleday, Doran and Co., 1941), 216.

23.   Elmer Winters, "Man and His Changing Society: The Textbooks of Harold Rugg," *History of Education Quarterly.* 7 no. 4 (Winter 1967): 505.

24.   Kenneth Benne. In M. E. James, ed., *Social Reconstruction through Education: The Philosophy, History, and Curricula of a Radical Ideal* (Norwood, NJ: Ablex Publishing Corporation, 1995), xxiii.

25.   George Counts. *Dare the School Build a New Social Order?* (Carbondale, IL: Southern Illinois University Press, 1932).

26.   Kenneth Benne. In M.E. James, ed. *Social Reconstruction through Education: The Philosophy, History, and Curricula of a Radical Ideal* (Norwood, NJ: Ablex Publishing Corporation, 1995), xxvii.

27.   Theodore Brameld. *Toward a Reconstructed Philosophy of Education* (New York, NY: Holt, Rinehart and Winston, 1971), 470.

28.   Allan Ornstein and Francis Hunkins. *Curriculum Foundations, Principles and Issues,* 3rd Edition. (Needham Heights, MA: Allyn and Bacon, 1998).

29.   George Counts. *Dare the School Build a New Social Order?* (Carbondale, IL: Southern Illinois University Press, 1932), 49.

30.   Allan Ornstein and Francis Hunkins, *Curriculum Foundations, Principles and Issues* 3rd Edition (Needham Heights, MA: Allyn and Bacon, 1998), 262.

31.   *Ibid.*

32.   Boyd Bode. *Progressive Education at the Crossroads.* (New York, NY: Newson & Co., 1938).

33.   Harold Rugg, ed. *The Twenty-Sixth Yearbook of the National Society for the Study of Education: The Foundations and Techniques of Curriculum Construction* (Bloomington, IL: Public School Publishing Company, 1926).

34.   Ibid., 151.

35.   Ibid., 154–155.

36.   Harold Rugg, ed. *Democracy and Curriculum: The Life and Program of the American School.* (New York, NY: Appleton-Century Company, Inc., 1939), 6.

37.   *Ibid.*, 7.

38.   Hollis Caswell, "Developing the Design of the Curriculum," in Harold Rugg, ed., *Democracy and the Curriculum: The Life and Program of the American School.* (New York, NY: Appleton-Century Company, Inc., 1939), 418.

39.   *Ibid.*, 414.

40.   *Ibid.*, 412.

41.   Hollis Caswell, "The Design of the Curriculum," in Harold Rugg ed., *Democracy and Curriculum: The Life and Program of the American School.* (New York, NY: Appleton-Century Company, Inc, 1939), 406.

42.   Ibid., 411.

43.   Ibid., 429.

44.   Ibid., 433.

REFERENCES

The early Reconstructionists would be extremely disappointed in the lack of progress made by our public schools in designing curricula that would assure the children of a brighter, more exciting, and democratic future.

William C. Bagley, "Supplemental statement." The twenty-sixth yearbook of the National Society for the Study of Education: Part II. The foundations and technique of curriculum making ed. Harold Rugg (Bloomington, IL:Public School Publishing Company, 1926) 29–40.

Kenneth Benne, "Preface." Social Reconstruction through Education: The philosophy, History, and Curricula of a Radical Ideal. ed. M. E. James (Norwood, NJ: Ablex Publishing Corporation, 1995), xxi-xxviii.

Franklin Bobbitt, "The Orientation of the Curriculum Maker." The Twenty-Sixth Yearbook of the National Society for the Study of Education: Part II. The Foundations and Technique of Curriculum Making ed. HaroldRugg (Bloomington, IL: Public School Publishing Company, 1926), 41–56.

Boyd Bode, Progressive education at the crossroads. (NY: Newson & Co., 1938)

Theodore Brameld, Toward a Reconstructed Philosophy of Education (New York, NY: Holt, Rinehard & Winston, 1971).

Hollis Caswell, "Developing the design of the curriculum." Democracy and the Curriculum: The Life and Program of the American School ed. Harold Rugg (New York, NY: Appleton-Century Company, Inc, 1939), 406–434.

Werrett Charters, "Statement." The Twenty-Sixth Yearbook of the National Society for the Study of Education: Part II. The Foundations and Technique of Curriculum Making ed. Harold Rugg (Bloomington, IL: Public School Publishing Company, 1926), 71.

George Counts, "Some Notes on the Foundations of Curriculum Making." The Twenty-Sixth Yearbook of the National Society for the Study of Education: Part

II. The Foundations and Technique of Curriculum Making ed Harold Rugg (Bloomington IL: Public School Publishing Company, 1926), 73–90.

George Counts, Dare the School Build a New Social Order? (Carbondale, IL: Southern Illinois University Press, 1932).

William Kirkpatrick, "Statement of Position." The Twenty-Sixth Yearbook of the National Society for the Study of Education: Part II. The Foundations and Ttechnique of Curriculum Making ed. Harold Rugg (Bloomington IL: Public School Publishing Company, 1926), 110–146.

Allan Ornstein and Francis Hunkins, Curriculum Foundations, Principles and Issues. (3rd Ed.) (Needham Heights, MA: Allyn and Bacon, 1998).

Harold Rugg, (ed.) The Twenty-Sixth Yearbook of the National Society for the Study of Education: The Foundations and Techniques of Curriculum Construction. (Bloomington, IL: Public School Publishing Company, 1926).

Harold Rugg, (ed). Democracy and curriculum: The Life and Program of the American School. (New York, NY: Appleton-Century Company, Inc., 1939).

Harold Rugg, That Men May Understand: An American in the Long Armistice. (New York, NY: Doubleday, Doran & Co., 1941).

William Schubert, Curriculum: Perspective ,Paradigm, and Possibility. (New York, NY: Macmillan Publishing Company, 1986).

Elmer Winters, "Man and His Changing Society: The Textbooks of Harold Rugg," History of Education Quarterly, 7 (Winter 1967): 493–514.

CHAPTER 11

SOCIAL RECONSTRUCTION IN EDUCATION

Searching Out Black Voices

William H. Watkins

INTRODUCTION

The Social Reconstruction movement of the 1930s was one of the most provocative and fascinating educational protest movements of the early twentieth century.[1] In broad terms, it connected education to the class struggle. Historically, it forever connected schooling to social protest.

The loose assemblage of university professors, teachers, school reformers, iconoclastic intellectuals, Progressives, Marxists-Leninists, (anti-Communist) socialists, and assorted radicals made for an interesting adventure in dissent. Although short-lived, this educational "movement" took up highly volatile and super-charged political issues of power, property, wealth distribution, knowledge selection, and societal reform as few other groups of educators, before or after, have dared.

The connection of African Americans to the Social Reconstructionist movement in the late 1920s and 30s is not clearly defined. Did the Reconstructionists reach out to African Americans? Did African Americans reach

Social Reconstruction: People, Politics, Perspectives, pages 211–234
Copyright © 2006 by Information Age Publishing
All rights of reproduction in any form reserved.

out to them? Was there a Reconstructionist response to the great racial dilemmas of the day, including American apartheid, lynching, race riots, and the Scottsboro Boys incident? What were Reconstructionist reactions to the racial scholarship of the time?

Clearly the race problem was not central in the writings, journals, and speeches of the Reconstructionists but neither was it absent. Several Reconstructionists or Frontiersmen, notably Harold Rugg, demonstrated interest in the "Negro question." Prominent African American scholars, discussed later, contributed articles to the Social Frontier, journal of the Reconstructionist movement. Of greater importance, African American theorists, such as W.E.B. Du Bois expressed views nearly identical to those of the Frontiersmen. Although we cannot make unimpeachable assertions linking the Social Reconstructionists to African Americans, the race problems or the "black liberation movement," we can identify some interesting connections for further consideration.

Since Reconstruction, educational dissent has become central in social protest.[2] This inquiry illustrates that notion. The discussion will move from the general to the particular. We will first explore the origins of Social Reconstructionism, summarizing the broad ideological platform of the movement. Second, we will illuminate the views of selected Reconstructionists on matters of race. The core of the work will explore Reconstructionist connections to the race issue and parallel Reconstructionist views that emerged among some African Americans.

SOCIAL RECONSTRUCTIONISM: THE SOCIAL AND POLITICAL CONTEXT

By the turn of the twentieth century several interconnected theaters of dissent were percolating in American society. Notable among them were concerns about corporate abuse, labor unrest, and the race problem. Each had expression and articulation in the social discourse and protest thought of the time.

Both reform-minded social scientists and elements of the popular media expressed concern about the inequities and impersonal nature of the intensifying corporate industrial organization of society. Thorstein Veblen's 1899 Theory of the Leisure Class[3] along with essays by muckraking journalists dramatized social and economic problems in the midst of plenty. An emerging Progressive movement with its themes of democracy, humanism, and social reform profoundly impacted the political environment.

Throughout the nation harsh working conditions, low wages, and intense exploitation were giving rise to worker unrest, strikes, and union organizing. Boyer & Morais described the activities of the Industrial Workers of the World (Wobblies), voices in labor dissent, as the following:

> The Wobblies probably never had more than 60,000 active members but they influenced millions as they moved into strike situations all over the country from McKees Rocks, PA., and Skowhegan, Maine, to Goldfield, Nev., and Portland, Ore. And as they led the huge mass strikes they were forever talking of one big union, of solidarity, of one for all and all for one; forever declaring that the working class, those who did the nation's work, should own the nation's industries.[4]

Within race relations, the promises of the post Civil War period had all but vanished. Harsh treatment, rigid segregation, and lynching threatened racial peace and endangered the politics of accomodationism. The demands for racial inclusion coming from civil rights activists, such as the participants of the Niagara Movement, alongside the demands for separation coming from Garveyism, established popular ideological platforms for a century of race dissent.

Joined by movements for women's rights, immigrant inclusion and environmentalism, a scattered, disparate twentieth-century protest ideology began to crystallize.

POLITICS, EDUCATION, AND RACE: CONVERGING DISSENT

Early twentieth-century industrial capitalism found corporate hegemonists using their wealth and the legal-legislative political bureaucracy to influence public policy and the political culture in new ways. Powerful forces shaped a stratified labor market, apartheidist race relations, and a system of public education which ideologically supported the corporate order.[5] The new corporatism called for a scientific society where managed social change, gradualism, and parliamentarianism would prevail over anger and radical insurgency. Corporate hegemonists desired class peace, efficiency, stability, and peaceful race relations.

Within education, dissatisfaction was becoming evident at several different levels. Deweyian progressivism opposed the scientific efficiency, essentialism, and rigidity of the time. Simultaneously Du Bois[6] was expanding his political and racial critique to include the "training" of black Americans. Interestingly, both Dewey and Du Bois were profoundly influenced by Charles Pierce and the European pragmatists. Strict segregation dictated two separate racial traditions in education. Black and white schools had separate curricula, different funding sources and different practices.[7]

While both Dewey and Du Bois favored "liberal" education, their critiques had separate platforms. Both would, however, reflect the emerging Social Reconstructionism.

PROGRESSIVE EDUCATION AND NEW STRIDENT VOICES

With John Dewey as one of its principal theoreticians, progressive education criticized mechanism, the efficiency movement, and the impersonal nature of education.[8] It offered new approaches to understanding the child, curriculum, and the processes of education. Progressive education gave us the "cult of the child." Through its organizational arm, the Progressive Education Association (PEA), progressive educators promoted child-centered education. They championed the rights of children and insisted that the fundamental interests of the learner be recognized. Dewey posited that the experience of the community should be the subject matter of education and that school ought to be the community in embryo. Progressive rhetoric talked of the whole child and working to create fully humanized individuals.

While progressive education made its influence felt in the post World War I period, the Progressive Education Association (PEA) was never a strong centralized organization. It had no single voice[9] and was always numerically inferior to the larger National Education Association (NEA). By the mid 1930s the intellectual climate of the country took a noticeable turn to the left. The social criticism of the early nineteen hundreds expanded. A significant section of the intelligentsia and politically conscious populace began to question the moral worth of the capitalist system insisting that human rights take priority over property rights. The educational community could not remain outside this discourse.

A discernibly dissident group began to make their voices heard from within the PEA. One rallying point for this group was the report of the Commission on the Social Studies within the American Historical Association.[10] The report, funded by the Carnegie Foundation, was presented in seventeen volumes between the years 1932 and 1937. Among those who contributed to the project were well known educators and social theorists like Charles A. Beard, Merle Curti, George S. Counts, and Jesse Newlon. The report both provoked and polarized.[11]

The year 1932 became eventful for this dissident group to become known as Social Reconstructionists or Social Frontiersmen. While the PEA remained committed to child-centered education, the Reconstructionists wanted more of Progressivism than the exaltation of the child. They wanted education to feature a "social point of view," that is, a descriptive and prescriptive examination of social problems.

When George S. Counts of the University of Chicago delivered his attention-getting lecture "Dare Progressive Education Be Progressive?" to the PEA in April 1932, the new movement took on identity. Counts criticized the Progressive Education movement as one of middle class dilettantes. He stated:

> The great weakness of Progressive Education lies in the fact that it has elaborated no theory of social welfare, unless it be that of anarchy or extreme individualism. In this, of course, it is but reflecting the viewpoint of the members of the liberal-minded upper middle class. . . .[12]

Further in this lecture, which was greeted by a stunned silence that sent shockwaves through the Progressive education community, he suggested that these Progressives were romantic sentimentalists not interested in addressing the economic and social crises. He called on Progressive educators to

> face squarely and courageously every social issue, come to grips with life in all of its stark reality, establish an organic relation with the community, develop a realistic and comprehensive theory of welfare, fashion a compelling and challenging vision of human destiny, and become somewhat less frightened than it is today at the bogeys of imposition and indoctrination.[13]

Counts continued on to speak about how our competitive capitalist society "must be replaced by cooperation" and "some form of socialized economy." This blockbuster lecture along with two others, "Freedom, Culture, Social Planning, and Leadership" and "Education Through Indoctrination," were issued in what R. Freeman Butts [14] called "perhaps the most widely discussed pamphlet in the history of American education, "Dare the School Build a New Social Order?"[15] In this work, which became the blueprint for Social Reconstructionism, Counts challenged the educational community to bridge the gap between school and society where schools create a vision of a new world based on the principles of collectivism.

The works of Counts in 1932, combined with the publication of the Commission on the Social Studies in the Schools' "A Charter for the Social Sciences in the Schools" (1932) drafted by Charles A. Beard,[16] served as a unifying framework to bring together such individuals as William Heard Kilpatrick, John L. Childs, R. Bruce Raup, and Harold Rugg. Additionally, other well-known progressives like John Dewey and Boyd H. Bode were attracted to the call of the Reconstructionists.

SOCIAL RECONSTRUCTIONISM:
AN EDUCATIONAL AND POLITICAL PROGRAM

While the dissident Social Reconstructionists remained within the PEA and enjoyed a measure of support it became clear that they had a different focus. In an effort to respond to the insurgents, particularly Counts, the PEA in 1932 established the Committee on Social and Economic Problems. This committee served to rally the Reconstructionists and further split the ranks of the PEA. Between 1932 and 1934 the Reconstructionist position became more clearly defined and more radical. Two more books joined the essays of Counts to advance their cause. One, A Call to the Teachers of the Nation [17] written by the PEA's Committee on Social and Economic Problems, summoned teachers to act, while the second, The Educational Frontier,[18] edited and partially written by the respected William Heard Kilpatrick, called for the politicalization of education. The Social Reconstructionists now had their own identity.

As the Reconstructionists more forcefully asserted their position, the larger sentiment within the PEA began to assert itself. Though still not tightly administered, the PEA focused its commitment and its journal, Progressive Education, on child-centered classroom techniques. Experiencing increased difficulties getting published,[19] the Reconstructionists founded their own journal, The Social Frontier, which first appeared in October, 1934. Now they could continue to develop their distinctive position. The "hard-core" of the Reconstructionists, that is, Sidney Hook, Counts, Harold Rugg, Jesse Newlon, Goodwin Watson, and John Childs,[20] best articulated their views.

Three socio-political and educational propositions formed the foundation of Social Reconstructionism.The first is the advocacy of a "collectivist" society. The capitalist system was seen as the source of human misery, unemployment, and divisiveness. Capitalism was to be replaced by "economic collectivism." Though Hook was a Marxist and Counts spoke of his serious study of Karl Marx, the beliefs and language of the Reconstructionists seldom suggested the "proletarian" revolution Marx had called for. The Reconstructionists instead spoke of evolutionary change. They, in fact, suggested that, given New Deal politics and the intellectual climate, the country had already evolved into an era of economic collectivism. For them, a benevolent and democratic socialist collectivism represented desirable social development. A redistribution of the wealth and resources would allow public morality and cooperation to reshape society.

Second, the Reconstructionists called for linking education with (collectivist) political ideology. They believed the attainment of a truly progressive society required an expanded role for education. Treating children humanely was fine but education must take on a major role in the plan to transform society. Education must be utilized to transform social institutionsand should be viewed as a form of social action. Schools must take an active role in determining the new social order.

Third, schools should participate in reshaping society to realize education's true mission. Kilpatrick[21] argued that the worn socioeconomic system was making it difficult for schools to produce worthy citizens. Schools should foster a broader social responsibility and work for the common good. By helping to transform laissez-faire capitalism, education could help make society more humane. Education should be at the cutting edge of civilization. In short, the process of schooling should be inextricably linked to social progress.

THE ROLE OF THE TEACHER

Among the most intriguing formulations presented by the Reconstructionists were their views on the role of the teacher. If education was to play a key role in changing the old social and economic order as well as an expanded role in the new collectivist order, educators could not remain neutral. John Dewey, in the pages of the Social Frontier, wrote of teachers as active participants in a new social order. Counts exhorted teachers to mobilize themselves into an activist force and take sides in the struggle to forge a new collectivist society.

Interestingly, the hard-core Reconstructionists clung to an optimistic yet unfounded hope that teachers would quickly adopt the Reconstructionist program as their own. As it turned out, this was to be a gross miscalculation emanating from an exaggerated reading of the political climate and a misreading of the social consciousness of the 10,000 teachers who were to serve as a core and the one million teachers they hoped to inspire.

Counts hoped that every teacher would be an agent for change. He suggested that teachers continue to unionize themselves and join ranks with the disaffected radical labor movement at large. Teachers should fight for social progress and reform both in the street as well as the classroom. In the January 1935 issue of Social Frontier, the editorial board articulated this position statement:

> The Social Frontier consequently proposes to the teachers of the country that they ally themselves with that conception of social welfare which may be expected to serve the many rather than the few–that they strive to substitute human for property rights, a democratic collectivism for an oligarchic individualism in economy, social planning and security for anarchy and chaos. Positively and consistently they should seek to develop in the population those values, attitudes, ideals, and loyalties consonant with the new way of life, as well

as habits of thought and action calculated to bring that way of life into being.[22]

REMAKING THE CURRICULUM

If education was going to significantly contribute to social change, schools must necessarily adopt a curriculum sufficiently critical of the old social order while supportive of the new collectivism. The Social Reconstructionists called on the curriculum community to support wholesale change in curriculum materials, activities, and outlooks.

A leading curriculum theoretician among the Reconstructionists was Prof. Harold Rugg of Teachers College, Columbia University. Long committed to change, Rugg, in The Scientific Method in the Reconstruction of Elementary and Secondary School Subjects,[23] argued for a curriculum that would combine critical socio-political inquiry with the life's experience of the learner. Above all, Rugg wanted to guarantee that any new curriculum was pedagogically sound. In the early 1920s Rugg began to publish his own social studies pamphlets. In his series, published by Ginn, entitled "Man and His Changing Society," Rugg offered a comprehensive social science curriculum based on democratic and humanistic values.

In the October 1936 issue of Social Frontier, Rugg challenged "commissioners, presidents, deans, superintendents, principals, supervisors, teachers . . . to stir the mass into action!"[24] Rugg went on to blast "professional Directors of Curriculum and a powerful behind-the-scenes body of textbook writers and publishers who have controlled the program of American education . . . primarily in the interest of the status quo."[25]

In his blueprint for a new curriculum Rugg suggested that schools focus on the "Social Scene," a "new psychology," and a "syllabi of activities and materials directly out of the crucial conditions, problems and issues of our changing social order."[26] He advocated confronting controversial issues, exploring alternative decision making, and teaching the basic issues of civilization in the classrooms.

THE END OF AN ERA

Nineteen thirty-four to thirty-five was a peak period for these Social Frontiersmen. However, by 1936 their unresolved internal contradictions could no longer be ignored. A shifting national and international mood revealed fissures in the movement. Although the Social Frontier had between 5,000 and 10,000 subscribers at varying times and claimed among its editorial board and spokespeople some of the most influential educational theorists in the country, its leaders could never agree on a single platform that could bind the movement. By 1936 the difficulties became glaring.

First, the issue of "indoctrination" would not die. Counts, all along, had held that the dominant "elite" groups exerted a monopoly on indoctrination in the schools and perhaps it was time that another voice was heard. Eventually detractors asserted that Counts wanted to brainwash students.

Second, and more important, by 1936, John Dewey and Boyd Bode, never fully in the radical camp, reaffirmed their commitment to experimentalism and Progressivism. Bode argued that schools were not the proper place to evolve public policy. Dewey, now no longer interested in radical Reconstructionist initiatives, turned his attention to a critical analysis of the pedagogy of Robert Maynard Hutchins.

As the Reconstructionists lost momentum, the newly formed John Dewey Society began to attract many of the old forces and actually absorbed the Social Frontier. During the war years a few halfhearted efforts were undertaken, particularly by Rugg, to rekindle the old vigor but without much success. By the mid-1950s even the PEA was in mortal decline.As the war years approached, radicalism gave way to patriotism. The fascist menace was so threatening it became the priority for conservatives and socialists alike. The resignation of Counts from the Social Frontiers editorial board in 1937 signaled the beginning of the end.

It can be concluded that the Social Reconstruction movement was very much a product of its time. While it attracted the attention of significant educational and curriculum thinkers, it never became the hoped-for mass movement of teachers. Energetic, though short lived, this body of thought left its indelible imprint on educational theorizing and curriculum reform. After World War II scattered efforts, such as the work of Theodore Brameld [27], the Society for Educational Reconstruction, and other individuals have kept this once lively movement in our memory.

Where did African Americans fit in the grand plans of the Reconstructionists to fashion a new world? The "Negro question" had emerged to significance long before the movement of Social Reconstructionism. How did they address it both as individuals and collectively?

HAROLD RUGG ON RACE

As mentioned, the race problem was not prominent in the writings of the Frontiersmen, however, Harold Rugg among others offered some thoughts in this area. Since this writing did not emanate from the Social Frontier editorial board, it cannot be viewed as collectively agreed upon, but rather a sample of sentiment.

As a central figure in the Reconstructionist movement, Rugg's writings on race cannot be ignored. His most developed essay on the subject, a book chapter, did not appear until 1955.[28] This is noteworthy because the influence of the Frontiersman had long ago waned while the modern Civil Rights Movement was now beginning to stir. Rugg offers no explanation of the timing except to note that discrimination and violence continue to plague the land and America must redress this problem if she is become a beacon of democracy for the world. Rugg (and Wither's) essay is entitled "Racial and Social Conflict in America."

The conceptual and contextual framework for this work is revealing. They introduce the chapter offering the contentious immigrant thesis. America was a country founded by disparate groups all fighting for their piece of the pie. They write:

> Rivalries, jealousies, and distinctions of rank-order developed in every phase of the culture. Economic rivalries developed for land and trade, wealth and comfort. Political rivalries developed for office-holding and control of parties and governments, social rivalries for prestige in community and national life, religious rivalries for the advancement of the contending churches-each for the supremacy of its special Word. Thus, disunity entered because of conflicts affecting every phase of the culture-economic, political, social, and religious.[29]

The essay then moves to a sociological discussion of race myth. Noting the Nordic supremacy arguments of Degobineau,[30] Rugg (and Withers) points to the counter discourses of Boas,[31] Ruth Benedict[32] and Otto Klineberg,[33] who all presented anthropological and sociological research attacking supremacy notions. Finally, the chapter ends with a concluding paragraph suggesting that Blacks, Catholics, Jews, Chinese, liberals, and others have been historically scapegoated in American national life.

While Rugg's analysis was politically correct for that time, it was at best shallow. Rugg had decades of Black protest thought and literature to draw upon. Certainly the strident protests activities of Du Bois, Marcus Garvey and other voices were known to all. Even the voices of black democratic socialist labor people, for example, A. Phillip Randolph and Bayard Rustin should have resonated with Rugg. More importantly, Rugg failed to connect the race problem to capitalist expropriation and labor economics.

Meanwhile, it can be argued that African Americans, in the first half of the twentieth century were evolving their own kindred version of Social Reconstructionism parallel to the more organized version. Du Bois' early educational polemics offers an example.

W.E.B. DU BOIS:
BLACK SOCIAL RECONSTRUCTIONIST EDUCATOR

Traditional educational scholarship has for too long overlooked the historical evolution of the "radical" black theorizing. More importantly, critical black pedagogy has often been viewed narrowly as protest thought. While there can be no doubt that the policies and practices of a racialized society have shaped black intellectual life, there remains a body of inquiry which needs further examination.

Black and white dissent have been as disconnected as black and white history. Typically the white radical intelligentsia is seen to be concerned with sweeping economic, political, and social change while black radical thinkers are associated exclusively with Black liberation. Without question there is a Black radical tradition within the education dialogue. W.E.B. Du Bois is a pioneer in that movement.

Though known in academia since the turn of the twentieth century, Du Bois has never been considered a force in the education or curriculum dialogue. While he lived through and was influenced by sweeping social transformations such as the Progressive movement and the radicalism of the 1930s, seldom is his contribution included as a factor in the discourse of his day. We have not yet come to fully appreciate or understand the work of this man who was so passionately concerned with the aims of education. [34]

If we proclaim Du Bois as the father of radical black educational theorizing, it can be said that his is an outgrowth of late nineteenth-century sociological inquiry. Pioneer black scholars such as George Washington Williams [35] and T. T. Fortune [36] early on examined the conditions of blacks in the reconstructed south. Du Bois, committed to activism and social change, linked social criticism to the emerging examination of black life. Armed with an education from Fisk, Harvard, and the University of Berlin, Du Bois was well prepared to take his place as a social theorist, critic, and radical educator. The educational views of Du Bois should be examined within the context of his time in order to understand their true impact.

The Progressives advanced a new examination and critique of the dynamics of schooling. They began to look at school as a social and political construct. The more radical Progressives began to explain schooling in terms of power and ideology. They viewed schools as linked to dominant political and economic ideologies, that is, the corporate state and its narrow objectives. It was at this chronological and political juncture that the interests of Du Bois overlapped the Progressive educational community in general and the Social Reconstructionists in particular.

DU BOIS AND SOCIAL RECONSTRUCTIONISM:
COMMON ORIGINS, COMMON VIEWS

Though the Social Reconstructionists never claimed Du Bois nor did he claim them, they were undeniably linked by virtue of their history, pedagogy, and views on the nature of society, socialism, and reform. While segregation dominated our socio-political processes, racial politics also influenced radical social theory.

Progressivism represented the common historical thread between Du Bois and the Reconstructionists. The democratic-socialist views of the left wing of the Progressive movement were consistent with Du Bois views between 1910 and 1930. A collectivist economic order without revolution is what Du Bois had long advocated. Consistently supporting and being supported by such progressives as Walter Lippmann, Jane Addams, and many others, Du Bois was comfortable with this company. Additionally, he was an unyielding supporter of educational reform, the suffrage movement, and trade unionism, all of which were Progressive platform issues. Marable[37] says of Du Bois' association with Progressivism:

> He sought to advance theoretical concepts on the meaning of each movement to the reconstruction of American democracy. But as a Negro, Du Bois was always aware of the veil of color that inhibited many white radicals from pursuing creative reform strategies challenging racial inequality. He believed that the central contradiction in democratic society was the barrier of racism, and that if left unchallenged, racial prejudice would compromise the goals of social reformers.

Because of Du Bois's intense concern with questions of race and class, his views on education are often overshadowed. It will be argued that Du Bois' views on the purposes of education coincide with those of George S. Counts, Harold Rugg, Sidney Hook, Theodore Brameld and others associated with the heyday of Social Reconstructionism during the 1930s.

While Du Bois wrote widely on character training and black college issues, the Reconstructionists did not. Regarding education for social change and the aims of education, the views of Du Bois are almost indistinguishable from those of Rugg, Counts, et al. during the early 1930s.

ON THE PURPOSES OF EDUCATION

It is in this area where Du Bois becomes the consummate Social Reconstructionist. Beyond cognitive development, the Reconstructionists saw a special role for schooling. That role was to assist the evolution of a new enlightenment and even a new social order. By virtue of their positioning in society, confrontation with ideas, dynamic nature, and the perceived leadership role of teachers, schools were viewed as having revolutionary possibilities.

Du Bois consistently upheld the notion that schooling was both personally and socially emancipatory. He noted that education should "give to our youth a training designed above all to make them men of power." Du Bois often said that education must prepare one to do the "world's work." What was the world's work? Du Bois answers thusly:

> The world compels us today as never before to examine and re-examine the problem of democracy. In theory we know it by heart: all men are equal and should have equal voice in their own government. This dictum has been vigorously attacked. All men are not equal. Ignorance cannot speak logically or clearly even when given voice. If sloth, dullness and mediocrity hold power, civilization is diluted and lowered, and government approaches anarchy. The mob cannot rule itself and will not choose the wise and able and give them the power to rule.[38]

Education, for Du Bois, became social capital, which can be utilized by marginalized people, especially African Americans, to influence and reform society. In an eloquent summary of his views on the power of education Du Bois noted in 1930:

> We are going to force ourselves in by organized far-seeing effort- by outthinking and outflanking the owners of the world today who are too drunk with their own arrogance and power successfully to oppose us.[39]

DU BOIS AND DEMOCRATIC SOCIALISM

Ultimately the social reconstructionism of Du Bois rests with his political and social philosophy. Like his radical counterparts in the 1930s, Du Bois advocated a (collectivist) democratic socialist organization of society's wealth, resources, and knowledge. He argued in 1942:

> In the period between 1860 and 1914, capitalism had come to its highest development in the European world, and its development meant the control of economic life and with that the domination of political life by the great aggregation of capital. It became, therefore, increasingly clear, as Karl Marx emphasized at the beginning of the

era, that there could be no real democracy unless there was greater economic equality.[40]

Du Bois, the socialist, looked for a vehicle to social reform. He, like many others, concluded that the dynamic nature of ideas and ideology could prompt change. For Du Bois there was an undying belief that ideas, when adopted by people became a force in the real world. It is that belief which continues to point reformers and radicals to the schools in their search of change.

BLACK VOICES: BEYOND DU BOIS

While data is scarce and the scholarship is limited, a radical Black reconstructionist critique of American public education beyond that of Du Bois throughout the twentieth century exists. Scattered writings in the Social Frontier, the ongoing activities of Harlem activists, and the widely known "local control" movement in New York during the late 1960s provide examples for consideration.

THE *SOCIAL FRONTIER* ADDRESSES RACE

The Social Frontier, journal of the Social Reconstructionists, experienced a name change in October 1939 to Frontiers of Democracy. The April 15, 1940 issue was dedicated to the race question. Articles by well-known white scholars such as Margaret Mead, William Heard Kilpatrick and Eugene L. Horowitz bemoaned the social inequality of the races and attempted to excavate the social roots of prejudice. Black philosopher Alain Locke offered a contribution entitled, With Science as His Shield: The Educator Must Bridge Our "Great Divides." Beyond the standard denunciation of segregation, Locke explored possibilities for the curriculum. He called for "intercultural studies" arguing that students needed a broader social science and social studies ideology that would promote tolerance, democracy, and humanity. He wrote:

> Presumably there would be a more humane and tolerant sense of solidarity in a society permeated with such social intelligence and less need and demand for the intolerant and chauvinistic varieties of patriotism and other group loyalties. The school, after all, cannot alone create democracy or be primarily responsible for it.[41]

The journal had a wide audience. The appearance of these essays in a special issue is open to interpretation. It suggests that this group possessed interest in the "Negro question" and specifically the education of blacks. Beyond the intellectual work of the time, a militant black critique of public education unfolded in certain communities, most notably New York City.

HARLEM: HOTBED OF EDUCATION DISSENT

Two groups exemplified the black radical protest of public education in Harlem during the 1930s, the Harlem Committee for Better Schools and the Teacher's Union (TU). The Committee for Better Schools was a mass organization that included parents, teachers, churches, and community reformers. Indignant about Harlem's neglected and deteriorating schools these activists recruited and attracted black teachers and radicals. Allied with the Teachers Union, they worked for the physical improvements of schools, free lunches, and better working conditions for teachers.

An incident in 1936 where a burly white school principal physically attacked a fourteen-year-old black schoolboy sparked community action. Here is how Naison describes the outrage:

> The Committee for Better Schools, with the aid of seasoned Communist street speakers like Audley Moore and Richard Moore, immediately established picket lines at the school and organized demonstrations designed to force Schoenchen's expulsion from the school system. These protests attracted thousands of participants, ranging from Harlem parents to top-ranking black politicians, to leaders of the Harlem branch of the NAACP, and culminated in a mass trial of the School Board at Abyssinian Baptist Church. Three months after the incident, Schoenchen was transferred to a school outside Harlem.[42]

Naison looks back at the work of the committee:

> In cooperation with the Teacher's Union, the committee sponsored workshops and forums on black accomplishments in American life and fought to remove racist textbooks from the city school system. Condemning the practice of channeling blacks away from academic careers, they agitated for the right of black students to participate in college-bound programs and to attend high schools out of the Harlem district.

The Party's presence pervaded the committee. Theodore Bassett, its secretary, and Emmet May, its vice-chairman, were both Party members, and conducted most of the committee's administrative tasks. Born in the south and trained as schoolteachers, they did their work with a quiet efficiency that won the respect of the black ministers and schoolteachers who composed the group's other leaders. In addition, Party neighborhood branches participated actively in the committee's work. Communists served as members of PTA's in most Harlem schools and placed their best street speakers at the Committee's disposal when it organized demonstrations.[43]

These events represent the development of a more strident variety of school protest. The joining of white radicals with African American community activists is particularly noteworthy as it provided an alliance for expanded activity.

THE TEACHER'S UNION

Founded in 1916 by the children of unionists committed to unionism[44] Local 5, Teacher's Union (TU) of the American Federation of Teachers was formed in New York City. During the 1920s the aggressive and expanding TU took up bread and butter issues such as salaries and working conditions as well as the broader issues of academic freedom, church-state relationships, and the "democratization" of the schools. By the 30s the TU counted many communists and socialists in its ranks. It became an active part of the broad social movement against fascism and reaction. As the hard left gained power within the TU, those opposing their views split and formed the Teacher Guild in 1935.

The more radical TU participated in campaigns against poverty, unemployment, and teacher firings. Markowitz attempts to assess the level of radicalism among New York teachers during the depression era:

As for the political beliefs of the city's teachers, while a number of Communist party members did teach in the city's schools, according to most accounts, including several of those interviewed, they apparently constituted only a very small portion of the teaching staff. . . . The results of a questionnaire for city teachers sponsored by the John Dewey Society for the Study of Education in 1936 showed that the general tendency of teachers was "leftish" with "pale pink" rather than "red" coloring. The study found that while there was predominance of teachers holding socialist convictions, only a small group actually voted for the Socialist party. This study noted that while the great majority of teachers saw the need for far-reaching economic and social reforms, their dissent from the status quo was of a gradualist rather than revolutionary approach.[45]

The Scottsboro Boys case led to Communist Party recruitment of, and alliances with, African Americans. Segregated and inferior schools had long plagued urban (and rural) black communities. By the mid-1930s radical public schoolteachers joined the community struggles of black schools. In Harlem, for example, largely Jewish female and African American Communist Party members joined with a broader number of teachers and parents to protest inferior schools. Markowitz chronicles the activities of teachers Alice Citron, Dorothy Rose, Mildred Flacks, Celia Zitron, and Minnie Gutride among others in this effort.

Containing both black and white communists and radicals, the Teachers Union continued its activities despite being battered by government red-baiting and defections. In the early 1950s they ambitiously challenged the established school curriculum. While it is difficult to sort out the exact role of black people, they were clearly an integral part of this endeavor. Here is how Biondi describes one event:

> In 1951 the left-wing Teacher's Union, with which the board had broken relations after its expulsion from the CIO, produced a remarkable study of textbooks currently in use in the public schools. In "Bias and Prejudice in Textbooks in Use in New York City Schools: An Indictment," the union took pains to clarify why its review did not constitute censorship. The Teachers' Union "makes a sharp distinction between censorship—which it opposes—and the elimination of material containing racist stereotypes, distortion of historical and scientific fact, and bias, whether conscious of unconscious, toward allegedly 'inferior' peoples." Prepared by the Harlem Committee of the Teachers' Union, the report reflected scholarship in U.S. history that had been ignored by the mainstream academy, and it anticipated the revisionism of the next generation of historians who came of age during the civil rights movement.[46]

Thus we observe that one of the first movements to revise racist curriculum included black voices. Biondi continues:

To compensate for the deficient materials used in city schools, the Teachers' Union created its own Black history curriculum, including "The Negro in New York, 1626–1865: A Study for Teachers." While this guide was not adopted by the board, it is possible that individual teachers used it. It began: "In New York City the Negro people constitute more than 10% of the city population. This is probably the largest Negro community of any city in the world with great and growing influence on the social and cultural life of the city and of national importance because of its leadership in the fight for civil rights throughout the country."[47]

LOCAL CONTROL IN NEW YORK: THE RADICAL RECONSTRUCTIONIST INFLUENCE

In the context of expanding affluence for some, differentiated and segregated schooling remained a target of Marxists and radicals throughout the 1950s. Unequal schools were viewed as symptomatic of the unequal society. On the heels of Brown v. Board and McCarthyism, radical agitation for improved schools continued and even intensified in many areas of the nation. The school wars described by Danns[48] in Chicago suggests continued widespread discontent with public education by people of color.

Every aspect of the "great divide," that is, the contradictions between black and white, affluent and poor, powerful and powerless, city and suburb existed in New York City in the 1960's. Within education concerns about racism, the achievement gap, relevant curriculum, effective teaching, and governance boiled over in Ocean Hill-Brownsville.[49] The demand for local control of schools was seen by its advocates as empowering, liberating, and democratizing the schools.

Reverend Milton Galamison, a leader in the Ocean Hill–Brownsville battle, emphasized Christian social obligation, telling his congregation that the dire situation created by class exploitation had created a special need for Christians. Followers of Christ must fight all forms of inequality. If one professes to be a Christian, one cannot sit idly by and allow innocent human beings to suffer from poverty, racism, and war. True Christians should be vehicles for change and social redemption. Taylor writes:

Ideologically, Galamison felt connected to Progressives and radicals, they worked for the same goals and criticized the same targets: the state and church. . . . On occasions he even praised Marxism. According to the Presbyterian minister, socialism has been an important "historic force." It has been a "definite attempt to define the nature of man. The ideas of human dignity and justice are the basis of Marx's writings and these ideas created modern socialism and Russian Communism." Galamison claimed that using communists as scapegoats was a diversion that takes people's minds off the real issues:[50]

SOCIAL RECONSTRUCTIONISM, SOCIAL DEMOCRACY AND RACE: A HYPOTHESIS

The Social Reconstructionists of the 1930s are best described as American social democrats. They were an intellectual expression of the widespread social and economic discontent of the time. More pointedly, they represented a social democratic stance among professional educators. Early twentieth-century American social democracy took up the causes of the laborer and the immigrant. Opposition to segregation, lynching and discrimination occurred elsewhere.

Broderick and Meier[51] locate the epicenter of early twentieth-century black protest in organizations and individuals such as Du Bois, Garvey, the National Association for the Advancement of Colored People, the Universal Negro Improvement Association, etc. Although African American social democrats such as A. Phillip Randolph and Du Bois connected the causes of race and labor, they were not joined in the larger social movement. The disconnect and confusion of how race and class protest fit, has plagued and even shaped American social protest.

Hence, the Social Reconstructionists may not have been able to rise above their ideological inheritance. This may explain, in part, their energetic engagement with issues of economic and social class combined with a lethargy on matters of race.

FINAL REFLECTIONS

School reform and race are now totally intertwined in the policy discourse. Several issues call out for further investigation and consideration. First, the unfinished nature of this body of research, second the need to further critique contemporary school reform and thirdly the urgent mandate to think about school reform and race in the unfolding techno-global society.

The early twentieth-century radical Reconstructionists, both Black and White, were the progenitors of contemporary critical discourse in education. The education community and the general public need to know this work. Their politicization of education contributed mightily to our expanding understanding of public schooling as a function of the political state, and an entity profoundly influenced by powerful economic forces undergirding the hegemonic order. While the Social Reconstructionists did not greatly illuminate the modern issues of race and education, they brought attention to the issues of power and equity surrounding racism. Their concepts of school reform and the role of school in society interjected a new dynamism, spirit, urgency and passion into the discourse.

Further exploration of primary source data as well as more exhaustive scholarship on radical Reconstructionist African American educational dissent needs to take place. We need to know more about how and where the Frontiersmen connected to African Americans.

We know, for example, Harold Rugg and John Dewey traveled to South Africa in 1934 with their African American colleague, Professor Mabel Carney. There, they all attended a conference hosted by the South African Institute of Race Relations.[52] How close was their relationship with Carney whose research[53] involved race, rural development, and African education? Did they interact with other African Americans in the 1930s? How wide was their influence?

Second, urban school "reform," with its powerful racial overtones, has become central to America's political drama. Current policy initiatives are often ahistorical and myopic. The conservative restoration and restorers, the religious right and powerful corporate forces are heavily invested in a concept of school reform moving toward privatization and "choice."

Their version of school criticism, especially in urban education, has turned our attention to mediocrity. The mediocrity argument suggests that urban schools suffer from permissiveness, inefficiency, poor funding, bigness, social promotion, denied access, indifferent teachers, exoticized curricula, limited home experiences, and lack of school choice. While many of these points are indisputable, their broader argument is simplistic and reductionist as explanation. The mediocrity thesis is often driven by political conservatism, Fordist efficiency, and partisan expediency. It lacks a historicized excavation of schooling. Today's corporate-minded and sponsored "reform" movement calls for the reversal of the aforementioned maladies. "Back to basics" and increased standardized testing are hardly remedies for structured inequity. We have yet to have an informed public dialogue that locates schools squarely within the context of power, ideology, race relations, property, and partisanship.

Additionally, popular criticism of urban schools focuses primarily on race and achievement. Even the well articulated reproduction arguments rarely join race to class. Perhaps we need new ways problemitize the intersection of race and class oppression within the capitalist system.

Finally, we are all witness to the deep restructuring occurring in the political arena, legal policy, neighborhood demographics, and perhaps most importantly, the labor market. The techno-global revolution is marked by imperialistic aggression, shifting power alliances, market "solutions", deindustrialization, displacements in the labor market, unforeseen automation, urban gentrification, the extreme pyramiding of wealth, and rudimentary changes in the "social contract." The safety net, formerly funded by social wealth, is being eroded by privatization. Concern exists that universal education might be undermined in this environment. There is also fear that people of color will be further marginalized in these shifting sands.

Related questions cry out for illumination. Will privatization efforts lead to increasingly stratified and tiered schools? Do "anti-racist pedagogy" and multicultural education have any real substance in this environment? How can we explore race and schooling in association with labor economics? What do the new demographics mean to public schooling? Perhaps a deeper understanding of Reconstructionist theorizing will contribute to a more developed analysis.

NOTES

1. Lawrence A. Cremin, *The Transformation of the School: Progressivism in American Education 1876–1957* (New York: Alfred A. Knopf, 1961).

2. William H. Watkins, ed., *Black Protest Thought and Education* (New York: Peter Lang. 2005).

3. Thorstein Veblein, *Theory of the Leisure Class: An Economic Study in the Evolution of Institutions* (New York: The Macmillan Co.,1899).

4. Richard O.Boyer & Herbert M. Morais, *Labor's Untold Story* (New York: United Electrical, Radio & Machine Workers of America, 1955), 172.

5. Joel H. Spring, *Education and the Rise of the Corporate State* (Boston: Beacon Press, 1972).

6. William Edward Burghardt Du Bois (1903/1969), *The Souls of Black Folk* (New York: New American Library, 1903).

7. William H. Watkins, *The White Architects of Black Education: Ideology and Power in America 1865-1954* (New York: Teachers College Press, 2001).

8. Daniel Tanner & Laurel Tanner, *Curriculum Development: Theory Into Practice* (New York: Macmillan Publishing Co., Inc., 1975), 351–364.

9. C. A. Bowers, *The Progressive Educator and the Depression: The Radical Years* (New York: Random House, 1969).

10. Commission on Social Studies of the American Historical Association, Conclusions and Recommendations (New York: Charles Scribners' Sons, 1934).

11. Ronald W. Evans, *The Social Studies Wars: What Should We Teach the Children* (New York: Teachers College Press, 2004).

12. George S. Counts, "Dare the Progressives be Progressive?" *Progressive Education* 9 (1932a): 257–63.

13. Counts, *Dare the Progressives be Progressive*, 259

14. R. Freeman Butts, *Public Education in the United States: From Revolution to Reform* (New York: Holt Rinehart & Winston, 1978), 385.

15. George S. Counts, *Dare the Schools Build a New Social Order?* (New York: John Day, 1932).

16. Charles A. Beard, Commission on the Social Studies in the Schools, *A Charter of the Social Sciences in the Schools* (New York: Charles Scribners' Sons, 1932).

17. Progressive Education Association's Committee on Social and Economic Problems, *A Call to the Teachers of the Nation* (New York: John Day, 1933).

18. William H. Kilpatrick, ed., *The Educational Frontier* (New York: Appleton-Century-Crofts, 1933).

19. Bowers, *The Progressive Educator and the Depression* (1969).

20. William H. Watkins, *The Social Reconstructionists* (1990). In T. Husen & T. N. Postlethwaite, eds., *The International Encyclopedia of Education, Supplementary Volume Two* (London: Pergamon Press, 1990) Reprinted in Lewy, A., ed., *The International Encyclopedia of Curriculum* (London: Pergamon Press, 1992).

21. William H. Kilpatrick. *Education and the Social Crisis: A Proposed Program* (New York: Liveright Publishing Corp., 1932).

22. Social Frontier,Editorial Board, (January 1935): 31.

23. Harold O. Rugg, *The Scientific Method in the Reconstruction of Elementary and Secondary School Subjects* (1921). This series was published in conjunction with school reviews and elementary school journals. The University of Chicago published some of the early work in Chicago: University of Chicago Press, 1918.

24. Rugg, *Social Frontier* (October 1936): 15.

25. Ibid., 15.

26. Ibid., 15.

27. Thedore Brameld, *Toward a Reconstructed Philosophy of Education* (New York: Holt, Rinehardt & Winston, 1956).

28. Harold O. Rugg & William Withers, *Social Foundations of Education* (New York: Prentice Hall Inc.,1955).

29. Rugg & Withers, Social Foundations of Education, 270.

30. A. Degobineau or deGobineau, *Essai Sur L'inegalite des Races Humaines (Essay on the Inequality of Human Races)* (New York: Fertig, 1967). Original work published 1854.

31. Franz Boas, *Anthropology and Modern Life,* (New York: W.W. Norton.,1928).

32. Ruth Benedict, *Race and Racism* (London: G. Routledge & Sons Ltd.,1959) and Benedict, R. *Patterns of Culture* (New York: Pelican Books, 1946).

33. Otto Klineberg, *Race Differences* (New York: Harper and brothers, 1935) and Otto Klineberg, *Negro Intelligence and Selective Migration* (New York: Columbia University Press, 1935a).

34. Eugene G. Provenzo Jr., ed. *Du Bois on Education* (Walnut Creek, CA: Alta Mira Press, 2002).

35. George Washington Williams, *History of the Negro Race in America* (New York: Bergman Publishers, Reprint 1968). Originally published, 1883.

36. Thomas T. Fortune, *Black and White; Land, Labor, and Politics in the South* (New York: Fords, Howard, & Hulbert, 1884).

37. Manning Marable, *W.E.B. Du Bois: Black Radical Democrat* (Boston: Twayne Publishers, 1986), 84.

38. W.E.B. Du Bois, Herbert Aptheker, ed.,. *The Education of Black People: Ten Critiques, 1906-1960* (New York: Monthly Review Press, 1973), 118.

39. DuBois, *The Education of Black People*, 77.

40. Meyer Weinburg, *W.E.B. Du Bois: A Reader* (New York: Harper Torchbook, 1970), 196.

41. Alain Locke, With Science as His Shield: The Educator Must Bridge Our "Great Divides," *Frontiers of Democracy* 6 no. 53 (13 April, 1940): 208–210.

42. Mark Naison, *Communists in Harlem During the Depression* (Urbana, IL: Univ. of Illinois Press, 1983), 215.

43. Naison, Communists in Harlem During the Depression, 216.

44. Ruth J. Markowitz, *My Daughter, The Teacher: Jewish Teachers in the New York City Schools* (New Brunswick, NJ: Rutgers University Press, 1993).

45. Markowitz, My Daughter, The Teacher, 158.

46. Martha Biondi, *To Stand and Fight: The Struggle for Civil Rights in Postwar New York* (Cambridge: Harvard University Press, 2003), 244–5.

47. Biondi, To Stand and Fight, 246.

48. DionneDanns, *Something Better for Our Children: Black Organizing in Chicago Public Schools, 1963-1971* (New York: Routledge, 2003).

49. Jerald E. Podair, *The Strike That Changed New York: Blacks, Whites, and the Ocean Hill-Brownsville Crises* (New Haven: Yale University Press, 2002).

50. Clarence Taylor,Knocking at Our Own Door: Milton A. Galamison and the Struggle to Integrate New York City Schools (New York: Columbia University Press, 1997), 36–7.

51. Francis L.Broderick & August Meier, *Negro Protest Thought in the Twentieth Century* (Indianapolis: The Bobbs Merrill Co., Inc., 1965).

52. R. Glotzer, "The Career of Mabel Carney, The Study of Race and Rural Development in the United States and South Africa", *The International Journal of African Historical Study,* 29 no.2 (1996): 309–336.

53. Mabel Carney (Forward) Albert David Helser, Education of Primitive People, (New York: Negro Universities Press, 1934), 7–10.

CHAPTER 12

SOCIAL RECONSTRUCTIONIST CURRICULUM IMPULSES

Pragmatism, Collectivism and "The American Problem"

Gerald Ponder

Social Reconstructionism in education shared time and historical context with the ideas and events driven by figures like Franklin Delano Roosevelt, Neville Chamberlain, Emperor Hirohito, Huey P. Long, Winston Churchill, Haile Selassie, Josef Stalin, Eleanor Roosevelt, Adolf Hitler, Benito Mussolini, Francisco Franco, Gertrude Stein, George Santayana, Thomas Mann, Sigmund Freud, Ernest Hemingway, Carl Sandburg, Virginia Woolf, Pablo Picasso, Frank Lloyd Wright, Paul Muni, Joe Louis, Jesse Owens, Joe DiMaggio, and The Marx Brothers.

The 1930s were not small times. Ideas for new social orders were everywhere, as this list of names from the covers of *Time* in that decade recalls.[1] These figures and their ideas personified a world in crisis, the turmoil of destruction, reimagining, and reconstruction. The stock market crash of 1929 and the subsequent and sudden depression in the United States snuffed quickly the prosperity of the 1920s, leaving 12 million people—24 percent of the labor force—out of work. The world joined

Social Reconstruction: People, Politics, Perspectives, pages 235–256
Copyright © 2006 by Information Age Publishing

in the economic misery. Fear, anger, and escapism ruled. Everywhere people sought scapegoats and saviors.

Franklin Roosevelt appeared on the cover of *Time* four times in the 1930s. George S. Counts and Harold Rugg never did. Nor did John Dewey. But by the end of the decade, the ideas and impulses of Social Reconstructionism—that the schools should contribute significantly to the building of a new social order—had become embedded in the discourse and lore of educational thought, and they received substantial attention and attack from outside observers.[2] The 1930s predated the times when faith in the power of education-as-schooling had become a commonplace in the American mind and culture. The United States was still transforming from agrarianism to industrialism, from rural to urban ways of living, from Victorian ways of seeing and thinking to modernism. For many—perhaps most—basic literacy and numeracy were the goals of schooling, and an eighth-grade education was the norm. In the early 1920s, only one in twenty American students went to high school. By the1930s, the numbers and percentages had increased steadily, and the high schools were experiencing a more diverse—at least economically and ethnically, if not racially—student body.[3]

Changes in the population, structures, and practices of American schooling fueled discussion and debate. John Dewey and his ideas of Progressivism in education had become, by the late 'teens, the most prolific set of alternatives to the subject-centered, rote and recitation practice of schooling that was commonplace throughout the country, as well as to the ideas of the cult of efficiency.[4] His apostles and translators, like William Heard Kilpatrick and members of the Progressive Education Association, had extended and popularized Dewey's progressive ideas in ways that focused on child-centeredness and the project method.[5] The processes of extension and popularization provided justifications for the private progressive schools sprinkled throughout much of the country in the 1920s; they also led to criticism that the child-centered and interest-based progressive notions of schooling were too narrow, that they failed to consider fully the Reconstructionist and Social Reconstructionist elements of Progressivism, that they unduly placed process over the content contained in the subject disciplines, and that they were potentially anti-democratic, as the progressive schools served nearly exclusively the children of the upper and upper-middle classes.

Criticism of the child-centered Progressives came from conservatives and skeptics, but also from the group of Progressives that were, in the 1930s, to form the Social Reconstructionist wing of Progressive Education—George S. Counts, Harold Rugg, and others—sometimes joined by Dewey himself.[6] Criticism and analysis of school, society, and culture were the hallmarks of Social Reconstructionist thought and writing. Counts first gained national notice with his critique of the high school curriculum and his charge that high schools, with their dominant population of children of the wealthy, were not serving to spread democracy.[7] The tone—social reconstruction leading to a utopian (if vague) vision of democratic collectivism—and focus—a greater concern with the high school—set the course for sSocial rReconstructionist thinking about the purposes and practices of schools through the decade of the 1930s.

By the time of Counts's address to the 1932 Progressive Education Association and the subsequent publication of his remarks and related materials as *Dare the School Build a New Social Order?*the ideas of Social Reconstructionism had been in discussion and development for some time.[8]

Explicit curriculum development or curriculum theorizing was not in the foreground of Social Reconstructionism. While Harold Rugg's writings, actions, and textbooks provide the clearest set of Social Reconstructionist curriculum products, and while the Social Reconstructionists and other Progressives did think about and write about issues related to the curriculum, explicit and exclusive thinking about curriculum as a policy and practice of schooling was still new. Most practitioners (with some notable exceptions such as Jesse Newlon's teacher-led curriculum work in Denver) probably equated curriculum development with textbook selection, at best. It had been less than two decades since Franklin Bobbitt published *The Curriculum.*[9] The most significant and broadly based consideration of curriculum to date, the 26th Yearbook of the National Society for the Study of Education, was published only a few years earlier, in 1926.[10] Ralph Tyler was, during the 1930s, leading the assessment team for the Eight Year Study and articulating his frustrations over the lack of stated goals and objectives and the variance among progressive schools and between progressive schools and public schools that later led to the "Tyler Rationale."[11] And Smith, Stanley, and Shores were still more than a decade from publishing *Fundamentals of Curriculum Development*, the most widely used of the first wave of texts *about* curriculum that spurred regular study of curriculum as a subject in professional schools of education.[12]

But the Social Reconstructionists did consider curriculum as part of their broader analyses of the purposes and practices of schools, the roles that schools and classrooms could and should play in American society, the character and qualities of teachers, the preparation of teachers, and their ideas of what we now might call "best practices" for teachers to use in promoting the aims of Social Reconstructionism for the greater good of their vision of needed social change. This chapter addresses the curriculum impulses of the Social Reconstructionists by asking three broad questions: Who were the Social Reconstructionists? What were the influences on their curriculum thought? What were their curriculum ideas?

THE SOCIAL RECONSTRUCTIONISTS:
THE TEACHERS COLLEGE DISCUSSION GROUP

". . . . [T]he United States of 1931 was a different place from the U.S. of the post-war decade; there was no denying that. An old order was giving place to new."[13]

That was Frederick Lewis Allen's succinct contrast between the 1920s and the still-unknown 1930s. While later historians would find that at least parts of the U.S. economy were in recession since 1926, the feelings of optimism in the country and among politicians during the 1920s were so rampant, and the fall of old boundaries—in culture, morals, thought, and finance— were so widespread that Herbert Hoover could consider campaigning for reelection on the promise of perpetual prosperity and the very real hope of ending poverty. October and November of 1929 ended that illusion. Three million men lost their jobs in one week in the fall of 1929, and the slide continued, introducing more and more displaced workers to the feeling of their "bellybuttons rubbing against their backbones."[14] Dramatic change in American society and its institutions was imminent.

By 1931, progressivism in education had become Progressive Education, with capital-letter designations and an organization that carried its banner.[15] Progressive education in practice had increasingly replaced the academic, separate-subject curriculum in schools with one divided into "units of work" or projects, with childrens' interests as the guiding principle of curriculum development and integration. During the 1920s, Progressive educators had been oriented primarily toward action rather than reflection, spending most of their time developing new teaching methods and promoting their guiding principles rather than considering carefully educational and philosophical issues. They were "zealous reformers, hardworking and sincere evangelists of a better childhood," as Harold Rugg described them.[16]

But the "sincere and zealous evangelists" of child-centeredness had their critics. Some Progressives worried that progressivism had become excessive and misdirected. Some feared that the reformist zeal had become too doctrinaire and ignored the Deweyan principle of experimentalism. Boyd Bode criticized progressive education for its failure to develop a cohesive program or sense of direction.[17] And John Dewey himself chastised the Progressives for allowing too much freedom in the schools and for making an anathema out of the academic disciplines.[18]

Among the most influential sets of critics of the child-centered progressives was a group of professors of education who met in an informal discussion group at Teachers College, Columbia. The group began meeting in 1927, when R. Bruce Raup suggested to William Heard Kilpatrick that they form a discussion group to discuss the influence of recent social changes on education.[19] "One by one after 1926 I had watched the new members of the group join our staff—George S. Counts, John L. Childs, R. Bruce Raup, Goodwin Watson, . . . Jesse Newlon, . . . and others," Harold Rugg recalled of the formation of the renowned faculty of Teachers College.[20]

This Teachers College Discussion Group was among the most identifiable incubators of Social Reconstructionism. William Heard Kilpatrick was the senior member of the group, and its convener. Kilpatrick was a southerner, born in 1871 in Georgia. He had attended Mercer University, a Baptist institution, before entering Teachers College in 1907 to do graduate work. At Teachers College, Kilpatrick studied under Dewey, and when he joined the Teachers College faculty himself in 1913, he began a long career of interpreting Dewey to his own students. Two important works, a 1918 essay titled "The Project Method," and a 1925 book, *Foundations of Method*, set out the philosophies and curriculum ideas for which Kilpatrick became best known and which established him as a leading theorist of progressive education.[21] The intent of the project method was to make "purposeful activity" initiated by the child in a social environment the center of the educational process. Kilpatrick supported Dewey's idea that the school should be an embryonic and nearly ideal community. He stressed his view that the project method was designed to integrate subject matter with the problems of life in a social setting, thus helping the student develop his abilities to carry out his plans in "life situations." The curriculum, Kilpatrick said, could not be planned in advance, because the emphasis was on the *process* of thinking and acting, rather than on the acquisition of the products of someone else's thought.[22]

George S. Counts, who became the leading and most visible spokesman of the Social Reconstructionists, was born in Baldwin, Kansas, in 1889. During his graduate work at the University of Chicago, Counts developed in two directions. One was his training in the scientific objectivity of tests and measurements. The other was sociology and social criticism. Two of Counts's early works, *The Selective Character of American Secondary Education* **(1922)**, and *The Social Compositions of Boards of Education* (1927) combined both facets of his graduate study as he used survey statistics to show that American secondary schools were populated by the children of the "more well-to-do classes" and that school boards were controlled by members of these same classes.[23] With these and other writings during the 1920s, Counts continued to assert that American education, especially through the high schools and the set of private—often Progressive—schools attended by upper middle class students actually was inhibiting the growth of democracy and perpetuating social and racial inequalities.[24] In 1930, he anticipated the thrust of his famous speech to the Progressive Education Association in *The American Road to Culture* by assailing the schools for failing to come to terms with the realities of industrialism and for drifting along without social goals.[25]

Jesse Newlon came to Teachers College in 1927, to direct the Lincoln School. He came from his superintendency in the Denver schools, where he had become nationally known for systematically including classroom teachers in the processes of policy making and curriculum development. Of the several members of the discussion group that influenced the development of Social Reconstructionism, Newlon may have had the greatest influence in public school circles due to his experience and his initiative involving teachers as decision makers for curriculum and policy.[26]

Born in Ohio in 1888, R. Bruce Raup had graduated from a Presbyterian seminary in Chicago. He first became a pastor and teacher in Nebraska, then a chaplain in World War I. After the War, he decided against a career in the ministry and entered Teachers College for graduate study in education. There he took "Kilpatrick's course" from Boyd Bode while Kilpatrick was on sabbatical; Bode introduced Raup to Dewey's theories and writing. Raup later recalled that his reading of *Democracy and Education* and Bode's explication of Deweyan theory left a deep impression on him, especially when he realized that Dewey had already synthesized many of the ideas that he only had begun to consider.[27]

Unlike most of his colleagues in the Teachers College discussion group, John L. Childs did not consider the ideas of sociologist Thorsten Veblen and historian Charles Beard as fundamental to his worldview. Instead, his social theory had been formed during his undergraduate days at the University of Wisconsin, where he became intrigued with the political thought of that state's progressive Senator, Robert M. LaFollette. From studying and discussing LaFollette's speeches and writing, Childs came to understand the relationship between education and politics and to believe in the power of education to impede or advance social change. By the time he joined the Teachers College faculty in 1928, Childs had come to believe that the United States was in the throes of a class struggle and that social planning was a practical necessity for social progress.[28]

Harold Rugg was unlike his colleagues in the discussion group and in the Social Reconstructionist camp in many ways. He was a New Englander, without strong religious affiliation. He trained first as a civil engineer and taught engineering for several years before earning his doctorate at the University of Illinois in psychology, sociology, and education. During World War I, he engaged in what he later called "an orgy of quantification" in his work with the Army's Committee on the Classification of Personnel. This experience led him to join the Teachers College faculty as director of research for the Lincoln School. During his early years at Teachers College and the Lincoln School, Rugg began reading the works of Veblen and Beard and to consider intensely the effects of industrialism on schools and society.[29]

Rugg's study of industrialism led him to conclude that public school students should have the opportunity to investigate the "great concepts" of American civilization : "The great human migrations of the world...man's increasing control over nature...the tendency in economic life toward concentration in ownership and control of wealth...the transportation of self-sufficient peoples into a fragile society of interdependent peoples."[30] During the 1920s, Rugg developed these "concepts" into a series of influential school texts that provided an integrated, if somewhat economics-oriented approach to the social sciences.

During the Depression of the 1930s, Rugg's writings took on an increasing emphasis on social analysis and the social theories of Social Reconstructionism. He promoted the use of the scientific method to resolve social problems and to develop the idea of a school-centered community where the frontier spirit could be kept alive and where the American dreams of democratic action and economic plenty could be realized. He became a lightening rod for general public concerns over the effects of Progressive ideas on American youth and specific fears about the influence of Social Reconstructionism itself. His writing, his theorizing, and his defense of his textbooks and the ideas they contained earned him his place as the most important curriculum figure in Social Reconstruction.[31]

While these sketches are brief, and while we can no longer know the full text or impact of the discussions among the members of the Teachers College group, they suggest some of the influences on the curriculum impulses of the Social Reconstructionists: great faith in the power of science and experimentalism to promote social and economic progress; faith in a better future, whether influenced by religious training or an optimistic upbringing; the influence of smaller, sometimes more rural communities; belief in the power of education to effect positive change; a strong belief in democracy; the ideas of John Dewey, especially the concepts of Reconstruction and Social Construction. Nor would it be easy or even possible to develop a complete "roster" of Social Reconstructionists beyond the most visible members of the "movement" that historical consensus has agreed upon. Some members of the TC discussion group would not include themselves among the "membership" of the movement. Many educators who were not members of the TC discussion group wrote for *The Social Frontier* or otherwise identified with the movement. Social Reconstructionism was more a set of ideas and perspectives than an easily identifiable and stable set of players.

The members of the TC discussion group, along with many of their contemporaries, shared a bent for social analysis and criticism, a deep concern for the future directions of American society, and a faith in the transforming power and social responsibility of education. They believed the school could—and probably should—play a significant role in building a new social order to replace the one rooted in 19th century ideas and events and severely damaged by the Great Depression. They also were influenced by some particular views of history, time, and world events.

INFLUENCES ON SOCIAL RECONSTRUCTIONIST CURRICULUM THOUGHT: SCIENCE, DEMOCRACY, AND INTERDEPENDENCE

Social Reconstructionist thought was influenced by several related intellectual traditions and historical interpretations. They were first, fundamentally American and situated broadly within the philosophical traditions of American pragmatism. John Childs explained that "pragmatism is more than a philosopher's philosophy. . . . Its emphasis on experience, on experimental activity, on the creative role of intelligence, and on the values and procedures of democracy brought these elements in the life of the American people into fuller consciousness. . . " and thus enhanced their influence in education.[32] Even Counts, a student of the Soviet socialist system, rejected the Soviet interpretation of collectivism and socialism, and instead envisioned and argued for American versions of collectivism and economic planning through consensus building.

Other significant influences on Social Reconstructionist thought were the sets of ideas represented in the writings of historian Charles Beard and sociologist Thorsten Veblen.[33] It was not that the works of Beard and Veblen set the ideological agenda for the Social Reconstructionists and others so much as they captured crucial ideas and provided an intellectual referent for them. Counts and other Reconstructionists themselves stated "It [*The Social Frontier*, the journal of the Social Reconstructionists] accepts the analysis of the current epoch . . . outlined . . . in *Conclusions and Recommendations, Report on the Social Studies*, of the Commission of the American Historical Association," a report authored primarily by Beard.[34]

The first of the ideas of pragmatism that especially influenced Social Reconstructionist curriculum thinking was the idea of experimental science and its attendant methodology. The Social Reconstructionists believed that the procedures of experimental inquiry—the method of laboratory science—applied by groups of people engaging in collective thought would lead to a "method of intelligence" that would provide a democratic basis for authority in decision making. The "method of collective intelligence" would thus be oriented toward solving real problems of concern to the group, and it would be self-regulating, in the sense that all "answers" would be tentative and subject to further inquiry. This idea of "science" as self-correcting process and as basis for authority countered the older authoritarian bases of tradition, position based on class, lineage, or family status, or appeals to religion.[35]

The second pragmatist idea, democracy, appeared more often than any other in Social Reconstructionist writings on the programs of the schools. The Social Reconstructionists relied heavily on Dewey's conceptions of democracy—especially as developed in *Democracy and Education*—for their own ideas of social organization and social authority. Dewey's studies of anthropology and social psychology had led him to realize that different cultures had produced different ways of education and social organization. Education, Dewey insisted, is a social process that develops distinctive modifications of learning and acting. For Dewey, no apparently natural or innately preferable modes of social organization had developed among the world's peoples, but he believed that the values of democracy could have universal authority because these values could be shown to rest on reason.[36]

The idea of interdependence was self-evident to Dewey and generally accepted as an article of faith by the Reconstructionists.[37] The idea of interdependence as an influence on Social Reconstructionist curriculum thinking also gained power as an antithesis to the forces of individualism and *laissez-faire* economics considered by many social analysts of the day to be outmoded, outdated, and even dangerous. "Cumulative evidence," the American Historical Association Commission reported, "supports the conclusion that, in the United States as in other countries, the age of individualism and *laissez-faire* in economy and government is closing . . ."[38] The American frontier had closed around 1890, historian Frederick Jackson Turner had earlier argued, and the end of free and open land, networks of railroads and telegraph wires, and increasing specialization by labor and agriculture and their increasing dependence on each other meant that the most striking tendency in American life was a "twofold tendency toward the closer physical unification of the nation and the ever-closer integration and interdependence of all branches of economy, social activity, and culture."[39] Historical forces had determined, in the Reconstructionist view, that "a new age of collectivism is emerging;" but since the age of collectivism had not yet occurred, their time had become "The Great Transition."[40]

The power of science and experimentalism, the promise and inevitability of democracy, and the trend toward interdependence that characterized the age of transition were more than articles of faith or interpretation to the Social Reconstructionists. They were inevitable and indisputable facts. As the American Historical Association Commission on the Social Studies stated, "At the present time, the trend has become so clearly apparent that to dwell on it is to labor the obvious."[41] These values and assumptions formed the foundational influences for the curriculum ideas of the Social Reconstructionists.[42]

SOCIAL RECONSTRUCTIONIST CURRICULUM IDEAS: DEMOCRATIC COLLECTIVISM, "THE AMERICAN PROBLEM," AND THE SOCIAL STUDIES

The social and economic problems brought on by the Depression were so large and so dominant, and their impact on educational discourse so pervasive that it is difficult to draw clear boundaries around Social Recostructionist curriculum thought. The Reconstructionists themselves were more devoted to their social analyses than to the curriculum implications of the analyses, leaving later curriculum historians to sift through volumes of their writing to glean ideas about curriculum processes. The Depression had pushed the efficiency movement and its theorists into the backgound, as the crisis had rendered debate about the directions of society—the ends—far more important than how quickly and efficiently it could arrive there. So the educational adversaries were less present to draw clear lines of contrast. And many educators from many perspectives began their advocacies with social analyses, so that writings about education often looked far more alike than distinct.

This section describes three sets of curriculum ideas—those of Counts, Rugg, and the NEA Department of Superintendence—to portray the curriculum impulses of Social Reconstructionism.

Counts wrote far more about social analysis and social action than curriculum. Four elements mark his thinking about the character of curriculum and the role of curriculum in schooling and education. First, Counts was most interested in the curriculum of the secondary school. His 1926 work on the high school curriculum marked his territory, and he continued that emphasis in much of his thinking about curriculum. He shared that interest in the high school curriculum with many Social Reconstructionists, perhaps because the high school was the closest in time to full participation in a society whose direction they hoped to influence.

Second, Counts approached curriculum issues primarily from the perspective of power and control: *who* should make the curriculum. Third, Counts was not as enamored of curriculum integrated around large themes as were Rugg and others. He retained a great deal of faith in the viability and usefulness of the academic disciplines and their related school subjects. He did, however, emphasize the need for social orientation in subject matter and instructional method. Finally, Counts argued that the overriding purpose of the curriculum and the program of the schools was to advance the cause of democratic collectivism in the United States.[43]

Like many educators of the period, Counts criticized what he considered to be the dominant historical feature of curriculum development, the evolutionary expansion of the curriculum by adding new courses. He opposed what he saw as the three dominant trends in curriculum making:

(1) efficiency models relying on the analysis of adult tasks to form the purposes of the curriculum, (2) basing curriculum on the perceived needs and interests of children, and (3) the use of the "great books" as an approach to curriculum content. Instead, he argued that education is always a function of some particular civilization at some particular time in history. Failure to recognize this "fundamental truth" had led, he believed, to confusion in curriculum and isolation of the school program from real life. The confusion and isolation had resulted from the power struggles among special interests—organized religion, chambers of commerce, and labor unions—as each sought to influence school programs.[44]

As an alternative to curriculum making that had exhibited "a hospitality to every form of human interest that is as broad as the Christian principle of charity," as Boyd Bode wrote, Counts repeatedly recommended that curriculum development be placed in the hands of professionally trained experts.[45] Further, the curriculum should be reorganized along lines congruent with the ideals of democratic collectivism. This would not, he said, require adding new subjects, but it would demand a spirit, orientation and approach different from that of the traditional curriculum. The primary objective of education, as he saw it, should be to establish dispositions that guided conduct. Selfishness and egotism should be sanctioned; cooperation and creativity rewarded.[46]

The needs of a society in transition and the demands of Social Reconstruction required, Counts believed, that curriculum content should be based on an analysis of the "emergent tendencies in civilization," including the passing of *laissez-faire* economics, the convergence of economics and politics, the rise of social planning, and the movement toward interdependence and cooperation on a worldwide scale.[47] The themes of interdependence and internationalism (often very like current discussions of globalization), along with social planning and collectivism permeated Counts' writings about society, education, and curriculum. Many of the Reconstructionists expressed great faith in and hope for progress toward democratic collectivism. The socialist idea of collectivism had great intellectual currency in the 1930s. It was a central idea in Marxist thinking, a set of ideas with perhaps their greatest power and appeal in the decades when the abuses of *laissez-faire* individualism and industrialism had become most apparent and before the collectivist failures of Soviet Russia and Maoist China. But while Counts and many of his contemporaries were clearly utopian and unrealistic in their thinking—citizens of "the pure realm of thought" as E.B. White would later label Ann Morrow Lindbergh and *her* utopian musings with Nazi sympathies—they were always American in their vision. As Counts would write later, "Our challenge is to preserve in [our children] the values and spirit of the American people."[48]

This same concern for preserving the ideals and spirit of America while seeking to fulfill the American dreams of peace and prosperity through control over industrialism and technology also marked the work of the most prolific among the social Reconstructionist curriculum theorists, Harold Rugg. Rugg was the great synthesizer among the Reconstructionists. He blended psychology, philosophy, sociology, economics, and history into social analyses and curriculum construction into a set of frequently revised textbooks that represented the greatest influence in schools of the values and views of Social Reconstructionism.

Rugg's credentials as a theorist and curriculum developer were well established by the 1930s. He had begun his curriculum work by leading the development of a series of social studies pamphlets for use in classes at Lincoln School in the early 1920s. He later expanded the pamphlets into a set of fourteen volumes of social studies texts for grades three through nine that were intended to "present American youth with a total word portrait of contemporary society as seen by scholars."[49] He also had led the committee of the National Society for the Study of Education that had attempted to resolve among other issues the conflict between the two most common approaches to curriculum development of the day, beginning with an analysis of the tasks and activities of adults or beginning with an analysis of the activities of children, an effort that had led to the well known 26th Yearbook of NSSE.

Rugg had never been entirely comfortable with child-centered Progressivism, and his angst over the conditions in American society and much of the world led him to spell out his stance in a 1931 article for *Progressive Education*. "Is it not clear," he asked, "that the schools are indeed the chief contestants in the battle between humanitarianism, international cooperation, and selfish nationalism? Does not the current situation demand of us Herculean efforts to avert world catastrophe?"[50]

For Rugg, the road to reconstruction lay in building an educated minority of citizens who would demand social and economic planning on the national level and a world economic council to monitor international trade and relations. The key to developing this "educated minority" was to build a new curriculum to study "the American Problem," which was distinct but related to the worldwide depression. As Rugg saw it, "the American Problem" for future generations was "to bring forth on this continent—in some form of cooperative commonwealth—the civilization of economic abundance, democratic behavior, and integrity of expression which is now potentially available."[51] Building a curriculum to study the factors involved in "the problem" and creating a new social order would require content derived from the problems and issues that characterize the changing society. The core of the content would be the twelve "great central concepts" that Rugg had begun to develop in his textbook series.

"No longer can the educationist remain aloof from the frontiers of social and artistic life," Rugg wrote, "for it is the problems on the frontier that constitute the nucleus of the educational program."[52] Those problems—Rugg's twelve great concepts—interdependence, accelerating change, the economic concepts of private property, economic gain, competition, forms of governmental organization including socialism, communism, and fascism, urban crowding and overpopulation, an awareness of the roles of the politician, the entrepreneur, and the artist in the acquisitive American society, formed his theme-based conception of curriculum content. He valued content—the "word portrait of society"—as the foundation of the curriculum, although he also insisted that the program of the schools, from kindergarten through adult education, should instill the methods of experimentalism.[53]

Rugg's curriculum ideas had shades of difference from those of other Social Reconstructionists, especially in his emphases on creativity, imagination, and artistic appreciation, and his consideration of the arts and the sciences as well as the social sciences as the subjects in the curriculum. But his curriculum ideas focused, as did other Reconstructionists, on the same concerns for democracy and experimentalism, the problems of industrial society, collective action, and preserving selected American values such as the love of freedom. Knowledge—organized around the great concepts or themes Rugg had developed—was to be the basis for reconstructing society. Students, whether they were in high schools or adult discussion groups, would have to first understand the problems society faced and their historical antecedents, then understand the possible alternative for solving the problems, develop the disposition to act, form a "great consensus," and finally, through their actions, shape governmental policy.[54]

The curriculum concerns of many Social Reconstructionists paralleled those found in three yearbooks published by the NEA's Department of Superintendence in the mid-1930s.[55] While the representatives of the Department of Superintendence rejected any advocacy of indoctrination (a major issue for the Reconstructionists and others in the 1930s[56]) in the precepts of a new social order, and while the group did not advocate any radical reconstruction of American society, it did insist that the problems of the Depression demanded a reconsideration of the program of the schools.

Social Change and Education, the first of the yearbooks, traced several broad social trends from the mid–nineteenth century, focusing on the rate of technological change and the rise of interdependence. The book advocated developing methods and materials that would produce "social intelligence" in students, so that "democracy in an age of cooperative living" could flourish.[57] The most important area of the curriculum for producing "social intelligence" was the social studies, the subject of the next yearbook. In *The Social Studies Curriculum*, the Department's Commission on the social studies set out their views on the purposes of the social studies, provided a set of "guiding principles" for developing curriculum materials in line with the purposes and philosophy they espoused, and gave some examples of actual school curricula they believed to be heading in the right directions.

The yearbook on the social studies began by citing three major influences on their thinking about the social studies curriculum: the first was the President's Research Committee on Social Trends, the second was the prior NEA yearbook on social change, and the third was the American Historical Association's Commission on the Social Studies. These were much the same sources claimed by *The Social Frontier* in its first issue. The similarities were not surprising, since both Counts and Beard were members of the NEA Commission on the Social Studies.[58] That set of influences, the yearbook committee wrote, led them to propose that social studies curricula should be designed to provide students with a more "realistic" view of the social situation and to prepare them for "promoting a wiser and more effective cooperation among regions...communities, states, and nations— a cooperation interracial, interreligious, and intereconomic."[59]

The yearbook committee advanced an "illustrative" set of guiding principles for curriculum construction. The second category of principles was called "the role of the school in social reconstruction," and contained in its list two that said, "the school is an agency of society for its improvement and continuous reconstruction," and "the school should participate in society's program of social reconstruction to the end of realizing a preferred social order, cooperative in its nature."[60]

Two proposed school curriculums—Fort Worth, Texas and the Virginia state curriculum—appeared as examples of the directions advocated by the Commission. The Fort Worth curriculum showed that the senior high school curriculum was organized into Ancient, Modern, World, and American histories. But the curriculum for grades four through eight was to be interdisciplinary and organized into themes, two of which were repeated at each of the five grade levels. These themes might have come from any Reconstructionist list of curriculum organizers. Grades four and six, for example, studied "Interdependence" of the "community and the world at large," while the fifth graders were to study "the increasing interdependence of the family and other social groups." Seventh graders learned that "national solidarity" had produced interdependence among the various states. The second theme, "The Progress of Democracy," appeared even more frequently than interdependence in the proposed curriculum guide. This theme also produced some interpretations as interesting as teaching about national solidarity and interdependence in a former Confederate state. Texas' war with Mexico, for example, was portrayed as a demonstration of "the tendency of people to demand democracy," and in grade seven, "how the raising of cotton in the United States has influenced the development of democracy" was to be used as an illustration of "the striving of man for social, political, and economic democracy." The eighth grade was to be devoted to nine-week units intended to develop "democratic attitudes and knowledge."[61]

It undoubtedly would be pure presentism to note the absence of slavery as a topic of study in the apparently unbroken march of American culture and civilization toward broad democracy.

The proposed Virginia curriculum guide corresponded even more closely to Harold Rugg's ideas. It was a broad fields model—in today's terms, a partially integrated curriculum—focused on the secondary grades and organized around the "major functions of social life," with a different "center of interest" for each grade. In the ninth grade, for example, "agrarianism and industrialism" formed the center of interest; grade ten's center of interest was "effects of a culture and changing social institutions upon our living," and grade eleven's proposed center was to be "effects of a continuously planning social order upon our living." Arranging the "major functions of social life" along one axis and the "centers of interest" along another yielded a grid from which curriculum questions could be generated. Thus in grade nine, the intersection of the *function* of "exploration" and the *center of interest* labeled "agrarianism and industrialism" led to the question, "How does the spirit of pioneering influence the development of equality of opportunity both in an agrarian and an industrial setting?" In grade eleven, crossing the *function* of "conservation" and the *interest center* of "effects of a continuously planning social order" was to be, "How can nations thru [*sic*] social planning guarantee to all the protection of life, property, and natural resources?"[62]

The last of the three yearbooks, *The Improvement of Education: Its Interpretation For Democracy* (1937) reverted to social analysis and criticism, and advocated change in the social studies, as well as other areas of the curriculum. The age of industrial affluence, the book argued, had become pervasive in all aspects of American life, including the schools. Business methods and efficiency models for organizing schools and the curriculum had led to "the mass production of educational superlatives and promises" by educational leaders who viewed high school and college diplomas as "certified pass[es] to material well-being."[63] But these goals and views of schooling were inadequate in their social emphasis, and the new social situation of the Depression placed new demands on the schools. The demands were that the schools "update" the content of their social studies curriculums, place greater emphasis on social analysis in all areas of the curriculum, promote the use of "intelligence" in social affairs, and adhere to the tenets of democratic problem solving in groups. All of these changes were necessary if the schools were to continue their "dynamic" role in providing guidance for the times.[64]

DISCUSSION: SOCIAL RECONSTRUCTIONIST CURRICULUM IMPULSES

All things pass. Social Reconstructionism and its curriculum ideas had their time as focal points for discussion in the 1930s before merging into the larger stream of thought about the purposes and programs of the schools. Counts, Rugg, and other Social Reconstructionists moved on to other areas of interest in their later lives, and even criticized themselves and others for the "inadequacy" of their ideas of the time.[65] There are plausible links between Social Reconstructionism and the life-adjustment education movement of the 1940s. The "Problems of Democracy" course that appeared in many high school social studies programs from the 1930s into the 1960s owed part of its impetus to Social Reconstructionist thought. Utopianism and criticism continue as strands of educational philosophy and debates over school purpose, now with Social Reconstructionism as part of the intellectual ancestry.

But what, really did the Social Reconstructionists seem to want and to expect of the curriculum? Harry Broudy may have said it best and most succinctly:

After all, where was the school supposed to lead American society in the 1930s and 40s? What did Rugg, Brameld, Counts, and the other Reconstructionists want the American society to become? It appears that the point was to make the benefits of a humane community, such as obtained in the small towns of America, accessible to the city dwellers and industrial workers of the [post-Depression and] postwar era. And this could be done, presumably, by instituting a social order that would be based on consensus achieved through collective use of the scientific mode of inquiry. . . . . What the muckrakers had turned up about the evils of American society would be "found out" by the pupils themselves, and thus pressure for liberal legislation would be created naturally in and by the schools.[66]

That seemed, indeed, the Social Reconstructionist view of curriculum and the purposes of the schools. Theirs was a thoroughly American notion of reform rooted in pragmatic patterns of developing new and widely shared knowledge about present ills and better ways. The schools—especially the high school (and adult discussion groups)—were to be the places where "updated" knowledge was acquired and "intelligence," defined as democratic problem solving within groups using the methods of science, was to be the means for change. The Social Reconstructionists did not advocate broad activism, marches or demonstrations, or wresting power from the elites.Instead they advocated study, the development of a consensus, and the restoration of a modernized version of the fundamental values of democracy, humanity, and collective plenty that they believed uncontrolled industrialism and industrialists had trampled and that they sensed must have once existed.

Social Reconstructionism waned partly because the Reconstructionists were far better at criticism and analysis than the politics of curriculum making. As historians have suggested, protest is not program, and the Social Reconstructionists knew more what they were against than what they were for. But Social Reconstructionism waned mostly because their time passed. The Depression continued, but Roosevelt and the New Deal—not the schools—carried the fight to reform or restore America until World War II brought full production, higher wages, and the pent up demand of induced shortages. John Levitt and his vision and versions of suburban prosperity and artificiality in the Levittowns of Long Island, Pennsylvania, and New Jersey came to characterize post-Depression and postwar America, not democratic collectivism. Levitt did appear on the cover of *Time* in the late forties. And television, not the schools or Social Reconstructionism, played a central role in creating a new social order, democratizing access to entertainment, but not promoting "intelligence," and engendering isolation, not collectivism.

NOTES

1. Editors of *Time Magazine, Time Covers History: 80 Years of Covers, 1923-2003*. New York: Time, Inc., 2003. *Time* covers can be accessed at www.time.com/archive.

2. See, for example, E.A. Winters, *Harold Rugg and Education for Social Reconstruction*, unpublished doctoral dissertation, The University of Wisconsin, 1968, for one account of attacks on Rugg, especially, and other Social Reconstructionists.

3. William Wraga, "The Comprehensive High School and Educational Reform in the United States: Retrospect and Prospect." *The High School Journal*. Vol 81, No. 3, 1998, pp. 121–135.

4. See, for example, John Dewey, *School and Society*. Chicago: The University of Chicago Press, 1902, and *Democracy and Education*. New York: The Macmillan Company, 1916. The ideas of the cult of efficiency are explored in Raymond E. Callahan, *Education and the Cult of Efficiency: A Study of the Social Forces That Have Shaped the Administgrations of the Public Schools*, Chicago: University of Chicago Press, 1962. For more complete analyses of Dewey's ideas

and place in historical context, see Lawrence Cremin, *The Transformation of the School: Progressivism in American Education, 1876-1957,* New York: Alfred A. Knopf, 1961; Herbert M. Kliebard, *The Struggle for the American Curriculum, 1893-1958,* Boston: Routledge and Kegan Paul, 1986; and Daniel and Laurel Tanner, *History of the School Curriculum,* New York: Macmillan, 1990. For a more presently politically drawn analysis of Progressivism and Dewey, see Dianne Ravitch, *Left Back: A Century of Failed School Reforms,* New York: Simon and Schuster, 2000. See also Paul Shaker's review of Ravitch's book, *"Left Back: Punditry or History?"* in the *Journal of Curriculum Studies,* Vol. 36, No. 4, 2004, pp. 495–507.

5. William Heard Kilpatrick, "The Project Method," *Teachers College Record,* Vol. 19, 319–335, 1918.

6. See, for example, Harold Rugg and Ann Shoemaker, *The Child-Centered School: An Appraisal of the New Education.* Yonkers, NY: World Book Company, 1929; George S. Counts, "Dare Progressive Education Be Progressive?" *Progressive Education,* Vol IX, No. 4, April, 1932; John Dewey, "Progressive Education and the Science of Education," *Progressive Education,* Vol VI No. 1 (January-March, 1929), pp. 62–63.

7. George S. Counts, *The Senior High School Curriculum.* Chicago: University of Chicago Press, 1926.

8. The text of Counts's address to the PEA was published under its original title, "Dare Progressive Education Be Progressive?" In *Progressive Education,* Vol. IX, No. 4, April 1932. The issue contained reactions to the speech by other members of the Association. The address apparently was unheralded, and most in the audience had no idea what to expect. Reports indicate that the immediate reaction to the speech was pervasive silence, followed by excited discussion. Many of the remaining activities of the PEA Convention were suspended or cancelled following Counts's address, and impromptu discussion groups sprang up and spent the remainder of the conference discussing the ideas Counts advanced. Counts later combined the text of the address with two other essays in a pamphlet bearing the more famous title, *Dare the School Build a New Social Order?* (New York: The John Day Company, 1933).

9. Franklin Bobbitt, *The Curriculum.* Boston: Houghton Mifflin, 1918.

10. Guy M. Whipple, Editor, *The Foundations and Technique of Curriculum Construction,* The Twenty Sixth Yearbook of the National Society for the Study of Education: Part I—*Curriculum Making: Past and Present;* Part II—*The Foundations of Curriculum Making.* Bloomington, Illinois: Public School Publishing Company, 1926. Harold Rugg was Chairman of the Committee that produced the yearbook, and the yearbook clearly bears his stamp in content and writing, but Whipple was the designated editor.

11. Ralph W. Tyler, *Basic Principles of Curriculum and Instruction.* Chicago: University of Chicago Press, 1949.

12. B. Othanel Smith, William O. Stanley, and J. Harlan Shores, *Fundamentals of Curriculum Development.* New York: Harcourt, Brace and World, 1950.

13. Frederick Lewis Allen, *Only Yesterday: An Informal History of the 1920s.* New York: Harper and Row, 1931. p.310 (Perennial Classics Edition).

14. Langston Hughes, "Waitin' for Mr. Roosevelt."

15. Progressivism (small "p") as a theory of society and politics that believed in the importance of human welfare, that wanted political and social reform to lessen the power of industrialists and big business, and that sought to extend political democracy through increased popular control of government, had lost much of its impetus in the prosperity and xenophobic reaction after World War I. The Progressive Party was no longer a force in American politics, a victim of the perils of prosperity. Progressivism in American education, however, had flourished, especially in the private schools attended by the children of the growing upper middle class, much as the Montessori method and schools would do decades later. Progressive Education thought and practice exerted an influence on educators' thinking far beyond the numbers the movement included in its ranks. The Progressive Education Association was founded in 1919.

16. Harold Rugg and Ann Shoemaker, *The Child-Centered School.*

17. Boyd Bode, *Modern Educational Theories.* New York: The Macmillan Company, 1927.

18. John Dewey, "Progressive Education and the Science of Education," *Progressive Education* VI, No. 1 (January-March, 1929), pp.62-63.

19. Gerald Ponder, *Conflict, Collectivism, and Consensus: A Historical Analysis of Social Reconstructionist Curriculum Theories.* Unpublished doctoral dissertation, The University of Texas at Austin, 1974. p.31.

20. Harold Rugg, *Foundations of American Education.* New York: World Book, 1947, p. 578.

21. William H. Kilpatrick, *Foundations of Method: Informal Talks on Teaching.* New York: Macmillan, 1925.

22. C.A. Bowers, *The Progressive Educator and the Depression: The Radical Years,* New York: Random House, 1969, pp. 80-81.

23. George S. Counts, *The Selective Character of American Secondary Education,* Chicago: The University of Chicago Press, 1922, and *The Social Composition of Boards of Education,* Chicago: The University of Chicago Press, 1927 .

24. Bowers, *The Progressive Educator and the Depression,* pp. 79-83.

25. Bowers, *The Progressive Educator and the Depression,* pp. 82-84. See also John L. Childs, *American Pragmatism and Education,* New York: Holt, Rinehart, and Winston, 1956, pp. 212-247.

26. Gary Lee Peltier, *Jesse H. Newlon as Superintendent of the Denver Public Schools, 1920-1927.* Unpublished doctoral dissertation, University of Denver, 1965.

27. Bowers, *The Progressive Educator and the Depression,* p.85.

28. Ibid, p. 85.

29. Peter S. Carbone, *The Social and Educational Thought of Harold Rugg,* Durham, NC: Duke University Press, 1977.

30. Harold Rugg, *That Men May Understand.* New York: Doubleday, 1941. p. 203.

31. Theodore Brameld, personal interview, November 20, 1973. Rugg's place as the leading curriculum theorist is based not only on his own works and the interpretations of those who have written about him, but also by the recognition of reconstructionists—like Theodore Brameld—themselves.

32. John L. Childs, *American Pragmatism and Education*. New York: Holt, Rinehart, and Winston, 1956. pp. 5–7.

33. Charles Beard, *An Economic Interpretation of the Constitution of the United States*, New York: the Free Press, 1913, and *The Rise of American Civilization* (co-authored with his wife, Mary Beard), New York: The Free Press, 1927. Thorsten Veblen was considered an influential, if idiosyncratic and sometimes quixotic writer among his students and other liberals and social critics. He coined, among other terms, the concept of "conspicuous consumption" in a long set of writings that included *The Theory of the Leisure Class* (1909) and *Essays in Our Changing Order* (1927).

34. George Counts, Mordecai Grossman, and Norman Woelfel, "Orientation," *The Social Frontier*, Vol. 1, No.1, October, 1932. Two volumes of the multi-volume report of the American Historical Association's Commission on the Social Studies were especially influential in focusing the thought of the Social Reconstructionists. The first was Charles Beard's *A Charter for the Social Sciences* (New York: Charles Scribner's Sons, 1932). The second was the Commission's *Conclusions and Recommendations* (New York: Charles Scribner's Sons, 1934). While neither of these works were intentionally supportive of the position of the Social Reconstructionists—Beard explicitly rejected the notion that the schools should lead the way in social reform in *Charter*—the interpretations of historical trends in these volumes represented the views of the Reconstructionists.

35. See, for example, John L. Childs, *American Pragmatism and Education*, New York: Holt, Rinehart and Winston, 1956, for a first person retrospective by a participant in the early discussions, and C.A. Bowers, *The Progressive Educator and the Depression: The Radical Years*, New York: Random House, 1969, for a later interpretation.

36. John Dewey, *Democracy and Education*, New York: The Macmillan Company, 1916; *Experience and Education*, Lafayette, IN: Kappa Delta Pi Lecture Series, 1938.

37. AHA Commission on the Social Studies, *Conclusions and Recommendations*, p.11–15.

38. AHA Commission on the Social Studies, *Conclusions and Recommendations*, pp. 11–13.

39. AHA Commission on the Social Studies, *Conclusions and Recommendations*, p.12.

40. The exact phrase, "The Great Transition," appears to have been coined by Harold Rugg during the mid-1930s, when he began writing his chapters for *Democracy and the Curriculum* (Harold Rugg, Ed., the 1939 Yearbook of the John Dewey Society, New York: Appleton-Century Company, 1939). Nearly all of the Social Reconstructionists, as well as the members of the AHA

Commission on the Social Studies, referred to the American society of the 1930s as a society in transition.

41. AHA Commission on the Social Studies, *Conclusions and Recommendations*, p.15.

42. Theodore Brameld indicated (personal interview, November 20, 1973) that these were important, but not the only sources of influence on the curriculum ideas or social analyses of the Social Reconstructionists. Reconstructionism, in his view, had its roots in the broad tradition of utopianism in Western culture dating back at least to Plato and other Greek and Roman utopian philosophers. He further argued that the modifier "social" severely limited the intent of reconstructionism, and that the Social Reconstructionists applied many of the concepts and principles of the broader understanding of Reconstructionism to social and educational analyses grounded in the events of the time. Brameld was a slightly later contemporary of many of the Social Reconstructionists, knew many of them and was influenced by them. His own version of a Social Reconstructionist curriculum was developed in the 1940s, added an element of futurism to the ideas of democratic social and economic planning and was published as *Design For America* (New York: Harper and Brothers, 1945).

43. Gerald L. Gutek, *An Analysis of the Social and Educational Theory of George S. Counts During the Depression of the 1930's,* unpublished doctoral dissertation, University of Illinois, 1964, pp. 259-262. For many of the outlines of Counts's curriculum thinking, see some of his earlier work, especially *The Senior High School Curriculum* (1926), *The American Road To Culture: A Social Interpretation of Education in the United States (*New York: The John Day Company, 1930), and "Who Shall Make the Curriculum?" *The School Review,* Vol. 35, No. 9 (May, 1927), p. 333.

44. Counts, "Who Shall Make the Curriculum?" and *The American Road to Culture.*

45. The quote is from Boyd Bode, "The Confusion in Present-Day Education," Chapter One in William Heard Kilpatrick, Editor, *The Educational Frontier,* New York: Appleton Century Crofts, 1933. Counts' views on curriculum makers were set forth most explicitly in his article, "Who Shall make the Curriculum?" *The School Review,* Vol. 35, No. 9, May, 1927, *The Senior High School Curriculum* (1926), and *The American Road to Culture: A Social Interpretation of Education in the United States.* New York: The John Day Company, 1930. Counts' writings related to curriculum in the 1930s implied that the "experts" should be people versed in social analysis and sympathetic to the Social Reconstructionist views.

46. Counts, *The Social Foundations of Education*, p. 541–544, and *The American Road to Culture,* p. 124.

47. Ibid.

48. George S. Counts, *Education and the Promise of America,* New York: the Macmillan Company, 1945, p. 11.

49. Harold Rugg, *That Men May Understand: An American in the Long Armistice.* New York:Doubleday, Doran, and Company, 1941, pp. 48, 193.

50. Harold Rugg, "Education and International Understanding," *Progressive Education*, Vol. VIII, No. 4, April, 1931, p. 299.

51. Harold Rugg (Editor), *Democracy and the Curriculum: The Life and Program of the School*. Third Yearbook of the John Dewey Society. New York: D.Appleton-Century Company, 1939, p.v.

52. Harold Rugg, "Social Reconstruction Through Education," *Progressive Education*, Vol. X, No. 1 (January, 1933), p. 11.

53. Rugg elaborated, justified, and reiterated his curriculum ideas in a number of his works, including *Democracy and the Curriculum* (1939) *That Men May Understand* (1941) (intended primarily as a defense of his textbook series, then under attack by conservative critics), *American Life and the School Curriculum: Next Steps Toward Schools of Living* (Boston: Ginn and Company, 1936), and *Foundations for American Education* (Yonkers, NY: World Book Company, 1947).

54. Rugg, *American Life and the School Curriculum;* Ponder, *Conflict, Collectivism, and Consensus*, pp. 172–173.

55. National Education Association, Department of Superintendence, *Social Change and Education: Thirteenth Yearbook* (1935); *The Social Studies Curriculum: Fourteenth Yearbook* (1936); *The Improvement of Education: Its Interpretation for Democracy; Fifteenth Yearbook* (1937). All published by the National Education Association, Washington, D.C.

56. The Social Reconstructionists and their critics engaged in a debate over indoctrination in the pages of *The Social Frontier* in 1935. Counts and others later declared that debate and others over the issues embedded in indoctrination a "waste of time."

57. NEA Department of Superintendence, *Social Change and Education*, p.242.

58. Ibid, p. 346.

59. Ibid, p. 57.

60. Ibid., p. 347.

62. Virginia State Board of Education, *Tentative Course of Study for Virginia Schools*. Richmond: The Board, 1934., pp. 16–19.61. Fort Worth, Texas, Board of Education, *Social Studies: A Tentative Course of Study*. Curriculum Bulletin No. 109. 1933, pp.11–19.

63. NEA Department of Superintendence, *The Improvement of Education: Its Interpretation for Democracy*. Washington, D.C.: National Education Association, 1937. p. 5.

64. Ibid, pp. 112–115.

65. See Harold Rugg, *Imagination*. New York: Harper and Row, 1963; George S. Counts, *Education and the Foundations of Human Freedom*. Pittsburgh, PA: University of Pittsburgh Press.

66. Harry S. Broudy, "Democratic Values and Educational Goals," in Robert M. McClure, editor, *The Curriculum: Retrospect and Prospect*. 70th Yearbook of the National Society for the Study of Education. Chicago: University of Chicago Press, 1971, pp. 132–133.

ABOUT THE AUTHORS

Murry R. Nelson

Murry R. Nelson is Professor of Education and American Studies at the Pennsylvania State University where he has taught since 1975. He received an M.A. in Anthropology and a Ph.D. in education from Stanford University and taught public school in Chicago. He was a Fulbright Senior Lecturer at the University of Iceland (1983) and was a Senior Fulbright Roving Instructor of American Studies attached to the Norwegian Ministry of Education (1990-91). He is a founding member of the Society for the Study of Curriculum History.

Gerald L. Gutek

Gerald L. Gutek is Professor Emeritus of Education at Loyola University Chicago. His academic specialization in the history and philosophy of education. He was co-founder of the Midwest History of Education Society. His books on Counts are *The Educational Theory of George S. Counts (1970) and George S. Counts and American Civilization: The Educator as Social Theorist,* (1984).

J. Wesley Null

J. Wesley Null is Assistant Professor of Education in the School of Education and the Honors College at Baylor University. Before serving on the

Social Reconstruction: People, Politics, Perspectives, pages 257–262
Copyright © 2006 by Information Age Publishing
All rights of reproduction in any form reserved.

faculty at Baylor, he taught social studies in public schools in New Mexico and Texas. He earned his B.S. and M.Ed. degrees from Eastern New Mexico University. In 2001, he completed his Ph.D. degree at The University of Texas at Austin, where he studied the history of education and curriculum. At Baylor, Null teaches interdisciplinary courses in the School of Education and the Honors College. He also teaches teacher education courses each semester at Waco High School. He is the author of *A Disciplined Progressive Educator: The Life and Career of William Chandler Bagley* (Peter Lang, 2003) and a co-editor of *Readings in American Educational Thought: From Puritanism to Progressivism* (InfoAge, 2004) and *Forgotten Heroes of American Education: The Great Tradition of Teaching Teachers* (InfoAge, 2006). He serves as Editor of the *American Educational History Journal.* He lives in Hewitt, Texas with his wife, Dana, and his daughter, Raegan.

Ronald W. Evans

Ronald W. Evans is Professor in the School of Teacher Education at San Diego State University. He is author of *The Social Studies Wars* (2004) and first editor of the *Handbook on Teaching Social Issues* (1996). He recently finished researching and writing a book manuscript on Harold Rugg and is currently collecting materials for a book on the history of the era of the new social studies of the 1960s and 70s.

Craig Kridel

Craig Kridel is Professor of Educational Foundations and Research and Director of the McKissick Museum of Education at the University of South Carolina. He is a former member of the Society for Educational Reconstruction and former member of the Board of Directors of the John Dewey Society and Editorial Board of the *History of Education Quarterly.* He has edited/co-edited *Teachers and Mentors, Writing Educational Biography, Education Books of the Century,* and *The American Curriculum.* His research interests include progressive education, biographical research, and documentary editing.

William B. Stanley

William B. Stanley currently serves as Professor and Dean of Education at Monmouth University in NJ. He is a former NJ social studies teacher who taught for 14 years before moving on to higher education. He received his BA in History and Social Science from Kean University and his MA in History and doctorate in Curriculum and Instruction from Rutgers University and has taught at Louisiana State University, the University of Delaware, the University of Colorado, Boulder and the University of Redlands, CA. He is the author of numerous articles, book chapters, two edited books, and Curriculum for Utopia (SUNY Press 1992). His research and publications have focused on social studies education, curriculum theory, and educational reform. Among his most recent work is an edited book, *Critical Issues in Social Studies for the 21st Century* (Information Age Publishing 2001). Over the past seventeen years, he has served as Department Chair and Interim Dean at the University of Delaware, as Dean of Education at the University of Colorado, Boulder and as Founding Dean at the University of Redlands, CA. He is a member of the National Council for the Social Studies, the American Educational Research Association, Professors of Curriculum honorary society, and currently serves on the NCATE Board of Examiners.

Karen L. Riley

Karen L. Riley is Distinguished Research Professor and Distinguished Teaching Professor at Auburn University Montgomery. Her research interests include the history of education, the politics of education, and curriculum history. She is also a consultant to the movie industry on the topic of the Holocaust.

Joseph Watras

Joseph Watras has been a professor of social foundations of education at the University of Dayton in Ohio since 1979. After serving with the U. S. Peace Corps in West Africa, he completed his doctoral work at The Ohio State University. Among the books he has published are *Social Education in the Twentieth Century* with Christine Woyshner and Margaret Crocco and *Philosophic Conflicts in Education, 1893–2000.*

Wayne Urban

Wayne Urban is Professor in the Department of Educational Policy, Leadership, and Technology Studies and Associate Director of the Education Policy Center at the University of Alabama, Tuscaloosa. He previously taught at Georgia State University and the University of South Florida and has held visiting appointments at several institutions, including universities in Australia, Poland, and Canada. He is author of *Why Teacher Organized*

(1982), *Gender Race and the National Education Association* (2000), and co-author of *American Education: A History* (1996, 2000, 2004).

Barbara Slater Stern

Barbara Slater Stern is an associate professor in the Secondary Education Program at James Madison University. Her research interests include the history of social studies education, integration of technology into social studies and curriculum history.

Susan C. Brown

Susan C. Brown is a visiting assistant professor of Educational Studies at the University of Central Florida in Orlando, FL. Dr. Brown served six years as the editor of *Curriculum Teaching Dialogue* and currently serves as associate editor of *Florida Educational Leadership*. She has co-authored *Applying Multicultural and Global Concepts in the Classroom and Beyond* and *What Every Teacher Should Know About Multicultural and Global Education*. Dr Brown's research areas include multicultural and global education and curriculum studies. Dr. Brown has presented nationally and internationally on her areas of research and has published numerous articles in national and international journals.

Marcella L. Kysilka

Marcella L. Kysilka is professor emerita in Educational Studies at the University of Central Florida in Orlando, FL. Her recent co-authored publications include *Applying Multicultural and Global Concepts in the Classroom and Beyond*, *What Every Teacher Should Know About Multicultural and Global Education*, *The Adjunct Professor's Guide to Success and Teaching College in An Age of Accountability*. Dr. Kysilka has presented nationally and internationally and has published numerous articles on curriculum studies, multicultural education, urban education and teacher education. Dr. Kysilka is past-president of Kappa Delta Pi, past editor of *The Educational Forum*, past-president of Florida ASCD and current editor of *Florida Educational Leadership*. Her current interest is working with a charter inner city high school in Cincinnati, Ohio.

Gerald Ponder

Gerald Ponder is Associate Dean for Academic Affairs in the College of Education at North Carolina State University, Raleigh. He previously served as Professor and Department Chair at the University of North Texas in Denton and The University of North Carolina at Greensboro. His interest in Social Reconstructionism began several decades ago with his doctoral dissertation on the curriculum theories of the Social Reconstructionists, and his interest in the history of schooling and education as part of American cultural history dates from studies during his M.A program in history. He is a founding member of the Society for the Study of Curriculum History.

Printed in the United States
48783LVS00001B/160-210

9 781593 112158